A Brief History of Liberty

Brief Histories of Philosophy

Brief Histories of Philosophy provide both academic and general readers with short, engaging narratives for those concepts that have had a profound effect on philosophical development and human understanding. The word 'history' is thus meant in its broadest cultural and social sense. Moreover, although the books are meant to provide a rich sense of historical context, they are also grounded in contemporary issues, as contemporary concern with the subject at hand is what will draw most readers. These books are not merely a tour through the history of ideas, but essays of real intellectual range by scholars of vision and distinction.

Already Published

A Brief History of Happiness by Nicholas P. White
A Brief History of Liberty by David Schmidtz and Jason Brennan

Forthcoming

A Brief History of Justice by David Johnston
A Brief History of the Soul by Charles Taliaferro and Stewart Goetz

A BRIEF HISTORY OF LIBERTY

DAVID SCHMIDTZ AND
JASON BRENNAN

A John Wiley & Sons, Ltd., Publication

This edition first published 2010
© 2010 David Schmidtz and Jason Brennan

Blackwell Publishing was acquired by John Wiley & Sons in February 2007.
Blackwell's publishing program has been merged with Wiley's global Scientific,
Technical, and Medical business to form Wiley-Blackwell.

Registered Office
John Wiley & Sons Ltd, The Atrium, Southern Gate, Chichester, West Sussex, PO19 8SQ,
United Kingdom

Editorial Offices
350 Main Street, Malden, MA 02148-5020, USA
9600 Garsington Road, Oxford, OX4 2DQ, UK
The Atrium, Southern Gate, Chichester, West Sussex, PO19 8SQ, UK

For details of our global editorial offices, for customer services, and for information
about how to apply for permission to reuse the copyright material in this book please see
our website at www.wiley.com/wiley-blackwell.

The right of David Schmidtz and Jason Brennan to be identified as the authors of this work
has been asserted in accordance with the Copyright, Designs and Patents Act 1988.

Library of Congress Cataloging-in-Publication Data

Schmidtz, David.
   A brief history of liberty / David Schmidtz and Jason Brennan.
      p. cm. — (Brief histories of philosophy)
   Includes bibliographical references and index.
   ISBN 978-1-4051-7080-2 (hardcover : alk. paper) — ISBN 978-1-4051-7079-6 (pbk. : alk.
paper) 1. Liberty—History. I. Brennan, Jason. II. Title.
   JC585.S365   2010
   323.4409—dc22

                                                                            2009033124

A catalogue record for this book is available from the British Library.

Set in 10.5/14pt Minion by Graphicraft Limited, Hong Kong
Printed and bound in Singapore by Ho Printing Singapore Pte Ltd

1   2010

Contents

Acknowledgments

In 1630, a troublemaker from London named Roger Williams fled to Boston, made more trouble there, preaching a radical separation between church and state, then fled again, to the colony that would become the state of Rhode Island. Williams made Rhode Island the first state in the world to be founded upon, and successfully to establish, a principle of freedom of religion. His efforts would inspire the First Amendment of the US Constitution. Some years after Williams settled in Providence, he learned that Joshua Winsor, an indentured servant of Massachusetts Governor John Winthrop, was having the same problems with religious orthodoxy that had driven Williams away. Williams wrote to Winthrop (I have seen a copy of the letter) and offered to pay the governor whatever the governor thought reasonable to take the troublesome Winsor off the governor's hands. Thus Williams purchased Winsor's servitude contract. Joshua Winsor moved to Providence. Within a year, he was no longer in debt: he had paid it off, or Williams had forgiven it. Winsor had a son, Samuel, who would one day marry Roger's daughter, Mercy Williams. I am grateful to Williams and Winsor, partly for their towering measure of devotion in the battle for religious freedom, but mainly for being great, great (11 times great) grandfathers of my wife, Cathleen Johnson. I also thank Cathleen and my mother in law, Sara Winsor, for their suggestions and encouragement.

Thanks to the Earhart Foundation for supporting each of us. Thanks to my colleagues at the University of Arizona for their unfailing trust and support over the years. I will single out my Department Head, Chris Maloney, and my former Dean, Ed Donnerstein, for being the two best administrators I've known; but I could name two dozen others who have been pivotal in making life and work in Tucson the joy it is. We thank Ian Carter and Stephen Davies, helpful and encouraging readers for Blackwell. We thank Nick Bellorini for originally proposing the book.

I thank Whitney Ball, Carolyn Cox, Fred Fransen, Steve Haessler, Cathleen Johnson, Randy Kendrick, the Charles Koch Foundation, Gerry Ohrstrom, Gayle Siegel, Menlo Smith, Thomas W. Smith, Elizabeth Volard, and Marty Zupan for helping to transform the Arizona Center for Philosophy of Freedom from an abstract concept into a functioning academic unit. Thanks to research assistants Nathan Ballantyne, Scott Boocher, Ian Evans, and John Thrasher for doing more than their share to make day-to-day operations run as smoothly as they do.

Thanks to Jim Rossi, Fernando Tesón, and Don Weidner at Florida State College of Law; Horacio Spector and Guido Pincione at Torcuato di Tella School of Law; Giancarlo Ibarguen at Francisco Marroquin University in Guatemala City; Bob Goodin, Geoff Brennan, and Jeremy Shearmur at Australian National University; Yoram Hazony and Josh Weinstein at the Shalem Center in Jerusalem; and Claire Morgan at George Mason University for arranging courses or multiple presentations on this material. Thanks for intense, constructive feedback from audiences at the University of Montreal, at McGill University, at Oxford University, at UCLA, at the University of Virginia, at the University of Miami, at the University of Toronto, and at Georgetown, Stanford, Tulane, Bowling Green, UNC-Chapel Hill, Kent State, Georgia State, Arizona State, Florida State, and the University of San Diego.

David Schmidtz

In addition, I would like to thank Sean Aas, Derek Bowman, Corey Brettschneider, Josiah S. Carberry, Katherine Erbeznik, David

Estlund, Christopher Freiman, Charles Griswold, Keith Hankins, Daniel Jacobson, Sharon Krause, Charles Larmore, Mark LeBar, Jesse Maddox, Christopher Morris, Emily Nacol, John Nye, Dennis Rasmussen, Douglas Rasmussen, Daniel Silvermint, Jed Silverstein, A. John Simmons, David Sobel, John Tomasi, Joshua Tropp, Steven Wall, Kevin Vallier, and Matt Zwolinski. Thanks also to the students from my first year seminars on freedom at Brown for helping to shape this book. Congratulations to my seminar students from fall 2006, who will graduate the semester this book is published.

Jason Brennan

Introduction:
Conceptions of Freedom

THESIS: *There are several forms of liberty. Whether they are conflicting or complementary is a matter of historical circumstance.*

"History, it has been said, is the field of study in which one cannot begin at the beginning."[1] Telling a story requires decisions that could have been made differently – in particular, where to start the story. For philosophers, the story often begins with the task of clarifying the topic. For many of them this is where the story ends, too, but this is not that kind of book. This is a history of liberty, not a history of *theorizing* about liberty. Still, the topic calls for a clarifying philosophical introduction.

Histories of Liberties

What, then, does it mean to be free? Like many core philosophical concepts, the concept of liberty is not easy to pin down. Ludwig Wittgenstein observed that we talk about games with ease, even though it is not easy to say what a game is. Solitaire, football, Dungeons and Dragons, chess, and hopscotch are games. But is there anything important that they all have in common? Do the things we call games share a common essence in virtue of which the term 'game' properly applies? Wittgenstein thought not. We could say that all games involve forms of play, but that is only to say that we use the word 'play' as we use the word 'game,' to refer to a range of activities whose differences are obvious but whose similarities are obscure. Part of Wittgenstein's point is that we often know *how* to use words like 'game' or 'liberty' well enough to communicate with no apparent difficulty, even when we lack a precise recipe for how to use these words. Languages evolve over centuries as tools we use to convey information and ideas about issues that actually arise in our living together. Moreover, we are constantly running into cases that are in some way novel or ambiguous, and our linguistic practices do not resolve them in advance. The historical fact about language in general is that we revise our categories as we go, as needed. The edges (if not the cores) of our categories are fluid, which is part of what makes our categories as adaptable, and thus as useful, as they are.

Part of our job as philosophers is to make our language, concepts, and questions more precise. This job is never easy. As Nietzsche once noted, only that which has no history is definable.[2] Liberty, however we define it, has a history. Partly because of that, defining it is indeed a serious problem. In ordinary discourse, we use the terms 'freedom' or 'liberty' to refer to various ideas; these are related in important ways, but there may not be any essence that the ideas all share. Or, if there is a shared essence, we may not be able to say exactly what it is. Perhaps the things we call freedom bear a 'family resemblance' to each other. That is, in a large family we may observe that two siblings have the same nose, while two others have the same chin or hair color. Even if no characteristic is shared by every sibling, overlapping patterns of family resemblance still mark the siblings as members of the same family.

Perhaps free speech and free trade are usefully viewed as members of the same family.[3] They may turn out to have a history of going hand in hand, even though they are logically separable. Here we categorize forms of liberty as much as our present purpose requires. We don't assume there is any essence awaiting our discovery; neither do we assume otherwise.

Freedom from and freedom to

Isaiah Berlin describes two kinds of 'freedom' or 'liberty.' (Berlin uses the terms interchangeably, and so do we.) We often equate being free with an absence of constraints, impediments, or interference. For instance, the American Constitution protects freedom of speech by prohibiting Congress from passing laws that constrain speech. Berlin called this a *negative liberty*. Negative liberty connotes freedom *from* – that is, from constraints or interference. The 'great contrast' between it and positive liberty is that the latter has to do with self-government. The positive sense of liberty, Berlin says, is in play when the question is not "How far does government interfere with me?" but rather "Who governs me?".[4]

Berlin is often interpreted as trying to draw the following contrast. Someone is free – free *to* as opposed to free *from* – when she has a relevant capacity. So, for a bird to be free *to* fly, it must have wings and energy to take off. It is not enough that no one stops the bird. For me to be in this sense free to fly implies that I have a working aircraft at my disposal, and not merely that flight control has cleared me for takeoff. Positive freedom in this sense – freedom *to* – connotes possession of a relevant resource or capability. But, however illuminating this contrast may be (and we will come back to it), Berlin's original aim seems to have been to draw a related but different contrast between being free from constraints, especially constraints imposed by others, and positive freedom, conceived of as exercising whatever capabilities one has in an autonomous way.[5] In different words, the distinction between positive and negative freedom is a distinction between being free to choose goals of one's own and being unimpeded in pursuing those goals.

Berlin sees negative (political) liberty as an absence of obstacles imposed by others.[6] Thus he says:

> If I say that I am unable to jump more than ten feet in the air, or cannot read because I am blind, or cannot understand the darker

pages of Hegel, it would be eccentric to say that I am to that degree enslaved or coerced. . . . You lack political liberty or freedom only if you are prevented from attaining a goal by human beings. Mere incapacity to attain a goal is not lack of political freedom.[7]

Berlin's negative/positive metaphor naturally suggests that the two categories are supposed, jointly, to exhaust the possibilities. Not so. Berlin says that historians have documented two hundred ways of using the term, and he is writing only about two central ones.[8]

According to human rights activist Natan Sharansky, the simple and ultimate test of whether you live in a free society boils down to the following question: can you speak your mind without fear?[9] The locutions 'free from' and 'free to' are merely handy figures of speech, and here is a case where they can mislead.[10] We would naturally speak of being free *to* speak one's mind; but what Sharansky means is being free from laws or tyrants who suppress opinions, rather than having the technological or rhetorical capabilities necessary for effectively expressing one's opinions to any given audience. Nothing stops us from being concerned about the latter, but as a matter of fact Sharansky's concern, and the concern of the framers of the US Constitution, was about freedom of speech as a negative freedom.

Benjamin Constant, writing in the wake of the French Revolution, distinguished the 'liberty of the ancients' from the 'liberty of the moderns.' Constant's idea is that the liberty of the ancients involves active participation in government, whereas the liberty of the moderns is more a matter of having control over one's own life within the rule of law.

According to Constant, a citizen of modern England, France, or America conceives of liberty as a

right to be subjected only to the laws, and to be neither arrested, detained, put to death or maltreated in any way by the arbitrary will of one or more individuals. It is the right of everyone to express their opinion, choose a profession and practice it, to dispose of property, and even to abuse it; to come and go without permission, and without having to account for their motives or undertakings. It is everyone's right to associate with other individuals, either to discuss their interests, or to profess the religion which they and their associates prefer, or even simply to occupy their days or hours in a way which is most compatible with their inclinations or whims.[11]

Constant continues:

Now compare this liberty with that of the ancients. The latter consisted in exercising collectively, but directly, several parts of the complete sovereignty; in deliberating, in the public square, over war and peace . . . But if this was what the ancients called liberty, they admitted as compatible with this collective freedom the complete subjection of the individual to the authority of the community.[12]

As we interpret Berlin and Constant, what Constant calls 'liberty of the ancients' is one example of what Berlin calls 'positive freedom.' Specifically, the liberty of the ancients is a collective form of freedom: people being free to deliberate and to choose their own goals. What Constant calls 'liberty of the moderns' is, by contrast, an example of what Berlin calls 'negative freedom'; it is, specifically, an individual form of freedom from external impediments.

A brief history of liberty cannot cover everything. We concentrate on liberty in its individual forms. However, we do not neglect the topic of collective freedom altogether. Our "Prehistory" chapter discusses a collective form of negative freedom, namely being free from subjugation by neighboring nations, while our "Civil Rights" chapter discusses a collective positive freedom – the empowering of subjugated groups.

Working toward an analysis of the concept of freedom is a theoretical task, but many claim that the consequences of the exercise are not merely theoretical. Constant wrote that confusing the two (that is, the ancient and the modern) conceptions of liberty was "in the all too famous days of our revolution, the cause of many an evil. France was exhausted by useless experiments, the authors of which, irritated by their poor success, sought to force her to enjoy the good she did not want, and denied her the good which she did want."[13] Likewise, after distinguishing between negative and positive liberty, Isaiah Berlin went on to say that the two are not merely different conceptual categories, but rival political ideals, with conflicting implications about the proper role and scope of government.[14] Right or wrong, Constant and Berlin make the debate more interesting, for their assumption that different conceptions of liberty entail different political regimes recasts the semantic issue as a political one, where the debate is not merely about how to use the language but about how to use the police.

The remainder of this chapter identifies some of the many forms of liberty. Later chapters discuss the histories of some (but not all) of these forms.[15]

Negative liberty

(a)   Hobbes describes liberty as an "absence of external impediments."[16]

By external impediments, Hobbes meant obstacles that "may oft take away part of a man's power to do what he would; but cannot hinder him from using the power left him, according as his judgment, and reason shall dictate to him."[17] On Hobbes's view, any obstacle whatever is an impediment to liberty.

(b)   More specifically, we can define 'liberty' as an absence of impediments imposed *by other people*.

Suppose some obstacle leaves me unable to move my car. Perhaps a tree fell on it. Or perhaps you parked in a way that boxed me in. I am impeded either way, yet the latter is a different kind of impediment; because, if you imposed it, then we can ask whether the law should forbid your imposing such obstacles. This is what Berlin seems to have had in mind when he discussed political freedom.

(c)   Even more specifically, we can define 'liberty' as an absence of obstacles *deliberately* imposed by other people.

Your unknowingly parking in my favorite parking spot is not the same as your deliberately parking there, in the knowledge that I always park there. Either act renders me unfree to park in my customary spot, yet they leave me in different situations. The accidental parking is a mere inconvenience. If I take this inconvenience personally, I am overreacting. To take my spot deliberately, though, is to send me some sort of signal – perhaps that I don't command as much respect as I thought. The accident may leave me feeling irritated in a way, but it does not leave me wondering what you are trying to tell me.

Consider another example. Your accidentally running over my bicycle is, morally, not the same as your deliberately running over it. Either act leaves me unable to ride my bicycle; but the *accident* requires you to apologize, me to accept your apology, and both of us to do the kinds of things neighbors do to make sure there are no hard feelings. (You should offer to fix the bike, at which point I should consider whether I was at fault to leave the bike in harm's way.) The deliberate assault, though, requires me to defend myself rather than to be a good neighbor. This example marks the difference between an accidental and a deliberate imposition; and now the moral overtones of the difference are unmistakable.

(d)   Accordingly, we can define 'liberty' as an absence of obstacles *wrongfully* imposed by other people.

Suppose you tow my car away because I was illegally and dangerously parked, and you are a duly appointed official hired to do such things. Compare this to a situation where you tow my car away because it is a lawless town and towing my car is your way of extorting money from me for the car's return. In the second case, I am furious and perhaps terrified. In the first case, by contrast, I am irritated and disappointed, but I cannot tell myself that the obstacle to my driving away was wrongfully imposed. I decided to park in a certain way, but I cannot tell myself that my decision to park in that dangerous and illegal way ought to have been respected. When you interfere with my deciding to park there, you are in the right, not me. So, the issue highlighted by this definition concerns obstacles that create *grounds for complaint.*

Although Locke and Hobbes had negative conceptions, each of them seeing liberty as an absence of obstacles, Locke's characterization of it is slightly moralized:

> the *end of law* is not to abolish or restrain, but *to preserve and enlarge freedom . . . where there is no law, there is no freedom*: for *liberty* is, to be free from restraint and violence from others . . . freedom is not . . . a *liberty for everyman to do what he lists*: (for who could be free, when every other man's humour might domineer over him?) . . .[18]

Two centuries later, in 1881, T. H. Green would agree that freedom, rightly understood, is not a mere absence of impediments. In particular, "We do not mean a freedom that can be enjoyed by one man at a cost of a loss of freedom to others."[19] Moreover,

> When we measure the progress of society by its growth in freedom, we measure it by the increasing development and exercise on the whole of those powers of contributing to social good with which we believe the members of the society to be endowed; in short by the greater power on the part of the citizens as a body to make the most and best of themselves. Thus, though of course there can be no freedom among men who act not willingly but under compulsion, the mere enabling a man to do as he likes, is in itself no contribution to true freedom.[20]

One way to understand Green is to see him as holding that real freedom has two parts: our having opportunities to perfect ourselves in cooperation with others, and our taking responsibility for pursuing such opportunities in a way that does not compromise the opportunities of others. On this reading, real freedom on Green's view is not freedom *from* responsibility but freedom *to* be responsible: responsible, namely, for pursuing our own perfection and for making sure we do no harm in the process. Note that Green's conception of freedom is not essentially individualistic. We can freely take responsibility for ourselves as individuals, to be sure, but we can also take responsibility for ourselves as a group (as members of a family, community, church, mutual aid society, or business). So long as we are not, as Green says, under compulsion, the form of responsibility we take will be a form of freedom.[21]

On any of these conceptions, we might want to say that potential as well as actual impediments could compromise our liberty. Suppose I am a slave, but my master never tells me what to do. If as a matter of fact I live as I choose, it makes sense to say I have more freedom than other slaves have. But it also makes sense to say I am not as free as people who similarly live as they choose but have no master, because mine could at any moment start ordering me around.

On a negative conception of liberty, it will be a matter of historical contingency whether a given liberty makes for happier or healthier or wealthier lives. Negative liberties are not guaranteed to make us better off, but neither is vitamin C, or exercise – so guarantees can be beside the point. The point of negative liberty has less to do with what liberty guarantees and more to do with what liberty gives people the chance to do for themselves.

There is a difference between guaranteeing in the sense of rendering inevitable (as when government price controls render shortages inevitable) and guaranteeing in the sense of expressing a firm intention (as when government declares no child will be left behind). Clearly, *guaranteeing* something in the latter sense is no guarantee in the former sense. A legal guarantee expresses the government's commitment to produce some result, but this doesn't mean that the government will in fact produce that result. Imagine a world where, every time a government legally guarantees that people will achieve a given level of welfare, an evil demon makes sure that people do not. In that world, if you wanted people to be well off, you wouldn't want to be issuing legal guarantees. You'd *permit* people to be badly off, because that would be their only chance to prosper in that demon-plagued world.

Of course, we don't live in a world of evil demons, so perhaps the example is irrelevant. Yet plenty of factors in this world can and do disrupt, corrupt, or pervert our best-laid plans and legal guarantees. Therefore imagining a world devoid of corruption and of unintended consequences is no more relevant than imagining a world of evil demons. We have to *check* how legal guarantees actually work in our world.

Despite the lack of guarantees, history may well reveal that respecting negative liberties has a long, successful, non-accidental track record of making for better lives. In any case, we won't settle any debate about what negative liberty does for people by conceptual analysis alone.[22] We need to investigate what happens to people when negative liberties are reasonably secure, and what happens when they are not.

Positive liberty

(e) In a more positive vein, we can treat freedom as an ability to do what we want rather than as an absence of impediments. Berlin would reject this notion in an analysis of political freedom (whether positive or negative). Berlin, as has been noted, would not label the inability to jump ten feet in the air a lack of *political* freedom, unless the inability in question were caused by other people.[23] Still, even if such inabilities have no bearing on political freedom, they remain a part of the conceptual landscape of positive freedom.

Many Greeks of Plato's time conceived of freedom as a capacity for living a certain lifestyle. Having to work for a living was close to being a slave. Wage workers work under duress, or so it was thought. But if this is a contentious idea (one that Berlin and quite possibly Constant would have rejected), its undeniable grain of truth is that there is a difference between being independently wealthy and not being so. In ancient times being independently wealthy meant having *time* – being able to enjoy leisure. Nowadays even average workers are independently wealthy in this sense. They work eight hours a day, not fourteen. Typically they work five days a week, not seven.

Even on this positive (in particular, capacity-oriented) view of freedom, though, it will be a contingent matter whether increasing freedom makes for better lives. Parents want better lives for their children, but does this mean that they want their child to be free to drive the family car? Not necessarily. Even when we are adults, some of our wants are self-destructive, and having the power to satisfy them won't necessarily be good for us: it will depend on the nature of these wants, or on our level of maturity. Maturity is partly a matter of being free to satisfy self-destructive wants without actually giving in to them. Maturity is, likewise, a matter of acknowledging that actions have consequences, and that the consequences of one's actions are something for which one should take responsibility.

For these sorts of reasons, Plato rejected conceiving of positive freedom as an effective license to do what we want. He worried that people could be slaves to their desires. He viewed freedom more as a capacity for effective self-governance than as a capacity to satisfy one's appetites.[24] Plato would have been more sympathetic to something like the following:

(f)   Moralizing the previous definition, we can think of freedom as a power to do what is right.

(g)   Kant distinguished between the grounds of dignity and the grounds of full moral worth.[25] A person's dignity consists of being at liberty to choose to respect the moral law, as per (f). By contrast, a person's full moral worth, and the fullest realization of freedom, involve not only possessing liberty in the sense of (f) but going ahead and exercising it, out of reverence for moral law. Rousseau in France, like his contemporary Kant in Prussia, spoke of freedom as "obedience to a law one prescribes for oneself."[26] Chapter 6 discusses what it takes to achieve something like (g) when one already has achieved freedom in the sense of (f).

(h)   We can define 'freedom' as a power to do what is right, free from all temptation to do otherwise.

Conception (h) leaves room for stressing that there are internal as well as external impediments to freedom. Moreover, it explicitly incorporates both positive (freedom *to*) and negative (freedom *from*) elements.[27] Where Hobbes's conception often is interpreted as being more like (a), Kant's conception of what it is like to be truly, fully free (to be a *holy* will) was more like (h). This Kantian conception (which has roots in Aristotle's discussion of weakness of will and in Plato's discussion of the tyrannical soul) is moralized; it is a power to do what is right, unimpeded by contrary desire.

These last two conceptions of freedom raise a question: Is living by morality a form of servitude or of freedom? Morality demands that I do some things and refrain from doing others. Does this make me unfree? We can answer this question in more than one way; but, here too, in order to answer the question clearly, we need to be clear about how we are using the terms. In this case, the question is not empirical. We settle the question by analyzing ordinary language together with some stipulation, not by gathering social scientific observations.

For example, we may choose to place weight on ideas like the following: A person of integrity (as we understand this notion) may be unwilling to act against her principles, yet the constraints under which she lives were not arbitrarily imposed by her parents or some other authority figure. Instead, they are self-imposed. She may not dictate the content of moral law. (She cannot simply *decide* whether telling the truth is moral law.) However, she does freely choose to respect it. In a way, she seems freest of all. You may have heard the legend of Martin Luther saying before a court, "Here I stand, I can do no other." If Luther really could not have brought himself to act against his principles, does this make him unfree, or free?

Consider a poetic remark of Viktor Frankl's. "It did not really matter what we expected from life, but rather what life expected from us."[28] Frankl's remark implicitly suggests that we are here on this earth for a reason. We have a mission. A typical reader finds remarks like Frankl's to be inspiring rather than stifling. Why?

(i)   We note the possibility of a whole family of related conceptions according to which liberty is a power to do what we want, without self-imposed baggage (in other words being free of commitments or, more generally, free of plans, promises, hang-ups, and self-conceptions that no longer fit the person one has become).

This conception of freedom (i), unlike (h), is not moralized. John Stuart Mill's idea of a free person is that of "a person whose desires and impulses are his own – are the expression of his own nature, as it has been developed and modified by his own culture . . ."[29] This conception of fully rational self-direction comes closer to what Berlin seems to have meant by positive freedom.[30] Persons who are free in this sense are autonomous: legally, politically, and psychologically in a position to decide for themselves what their lives are for.

This sort of psychological freedom, and the way it relates to other forms of freedom, is the subject of our final chapter. Here we leave the discussion with a question: Insofar as freedom involves being able to do what one wants, does this mean that we can be more free simply by not wanting very much? If we are not at liberty to emigrate, can we avoid this being a limitation on our freedom simply by talking ourselves into not wanting to emigrate?[31] The connection between being free and getting what we want is subtle, and only partly a matter of linguistic convention.

Republican freedom

Philip Pettit says: "The negative conception of freedom as non-interference and the positive conception of freedom as self-mastery are not the only available ideals of liberty; a third alternative is the conception of freedom as non-domination which requires that no one is able to interfere on an arbitrary basis – at their pleasure . . ."[32] Pettit adds that this republican ideal of freedom as non-domination "regarded all those who are subject to another's arbitrary will as unfree, even if the other does not actually interfere with them; there is no interference in such a case but there is a loss of liberty. The non-interfering master remains still a master and a source of domination."[33]

We have discussed some elements of this republican conception already. The negative conception of liberty as absence of impediments wrongfully imposed by others is a related notion. Another related notion is the positive conception of liberty as self-mastery – that is, as the power to do as we will. As Pettit draws the distinction, republican freedom shares with negative freedom the idea that freedom is an absence, and with positive freedom the idea that freedom is about mastery.[34] Republican freedom does not, however, entail self-mastery, but merely its most crucial political prerequisite: the absence of mastery by others.

We will continue to speak of positive and negative liberty in the pages to come, but we remain aware that, as Berlin and as his critics stressed, positive versus negative liberty is a false dichotomy. As noted, negative and positive liberty can themselves be viewed as clusters of related concepts. Moreover, there are other fruitful ways of carving up the conceptual landscape, and Pettit's is one of them.

Responsibility

Any freedom worth defending has responsibility as a corollary. (There is an existentialist conception of freedom, associated with Jean-Paul Sartre, according to which a person is responsible for literally everything, including events that occurred before the person was born.)[35] Societies that allow their citizens latitude for self-governance also need to trust citizens with some level of responsibility for their own conduct.

Having a lot of liberty starts to sound like having a lot of responsibility. Liberal societies give people a chance to choose a conception of the life worth living; but such opportunity to invent ourselves is at the same time a responsibility. What makes liberty good, then? Perhaps having a lot of liberty and a lot of responsibility simply goes with being fully human. Or perhaps it is the prerequisite of living a dignified, *adult* human life – accepting, and not cowering from, the fact that a lot can go wrong when we have a lot of freedom.

In sum, making the best of one's prospects for living a good life – the kind of life one considers happy, or inspiring, or whatever – is inevitably a personal responsibility to a great extent. We operate in a framework of largely self-imposed constraints. We embrace some goals as realistic yet inspiring, and we reject others. We narrow down our options so that what we have left is a manageable set.[36]

Picking a conception

Time-honored conceptions of liberty tend to be time-honored for a reason. They play different, often complementary roles in common-sense thinking. So we see a point in trying to narrow down the list. If the word 'liberty' is used in so many ways, this might reveal a confusion in common language. Alternatively, the differing uses might reveal something important, such as the fact that context matters. Particular historical contexts will make some aspects of freedom (social, political, economic, religious) more salient than others. Victorian-era social pressure is one context. Slavery is another. The Protestant Reformation is another. Freedom from the risk of polio is another. President Roosevelt's call for moving toward a society that achieves "freedom from want" is another. Seeking freedom from the stress of overcommitment is yet another. There is value in trying to identify the essence that these various freedoms all share, but there is also much to gain from acknowledging the differences. Each of these freedoms is something people have for good reason struggled to secure. One is concerned with liberty in all such contexts, but the concerns one aims to mark by using the word are only related, not identical.

Although these various conceptions of liberty are sometimes treated as competitors, we often see them as being complementary. Some theorists see a minimal set of protected negative liberties as being all we need in order to launch a society that, over generations, produces explosive gains in positive liberty. Other theorists seek guarantees and do not find them in a system of mere negative liberty. I might be free from interference by government, free from oppression by a rigid caste system, and so on, yet I might remain unable to do much because of lack of wealth. Negative freedom, some would say, is the freedom to be poor, to sleep on a public sidewalk, and the like.

We would not want to let debate about negative freedom's real effects degenerate into a terminological dispute. Perhaps, as a matter of fact, negative freedom often leads to poverty. How would we know? Manipulating definitions would not tell us much. The point of defining terms is not to cut off debate about whether negative freedom leads to poverty – but to facilitate debate: not to *stipulate* that negative liberty leads by definition to prosperity, but to be precise enough to make a question answerable. For example, where there are fewer obstacles to seeking employment of one's choice (fewer migration restrictions, fewer licensing or union membership requirements), are there fewer unemployed people? If so, then we can infer (not in the way a logician deduces but rather in the way a scientist guardedly infers causal connections from empirical regularities) that negative freedom is positively liberating in that particular way. We can ask well-defined questions about the consequences of specific forms of negative freedom, such as freedom from trade restrictions or from state-mandated religion. If we can document trends, making the debate less about whether a trend is real and more about why the world sometimes departs from it, we have made progress in lowering the barriers of understanding – which is what we realistically hope for from philosophy.

Isaiah Berlin and many classical liberals are suspicious of 'positive liberty,' thinking that acknowledging its value can be misinterpreted as licensing socialism – or, more generally, as licensing bureaucrats to force us to be "free." Nevertheless, simply acknowledging positive liberty as a valuable species of the genus liberty does not commit us to any particular view about what regime promotes it best. We share Berlin's concern about giving governments a license to do whatever it takes in order to promote positive liberty. (In the real world, to give government officials the power to do x is to *hope* that officials will use it to do x, knowing that, no matter who actually ends up holding such office, the person in question will duly pay lip service to doing x, then will use the power for purposes of her own.) None of the conceptions of freedom discussed earlier entails that it should be the government's job to secure that kind of freedom. Defining terms cannot settle a government's proper role as protector or promoter of particular liberties. We must examine historical, sociological, and economic evidence to see what actually happens when people rely on any institution, including a government, to play a given role.

At the risk of oversimplification, each of the first four chapters starts with negative liberty, treated as freedom from external impediments deliberately imposed. We argue that, in various ways, securing this freedom has a history of enabling people to achieve positive freedom. That is to say, in (negatively) free countries, people generally have more *real choice*. What is real choice? Charles Taylor (1979) distinguishes between negative freedom as an opportunity concept (that is, as a state of having options) and positive freedom as an exercise concept (that is, as a state of having exercised one's options in such a way as to achieve self-realization). In speaking of "real choice," we intend to encompass both an opportunity and an exercise concept: to have real choice is to have options together with the capacities to exercise these options successfully.[37] Chapter 5 (on civil rights) might be seen mainly as starting from a republican conception of freedom as non-domination and working toward the conclusion that non-domination, too, has a history of fostering positive freedom in the sense just defined. Chapter 6 (on psychological freedom) turns to an awkward, by no means merely theoretical, puzzle lying at the core of (one sense of) positive freedom. The puzzle: we could be, as they say, our own worst enemy. We might have an enviable set of options, yet we might want too much, or too little, or know too little about what we truly want, to be able to handle our world of options as it is. In sum, not all impediments to freedom are external.

Institutions

This book's overall purpose is to tell a story of liberty, and to tell it briefly, not to *argue* for liberty or for any particular way of defining the term 'liberty.' The claims we make here are not ideologically neutral, but neither are they ideologically loaded. They don't tell you how to vote. They don't settle debates between socialists and capitalists, communitarians and liberals, modern liberals and classical liberals.

When we ask, "What sorts of institutions promote liberty?", the only answer that does not admit of counterexamples and cannot be accused of oversimplification is: it depends. Naturally, we want better answers than that. So we will risk saying more, knowing that, in a world of general trends and exceptions to the rule, whatever we go on to say will be subject to counterexamples, will run the risk of oversimplification, and of needing correction in light of new information, as historical research always is.

We focus on western Europe and on the English-speaking world partly because this is where we and most of our readers are, but more importantly because this is where most of our information is. We wish we knew more about the history of liberty in non-western cultures, but we incorporate what we know as best we can. We find the history of liberty fascinating regardless of what culture it comes from. We hope that readers will feel the same way.

The role of government

Whatever Constant and Berlin meant to be doing by warning that different conceptions of liberty are also different political ideals, the takeaway value is not that different conceptions of liberty automatically translate into different government mandates, but rather that naïve conceptions of what is possible or what is at stake can leave people vastly overconfident about the likelihood of achieving a result by creating the political power to obtain that result by force.

Constant and Berlin would have agreed. Constant, for example, writing after the French Revolution, was aware of the potentially tyrannical nature of government. Even a democratic government needs to be sharply limited by a constitution.

> The holders of authority are . . . ready to spare us all sort of troubles, except those of obeying and paying! They will say to us: "what, in the end, is the aim of your efforts, the motive of your labours, the object of all your hopes? Is it not happiness? Well, leave this happiness to us and we shall give it to you." No, Sirs, we must not leave it to them. No matter how touching such a tender commitment may be, let us ask the authorities to keep within their limits. Let them confine themselves to being just. We shall assume the responsibility of being happy for ourselves.[38]

Thus, only so much of practical consequence hangs on how we define our terms. By contrast, a lot depends on what we want out of our lives and our communities – whether we want to be free to stand or fall by our own merit, or whether we want to be free from the risks and costs that go with personal responsibility. A lot depends on how big a hammer we want our government to be, which in part turns on how confident we are that the hammer will be used by, rather than against, our children.[39] In sum, it matters that we understand: a) what our options are; b) that we did choose among them; and c) that in many ways large and small, as individuals and as societies, we will face the choice again.

Beyond ideal theory

What makes a hammer good? One answer is: hammers are good insofar as they serve a purpose.[40]

To say what makes a hammer good, we wouldn't normally think we'd need to know what an *ideal* hammer is. Neither would we need to learn what sort of hammer would be useful to angels or giants, as intermediate steps in evaluating our own hammers as pale imitations of tools fit for the hands of angels or giants. All that matters for our purposes is whether the hammer works for us just as we are.

Institutions, as we see them, are like hammers. Institutions are tools. Institutions that help real people live together in peace and prosperity are to that extent worth preserving. Institutions that do the opposite, whatever they might symbolize or however blameless or famous their creators may have been, leave us without a reason to preserve them.

John Rawls, the author of *A Theory of Justice*, has another approach to evaluating institutions. He thinks that political philosophers who study institutions ought to start with what he calls 'ideal theory,' which involves asking "what kind of regime . . . would be right and just, could it be effectively and workably maintained?"[41] He assumes that people are motivated by a sense of justice, fully understand what they are doing, and will accordingly be competent and uncorrupted. Rawls then asks which institutions are the most just under those conditions. His question is probably worth answering at some point. We, likewise, might want to know at some point what sort of hammer would be best for a giant or an angel. We learn something about hammers when we answer that question. But a theory of institutions, for us, is about how people achieve peace, a rising standard of living, and mutual respect in our actual complex world. Thus Rawls's question has little (possibly nothing) to do with ours: "Which institutions have a history of enabling people to achieve peace, a rising standard of living, and mutual respect under real-world conditions, where the willingness and the ability to comply are variable, and very much depend on what citizens are being asked to do?"[42]

One misuse of ideal theory would result from inferring that, if some institutions are best under 'ideal' conditions, then our real-world institutions ought to come as close as possible to those institutions. Not so. Different conditions call for different tools. Ideal conditions might call for a wrench where non-ideal conditions call for a hammer. In other words, ideal theory is like designing cars on the assumption that they'll never encounter slippery pavement, or will never be driven by bad drivers. If we had no such worries, we might not bother installing air bags. Here and now, though, we have compelling practical reasons not to build cars like that. Analogously, if power didn't corrupt, if people were omniscient and unfailingly altruistic, we might want to entrust government with a great deal of power. But, if people are corruptible, if power is above all what corrupts, if people's generosity depends very much on circumstances, and if those who hold power never know exactly what will happen when they implement a given policy, the kind of government we have reason to favor might be far more limited.

Someone trying to do non-ideal theory would ask: How much power do we want our leaders to have, given that they are going to be about as good as actual leaders have been, historically speaking?[43] Both of us have heard students say: "This goal of social justice is so important that, if we need something like a KGB to achieve it, so be it. We'll just have to make sure the right people run the KGB." But there is no such thing as making sure that the right people run the KGB. People who gravitate toward KGB jobs do so for reasons of their own. Philosophers don't get to stipulate that their reasons are noble.

Beyond non-ideal theory

This book is not about ideal theory. It is not really about non-ideal theory either. We are not trying to say how the principles of justice for an ideal world would have to be modified so as to be fit for the non-ideal world we actually live in. Our first aim is simply to tell a story about liberty. This is not easy. First, it is no easy matter for historians to get their facts right. Even celebrated experts sometimes misinterpret archeological evidence that falls squarely within their area of greatest expertise. Second, there is no such thing as saying every true thing under the sun. We have to be intensely selective, and, as we judge what to say, our story inevitably will not be the same as the one that someone else would have told.

As we go through the history, we will be theorizing from the bottom up, building toward conjectures about why histories unfold as they do. When we imagine an ideal we at the same time try to imagine what it would be like to get to that ideal starting from where we are.

Finally, we offer piecemeal hypotheses about what worked and what didn't. As we discuss in our final chapter, it is hard to avoid being biased; indeed few succeed. In particular, people often decide what to believe, then look for evidence that seems to confirm that they decided correctly. This bias is hard to avoid; but some books are a joy to read because they simply ask a question, then follow the trail of evidence wherever it may lead, celebrating such surprises as come the author's way. Not many books are like that. But that is our model.

So what sorts of institutions tend to make people free? Which ones make people better off? Many works on liberty try to answer these questions from the armchair, by imagining how potential institutions might do. In this book we look at how real institutions have done.

We conclude that the rule of law is needed in order to provide a framework that encourages experimentation and entrepreneurship. Historically, societies that get their property rights more or less correct tend to achieve prosperity; societies that do not always fail. Cultures of tolerance and openness to change lead to greater prosperity than do closed, intolerant cultures. Societies that economize on moral motivation – working with, rather than against, self-interest – fare better than societies that do not.[44]

The result of freedom of thought, of freedom of association, of the division of labor within firms and of the specialization of roles that evolves between firms is that society becomes an unimaginably complex web of cooperation, moving ever further away from individual self-sufficiency. Although it may sound somewhat paradoxical, this is actually a contribution to positive freedom, because, as particular roles within society become redundant, a given individual grows less dependent on particular providers of a given service. Freedom in the positive sense can and sometimes does burgeon along with the increasing complexity of this web of interdependence. This book is a story of those preconditions of real choice slowly coming together.

Discussion

1 What promotes positive freedom? What is the historical record? Are there cases where people had to choose between respecting negative liberty and promoting positive liberty? If so, what happened? When people have to choose between these two forms, do they end up getting neither?

2 Are there circumstances where simply respecting negative liberty is a way (perhaps even the best way) of promoting positive freedom? If so, what would those circumstances be?

3 A constitutional framework is a set of relatively fixed rules formulated at a high level of generality. What else does a society need so as to promote positive freedom effectively?

4 Suppose we say the point of government is to promote liberty, and the point of liberty is to promote welfare. What would we need to show in order to turn these premises into a solid argument for some form of welfare state?

5 To Marx, your degree of freedom in exercising an option depends on how unacceptable your next best alternative is. Suppose Alf does not mind working, whereas Betty would (almost) rather die than have to work for a living. Does this mean that Betty, by virtue of having to work, is more *unfree* than Alf, or simply that Betty *resents* her unfreedom more than Alf does?

6   In a marketplace governed by voluntary exchange, there is a general truth that, if you want to induce others to provide you with goods and services, you have to reciprocate, which is to say that you have to work in return for the work others do for you. In some sense, we would be more free if we did not have to reciprocate – if we could consume products of other people's labor for free, without having to offer our own labor in return. Having to reciprocate – to pay for what we consume – makes us less free than if we could consume for free, where 'free' means at someone else's expense. Along this dimension, how free is it good to be?

Acknowledgments

For helpful comments, we thank Jerry Gaus, Benjamin Garcia Helgado, Jeff McMahon, Guido Pincione, and Horacio Spector.

Notes

1. Spiegel 1983, 2.
2. Nietzsche 1994, 57.
3. Gerald MacCallum has argued that all conceptions of freedom have something in common. Ian Carter summarizes:

> MacCallum defines the basic concept of freedom – the concept on which everyone agrees – as follows: a subject, or agent, is free from certain constraints, or preventing conditions, to do or become certain things. Freedom is therefore a triadic relation – that is, a relation between *three things*: an agent, certain preventing conditions, and certain doings or becomings of the agent. Any statement about freedom or unfreedom can be translated into a statement of the above form by specifying *what* is free or unfree, *from* what it is free or unfree, and what it is free or unfree *to do or become*. Any claim about the presence or absence of freedom in a given situation will therefore make certain assumptions about what counts as an agent, what counts as a constraint or limitation on freedom, and what counts as a purpose that the agent can be described as either free or unfree to carry out. (Carter 2003, 9)

4. Berlin 1997, 177.

5. See Horacio Spector 2009, "Two Dimensions of Freedom," manuscript, 2ff. To the contrast between negative and positive freedom, Horacio Spector adds an orthogonal contrast between natural and civil liberty. The two distinctions, conjoined, define four conceptions of liberty: (1) negative natural liberty is freedom as non-interference (mere liberty); (2) negative civil liberty is civil liberty (which adds rights and immunities to mere liberty so as to secure non-domination, that is, freedom from arbitrary power); (3) positive natural liberty is the capacity for individual self-government (which adds powers); and (4) positive civil liberty is the capacity for civil (collective) self-government.

6. Carter's entry in the *Stanford Encyclopedia of Philosophy* (Carter 2007) distinguishes between the location and the source of obstacles.

7. Berlin 1997, 169.

8. Ibid., 168. Berlin's reference to historians may be to Lord Acton, who said much the same thing.

9. As related by legal scholar Isaac Lifshitz in conversation, Jerusalem, 2008.

10. Again, the technical distinctions we use, such as positive versus negative, are getting at something, but our subject here is not technical. The edges of these concepts are notoriously hard to illuminate. We are seeking to minimize the vagueness and the potential for misunderstanding, even as we accept that eliminating all possibility of vagueness and misunderstanding is not a realistic goal. Success consists in being able to use various distinctions so as to triangulate and to develop a *fairly* accurate sense of what we are talking about.

11. Constant 1988, 311.

12. Ibid.

13. Ibid., 309.

14. For a superb discussion of Berlin, see Carter 2007.

15. Miller (1991, 10) gives a shorter, differently organized list. We do not pretend that ours is the best list for all purposes, but merely that it serves present purposes well enough.

16. Hobbes 1994, 79. The context is that Hobbes is describing the impediments to the Right of Nature as the liberty of people to do whatever they judge to be most conducive to self-preservation.

17. Hobbes 1994, 79.

18. Locke 1980, 32. We say that Locke's characterization is 'slightly' moralized insofar as the idea is not to define the moral so much as the practical limits of liberty. It takes a certain mutual forbearance for us to be truly free to achieve what we want to achieve.

19. Green 1986, 199.

20. Ibid.

21. Green is often seen as a transitional thinker, situated between the classical (individualistic) and the modern (welfare statist) forms of liberalism. On our interpretation, though, Green's conception of freedom does not beg the question against classical liberalism; rather, it is neutral between these broad categories of liberalism.

22. We acknowledge the possibility that conceptual analysis alone might establish a given liberty's intrinsic value.

23. Berlin says this in a discussion of negative liberty, but he never suggests he would categorize such inability as a lack of liberty of any kind.

24. This seems to be the sort of conception that Locke was rejecting when he asked readers to consider the circumstance of a man finding himself in the same room with a person he longs to be with. Without question, he is in the room willingly; but, unknown to him, the door to the room has been locked from the outside, so that he could not leave if he wanted to. Locke is arguing in this passage that liberty is not a matter of doing what one wills, but a matter of having the power to do or forbear to do what one has a mind to do (Locke 1996, 96).

25. Kant 1996, 61–2 and passim.

26. Rousseau 1968, 65.

27. MacCallum (1967) argues, plausibly, that the best way of analyzing freedom is as a three-place relation specifying what agent is free from what impediments to achieve what end.

28. Frankl 1997, 122.

29. Mill 1978, 57.

30. Berlin took a dim view of rationalism in politics, though, so he would not have wanted to be seen as endorsing rational self-direction as an ideal of *collective* self-determination.

31. Berlin claims that "every form of autonomy has in it some element of this attitude. I eliminate the obstacles in my path by abandoning the path" (1997, 182). He goes on to say that "the definition of negative liberty as the ability to do what one wishes . . . will not do. . . . Ascetic

self-denial may be a source of integrity or serenity and spiritual strength, but it is difficult to see how it can be called an enlargement of liberty" (186).

32. Pettit 1997, 271.

33. Ibid.

34. Ibid., 22.

35. The idea is, on its face, absurd, yet there is something interesting here. When someone says, "I am *not* responsible for the Holocaust. I descend from Germans, but the Holocaust happened before I was born," the person is freely *choosing* to regard her responsibilities as limited in this way. There are of course reasons for so choosing. On the other hand, it would be equally intelligible for someone to say, "I claim responsibility for the Holocaust in the sense that, even though it happened before I was born, I choose to take responsibility for making amends, for making sure it never happens again, and simply for remembering what happened." What existentialism should insist on is that people are *not* at liberty to see themselves as not responsible for *their choices*. Seeing oneself as responsible for one's choices is a core constituent of being of good faith.

36. See our final chapter.

37. See also Kant's distinction between *Wilkur* (autonomy as a capacity to choose to be moral) and *Wille* (autonomy as the actual choice to be moral). As Horacio Spector notes in his unpublished paper of 2009 (see above, n. 5), Locke distinguishes a collective form of autonomy when he defines civil liberty. "The Natural Liberty of Man is to be free from any Superior Power on Earth, and not to be under the Will or Legislative Authority of Man, but to have only the Law of Nature for his Rule." Civil liberty is a liberty "to be under no other Legislative Power, but that established, by consent, in the Common-wealth, nor under the Dominion of any Will, or Restraint of any Law, but what the Legislative shall enact, according to the Trust put in it" (Locke 1980, opening paragraph of chapter IV). Spector also notes that Rousseau likewise adopts a collective conception of positive political liberty as democratic self-government. According to Rousseau, in the civil state we acquire *moral freedom*, "which alone makes man the master of himself; for to be governed by appetite alone is slavery, while obedience to a law one prescribes to oneself is freedom" (Rousseau 1968, 65).

38. Constant 1988, 326.
39. When someone rejects a cherished government program (e.g. rent-control), it is tempting to assume that the person rejects our values (such as affordable housing for the poor). However, even if you conclude that the government ought to promote some end, this doesn't tell you how it ought to do it. In particular, your conclusion doesn't prescribe direct or indirect means for the government to promote the end in question. For example, a government might attempt to promote commerce directly, by creating new corporations, offering subsidies and grants to businesses, providing tariff protections, and buying products; or indirectly, by providing a basic institutional framework (such as the rule of law, constitutional representative democracy, courts, and a well-functioning property rights regime). Once you settle on an end for the government, which way of achieving it – direct or indirect – works best is always an empirical question. Aiming at something directly is no guarantee of getting it.
40. What would make this a good answer? Perhaps the answer itself is good or bad insofar as it gets the job done or not – and whether it gets the job done depends on the nature of the job. It is one thing if our purpose is to start a conversation. But, if our purpose were instead to provide a definition which even the cleverest philosopher could not devise a counterexample for, we would be a long way from getting *that* job done. A hammer is a tool; in a less obvious way, so are the words we use to describe it.
41. Rawls 2001, 137. Rawls imagines away corruption and moral hazard. So, while he is asking what is possible, he is not asking what is likely. Elsewhere Rawls asks: "what would a just democratic society be like under reasonably favorable but still possible historical conditions allowed by the laws and tendencies of the social world? What ideals and principles would such a society try to realize given the circumstances of justice in a democratic culture as we know them?" (Rawls 2007, 11).
42. Rawls disagrees. He thinks the answer to his question tells us that certain types of social regimes (which Rawls calls property-owning democracy and liberal socialism) are intrinsically more just than others (state socialism, welfare state capitalism, and laissez-faire capitalism). His theory leaves it open that, in the real world, we might have to choose

one of the latter three regimes over the others, if it does the best real-world job of bringing about justice. However, Rawls's way of evaluating social regimes appears inconsistent, as he treats property-owning democracy and liberal socialism under ideal conditions – for instance he assumes that economic efficiency is achievable without private ownership of the means of production (see Rawls 1971, 239); then he compares these idealizations with the two capitalist systems and with state socialism as he takes the latter alternatives to work in real-world conditions. For instance he puts enormous weight on his assumption that, in the real world, the economic inequality allowed by capitalism compromises political liberty (see Rawls 1993, 329). For an especially careful consideration of the empirical grounds for this assumption by an especially acute philosopher, see Gaus (2010).

43. "A sound argument for institutional change must avoid jumping between the real and the ideal. An argument that an institution is bad or unjust in some way is presumably about a real institution. Hence, an argument for changing or abolishing that institution must specify a real or realistic alternative" (Shapiro 2007, 6).

44. See Brennan and Hamlin 1995.

Chapter 1

A Prehistory of Liberty:
Forty Thousand Years Ago

THESIS: *The greatest threat to and the best hope for a better life, in the long run, comes from other human beings. Historically, trade has been a great liberator.*

Prehistory of Commerce

Homo sapiens became the wisest of primates around forty thousand years ago, when we learned to make deals with strangers.[1] Many steps in our social evolution involved expanding the spheres of mutually advantageous commerce. Paradoxically, we are inclined, perhaps even biologically programmed, to see commerce as a zero-sum game: that is, we see people who profit by selling us food or tools as getting rich at our expense. Eons ago, though, brave souls began to imagine what human beings could do, and saw that the key to a better life was trade. Thus began our liberation from the brutality of life as cave-dwellers.

As we spread, our closest cousins, the Neanderthals, went extinct.[2] Why? Neanderthals were stronger than *Homo sapiens* and had larger brains. They existed for half a million years, far longer than *Homo sapiens* has existed so far. What drove them to extinction? One theory is that *H. sapiens* had better weapons and systematically exterminated the Neanderthal. Archeologists now consider this unlikely, for there is no evidence of such slaughter: no evidence of such weapons, no mass graves, no battlegrounds.[3] Another theory is that *H. Neanderthalensis* was absorbed into the human genome via interbreeding: a not uncommon path to extinction. However, geneticists have recently said that this didn't happen either, since Neanderthal genes are being reconstructed, and so far no genetic mark of our inheriting them has been found.[4] On the other hand, evidence from paleontology is suggestive. Recently found skeletal remains dating back 30,000 years bear both modern human and Neanderthal characteristics.[5]

Another possibility is that we may be trying to explain the wrong thing. Extinction is, after all, normal. The real question may be, not "Why did Neanderthals go extinct?" so much as "Whatever drove *H. Neanderthalensis* to extinction, why didn't it take out *H. sapiens* at same time?"

Learning to cooperate

Ian Tattersall speculates that modern social and economic behaviors express an underlying capacity – a capacity recently acquired, which Neanderthals did not have.[6] Recent research speculates that the ascent of *H. sapiens* may have been less about developing superior military gear and more about something relatively mundane: an evolving propensity to truck and barter. There is no evidence of major technological progress in Neanderthal societies. Neither is there evidence of trade between groups. Neanderthals did not experiment much, nor did they learn from each other's experiments. Neither their technology nor their social organization changed much over hundreds of thousands of years. Five hundred thousand years ago, Neanderthals formed hierarchical hunter–gatherer groups of about two dozen. Forty thousand years ago, Neanderthals were still living in isolated groups of two dozen hunter–gatherers. It is hard to imagine a human society remaining so static for 460 years, let alone 460,000.

Thus Horan's, Bulte's, and Shogren's explanation of why Neanderthals disappeared and modern humans flourished is that the former were not entrepreneurs. Cultural cross-fertilization did not occur. By contrast, modern humans evidently practiced some rudimentary division of labor almost from the start, engaging in both intra- and inter-group trade.[7] They were innovators.

If Neanderthals were so smart, why did they not learn the way humans learned? George Grantham's explanation is that what distinguished humans from Neanderthals "was not their respective cranial volumes, which overlap, but modern man's capacity to articulate consonants and vowels required to sound an extensive vocabulary of distinct words."[8] Human adaptations for speech – such as a descended larynx that increased the risks of choking and a flattening of the 'snout' that increased the airway's curvature and thus reduced aerobic efficiency – were costly in terms of natural selection, so the benefits of speech had to be substantial. And, of course, they were. In a more recent paper, Horan, Bulte, and Shogren explain the benefits of speech in terms of incremental gains in the ability to make one's intentions known in an environment where cooperation was literally a matter of life and death.[9]

As the faculty of speech evolved, so could complex trading relationships built on a mutual understanding of such variables as the time and place of one's next meeting, the exact nature of what was to be delivered, contingency plans, and so on. Grantham notes that "Adam Smith was the first, and long the only, economist to observe that the ability to communicate is a precondition for voluntary exchange. That capacity is tightly linked to the faculty of speech."[10] As the potential benefits of trade mushroomed, so would the selection pressure on the ability to articulate one's thoughts and intentions. This pair of capacities – for cooperation and for articulate speech – would have evolved together.

Neuroeconomist Paul Zak writes:

> One hypothesis for the rapid and extraordinary growth of the human brain is that this occurred to support increasingly complex social behaviors. In particular, cooperation with nonkin is the hallmark of modern civilizations. Cooperation between unrelated individuals enabled the specialization of labor and the generation of surplus in societies, fueling technological advance and increasing living standards.[11]

As human society grew, cooperation increasingly became a matter of communicating and working with strangers. Thus the capacity – and the need – for gossip evolved, together with the possibility of having a reputation. One needs to be able to receive and to transmit information regarding whether particular trading partners play fair. As the possibility of relying on a partner's reputation evolves, so does the possibility of having extended trading networks.[12] At human sites (but not at Neanderthal sites), archeologists find tools made hundreds of miles away. Trade goods, then, traveled long distances, linking together different language groups and different cultures, contributing massively to the spread of ideas and cultures. To see how other groups do things is to see new, and sometimes better, ways of doing things. This very idea – that there may be better ideas out there – may itself have been the most inspiring of all.

Prehistory of Technology

Many advances began with experimentation and were spread by traders and other travelers who knew a successful experiment and a better idea when they saw one. For example:

> The shift to plant-rich diets is complicated because plant foods are typically deficient in essential nutrients, have toxic compounds to protect them from herbivore attack, and are labor-intensive to prepare.

Finding a mix of plant and animal foods that provides an adequate diet at a feasible labor cost is not a trivial problem. For example, New World farmers eventually discovered that boiling maize in wood ashes improved its nutritional value. The hot alkaline solution breaks down an otherwise indigestible seed coat protein that contains some lysine, an amino acid that is low in maize relative to human requirements. . . . The value of this practice could not have been obvious to its inventors or later adopters [they had no idea what lysine is] yet most American populations that made heavy use of maize employed it.[13]

Herbert Muller says:

The range in choice was widened by trade; for if the Neolithic village was basically or potentially self-sufficient, it chose not to remain so. The earliest villages have yielded materials (such as obsidian) the nearest source of which was hundreds of miles away; and trade grew ever brisker as Neolithic culture developed.[14]

Nevertheless, to move trade goods over long distances, people had to be able to count on potential trading partners being willing to deal on consensual terms. They needed a rudimentary rule of law, and of property rights in particular – you had to identify and respect the difference between what you brought and what someone else brought to the table – or trade would never get off the ground.

Trade gets off the ground when people feel so secure in their possessions that a transformation occurs: people begin to think of themselves as being able simply to count on having a right to say no. They can spend less of their time defending what they produced and more time producing it. People no longer see themselves as needing to be careful to conceal any valuables they possess. They cart their product to the market and literally *advertise*, displaying their valuables for all to see. Indeed there comes a time when, far from needing to hoard possessions and to keep them secret so as to avoid being a target for pirates, people need laws to curb the incentive to *exaggerate* the value of one's possessions.

In short, as society evolves, people begin to offer their goods in trade, insofar as they feel secure in their right to decline offers they do not welcome. The phenomenon of people advertising the fruit of their productivity heralds revolutionary progress in achieving a degree of security of possession that is the hallmark of a liberal, commercial society.[15]

We tend to imagine a history of nomadic tribes gradually settling down as they began to develop crops, then coalescing into villages and finally into cities. According to Jane Jacobs, though, cities must have come first, for "agriculture is not even tolerably productive unless it incorporates many goods and services produced in cities or transplanted from cities. The most thoroughly rural countries exhibit the most unproductive agriculture. The most thoroughly urbanized countries, on the other hand, are precisely those that produce food most abundantly."[16]

On the other hand, Paul Seabright remarks:

> Citizens of the industrialized market economies have lost their sense of wonder at the fact that they can decide spontaneously to go out in search of food, clothing, furniture, and thousands of other useful, attractive, frivolous, or life-saving items, and that when they do, somebody will have anticipated their actions and thoughtfully made such items available for them to buy. For our ancestors who wandered the plains in search of game, or scratched the earth to grow grain under a capricious sky, such a future would have seemed truly miraculous, and the possibility that it might come about without the intervention of any overall controlling intelligence would have seemed incredible. Even when adventurous travelers opened up the first trade routes and the citizens of Europe and Asia first had the chance to sample each other's luxuries, their safe arrival was still so much subject to chance and nature as to make it a source of drama and excitement as late as Shakespeare's day.[17]

But the emerging class of merchants, who made it their business to develop commercially viable grains and to domesticate livestock, was even more vulnerable than were relatively mobile traders. They and their crops were sitting ducks. Farmers had to count on the rule of law even to a greater extent than did other traders. They needed others to respect their right to make a living in peace.

Alternatives to war

However, peace was not easy to find. Steven Pinker says,

> many intellectuals have embraced the image of peaceable, egalitarian, and ecology-loving natives. But in the past two decades anthropologists have gathered data on life and death in pre-state societies rather than accepting the warm and fuzzy stereotypes. What did they find? In a nutshell: Hobbes was right, Rousseau was wrong.[18]

Pinker means that hunter–gatherers tend also to be warriors and raiders.[19] As states and civilizations grow, the propensity to make wars against neighbors does not disappear. States can and do organize warfare on a more massive scale, and technology enables warriors to be more lethal. Even so, wars have (by some measures) become less destructive. Lawrence Keeley and other archeologists note that, in contemporary hunter–gatherer tribes (our best approximation of our past), the percentage of males dying in war can be as high as 60 percent, as compared to just a few percent among Europeans in the twentieth century despite two world wars.[20] Why? One explanatory factor is that civilized societies find occupations for adult males other than hunting and fighting. Soldiering becomes a specialized vocation and most adult males belong to classes of non-combatants. When people turn to agriculture and begin to make a living in ways that render them sitting ducks to raiders, the imperative to develop a rule of law so as to protect these more settled ways of life becomes pressing. In the process, advancing societies make the life of peaceful trade ever more interesting, more secure, and more rewarding.

Written language

So, we believe that trade emerged about 40,000 years ago, and farming about 10,000 years ago. Closer to historical times, a new set of possibilities arose with written language. Language in general, whether written or spoken, is an unimaginably elaborate, delicate, rapidly evolving form of cooperation, and its evolution is typically spontaneous: that is to say, it is law-like and rule-governed, yet not the product of any legislature. Muller describes Sumeria as the earliest of the civilizations of the Near East.[21] Samuel Kramer describes how Sumerians invented a large-scale drainage system, a large-scale bureaucratic government, formal laws, standard weights and measures so as to facilitate markets, a medium of exchange, institutions of credit, and devices for keeping time.[22] They developed cuneiform writing around 3000 BC. They invented 'schools' around 2500 BC.[23]

In the late 1870s, a set of stone tablets of Sumerian provenance was discovered and dated back to 2350 BC. Some of the tablets chronicle people's complaints about a massive, ubiquitous, and rising tax burden.[24] Not much is known about this culture, and many of the conjectures made are contested; but in any case one word from these tablets, rendered as *amagi*, is thought to be the earliest instance of referring to the concept of freedom in a written language. *Amagi* means literally 'return to the mother.' It is a matter of conjecture how this came to be used as a word for freedom. However, J. N. Postgate notes that the word was used to denote the freeing of persons enslaved for debt. So, when a document testified that one's debt was repaid, in some cases this was tantamount to affirming a person's status as a free citizen. People would speak of a man freed from debt servitude as having been returned to his family, or returned to his mother.[25]

In the tablets discovered in the 1870s, the word *amagi* was used to pay homage to King Urukagina, whom Muller describes as the first social reformer known to history. Urukagina became king when the citizens of Lagash in Mesopotamia (a Sumerian culture) revolted, threw off their hereditary dynastic rulers, and appointed him instead. In addition to cutting or abolishing many taxes, Urukagina developed a series of reforms that may represent the first instance of a judicial code and of a formal rule of law. Although no record of the code's exact content survives, some of its elements (1) upheld the rights of peasants to refuse to enter into business deals with citizens of higher ranks; (2) obliged higher ranking citizens to pay in silver for what they purchased from people of lower ranks rather than to intimidate their fellow citizens into accepting unenforceable promises in lieu of actual payment; and (3) established rights for widows and orphans.[26]

Muller also reflects on the ups and downs of Sumer's invention of the city:

> The inevitable constraints imposed by the more complex life of civilization may likewise obscure the positive gains in freedom. . . . The young in particular might enjoy such opportunities; whereas education in the village trained the child to do and to be just like his father, education in Sumer might train him to do something different or to become something better. . . . The always crowded, restless, noisy, wicked city would in time be deplored by many writers, denounced by many more preachers; and it would always remain the mecca of bright, ambitious young men from the countryside.[27]

Mycenaean Greece, roughly from 1400 to 1200 BC, was a cluster of small states in which a rural population was dominated by a fortified palace.[28] However, the Mycenaean kingdoms collapsed and the eastern Mediterranean region regressed to tribalism. The reason for the collapse is not known. Conquest or natural cataclysm may well have played a role, but Lewis Mumford suggests that one of the key problems was cultural: the Mycenaeans glorified war and piracy, and had an aristocratic contempt for work and for trade. Mumford claims that "the Mycenaean ascendancy seems never to have developed the permanent urban forces essential to further growth: the code of written law, the bureaucratic controls, the system of taxation, that would have ensured its continuity for even a millennium. Power, dependent chiefly on personal force, soon crumbled."[29] From 1200 to around 900 BC, literacy, trade, architecture, and urban life in general disintegrated along with the rule of law.

One benefit of this collapse is that the disappearance of written language in cuneiform script set the stage for the eventual emergence and triumph of the alphabet, as it was developed and spread by Phoenician traders.[30] Cuneiform writing survived in various cultures, but the symbols were clumsy and hard to learn by comparison, so the people involved in commerce, or more generally those who wanted to be literate, "naturally preferred the much more economical and efficient alphabet. Common men could now easily learn to read and write, little artisans and merchants to keep their own accounts. The aristocratic monopoly on learning might be broken."[31] Literacy remained for a long time the trademark of a particular profession – scribes; but these were becoming numerous, laying the foundations of literacy as a general phenomenon.

Toward the end of this period long-distance shipping was reinvigorated through improvements in hull construction and through the development of a rigging that permitted sails to be furled or unfurled (like a Venetian blind), thus allowing for larger ships, which could respond well to changing wind conditions.[32] Rudimentary states reappeared around 750 BC. Mumford writes:

> The Greeks, it seemed, had in some degree freed themselves from the outrageous fantasies of unqualified power that Bronze Age religion and Iron Age technology had fostered: their cities were cut close to the human measure, and were delivered from the paranoid claims of quasi-divine monarchs, with all the attending compulsions and regimentations of militarism and bureaucracy.[33]

Populations began to grow. Mumford adds: "The transposition of the village into the polis, the place where people come together, not just by birth or habit, but consciously, in pursuit of a better life, takes place before our eyes in Greece."[34]

Bronze and iron

Muller says that the Bronze Age was one in which metal was largely
the preserve of the ruling class, owing to the scarcity of the basic ingredients – namely copper and tin. Ordinary peasants continued to use
tools made of stone. The Iron Age began in the Near East and Greece
in the twelfth century BC, and it was revolutionary. Although copper
and tin are scarce, iron is common. A smith needs higher tempera-
tures and greater expertise to smelt iron, but, once people developed
a workable process – and this was spurred by the aforementioned
collapse of Mycenaean trading networks, which made tin so much
harder to acquire – iron tools became cheap.[35]

> An unprecedented number of new tools were fashioned, among them
> spaces, tongs, shears, and planes, while oxen were made to work corn
> mills and olive crushers. . . . Above all, iron was a boon to the little
> man. Able to possess his own metal tools, he might now become an
> independent farmer or artisan, thereby providing more opportunities
> for small merchants too. A growing middle class, accustomed to
> individual enterprise, might grow critical of ancient traditions that
> impeded such enterprise . . . The Phoenicians, who anticipated the new
> age by living chiefly on trade, were inspired by commercial needs to
> invent their alphabet shortly before its dawn.[36]

In short, rich people could switch to iron from *bronze* tools; poor
people could switch to iron from *stone* tools. Iron was thus an equal-
izer; but, more relevantly for our present purpose, iron was a liberator. For people unable to afford bronze, iron was literally their
ticket out of the stone age.

Prehistory of Slavery

Early Greek city–states were relatively weak. For most, the main
political unit was the *oikos*, a large agrarian household or estate

consisting of the master, his immediate family, some extended family members, and a host of slaves and servants. The reward system of the *oikos* shows freedom's lack of value for the archaic Greeks. Status in the hierarchy was defined in terms of closeness to the master. A slave would be rewarded not with manumission but with increased responsibility, independence, and with being moved closer to the master's family.[37] There was no safety in, and no desire for, leaving the *oikos* in order to be independent. More generally, there is little evidence from the Homeric and archaic periods of Greek society reflecting on the value of freedom. But this was about to change.

Beyond barter, for better and for worse

Coinage emerges in the seventh century BC in Lydia, and the frontier of possibilities for production and trade expands yet again.[38] As Muller says,

> The Greeks, who most fully exploited the democratic potentialities of the alphabet, were also quick to exploit the invention of coinage, about 600 BC, which they credited to the Lydians, founders of a new kingdom in Asia Minor. Replacing bars of metal, standardized coins facilitated trade and encouraged industry, but the more revolutionary innovation was *small change*. Early coins, of silver and gold, had been in denominations too high for the daily transactions of the poor; with small change the little man could buy and sell things, in small quantities.[39]

Concerning these two inventions – coined money and a written alphabet – Mumford writes that these "refinements of number and writing were prime tools of the mind, though they first developed as essential notations in long-distance trading and commercial accountancy."[40]

Both Patterson and Muller note, however, that, in the immediate aftermath of the full monetization of the marketplace, inequality began to grow and some people's investments left them descending into debt servitude, while others were accumulating substantial wealth. According to Patterson, toward the end of the seventh century the situation worsened, and a new phenomenon emerged: the selling of Greek debtors into slavery, including selling them abroad. We infer from the phenomenon of slaves being bought and sold on international markets that this was full-blown slavery, as we understand it today. Presumably the advent of slavery in this horrific form, whose victims included unlucky neighbors and not merely 'barbarians' from non-Greek lands, sharpened the awareness of the difference between being and not being free.[41]

One may expect a rule of law to evolve into a framework for the emergence of predictable prices. This is a crucial historical moment, because predictable prices tell us more efficiently than anything else how to be of greatest service to other people and how to prosper in the process. But in the seventh century BC, it seems, the rule of law needed to catch up with the commerce for which it was supposed to provide a framework. Money, in its early inception in Lydia, seems not to have been a win–win game. It is reminiscent of the contemporary scare with subprime mortgage lending. Mortgage lending is a massively liberating institution, one of the primary factors enabling average people to become home owners. Yet credit is also a proverbially dangerous servant and a terrible master.[42]

Many societies experiment with debt servitude, but this quasi-voluntary slavery is not what a lover of liberty wants to see in practice. The philosophical question here is: should people be free to give away their liberty? Should people be free to *risk* giving it away, in effect putting up their liberty as collateral to secure a loan? Or should the status of free citizen be treated as an *inalienable* right?[43] No matter how, or how much, we value liberty, it is not obvious how to answer this question. Interestingly, though, the places we call free countries today all repudiated the right of citizens to sell their freedom, or even to put their freedom at risk by offering it as collateral to secure a loan. It seems that all western societies eventually opted in favor of inalienable rights, refusing to enforce unconscionable contracts. In any case, the question is fundamental, and seventh-century BC Greeks had not yet come to grips with it.[44] The market had run ahead of the rule of law, and members of all classes began to appreciate the danger.

Villages a few miles inland, like Athens and Corinth, with access to the sea yet defensible against pirates, became great cities.[45] Population increases over the next couple of centuries meant increasing demands for wood used in building, and also for land and agricultural products. In turn, this implied an increasing pressure not to become agriculturally self-sufficient but to do precisely the opposite: to use the land so as to produce whatever crop could be used to *purchase* the greatest quantity of food. Under the circumstances, producing enough food domestically to feed everyone was becoming out of the question. Increasingly, Greeks had to import food, which meant that they had to have something to sell. The more their products could command in exchange for foreign agricultural products, the better. So the increasing demand for foreign trade led Greeks to turn their own agricultural land over to producing fruit and olives for export.[46] As monocrop plantations came to dominate the rural landscape, slaves began to play a larger economic role.

Freedom became a political issue around the turn of the sixth century. Solon was elected *archon* (chief magistrate) in Athens in 594/3 BC. Athenians along with people from all over Attica were defaulting on their loans, so freemen were being turned into slaves. In response to a growing crisis and a potential political upheaval, Solon cancelled all existing debts and introduced legal reforms guaranteeing that freemen could no longer be enslaved for failing to pay a debt. Solon's laws forbade citizens from using their freedom as collateral to secure their loans. Solon thus introduced the first *inalienable* right of freedom. Apparently, Attica's experience with debt-bondage was repeated in Rome, and with the same result: a prohibition was passed against debt-bondage for freemen.[47]

In Persia, Cyrus the Great became king in 546 BC and proceeded to build an empire marked by general toleration for cultural differences, especially where religion was concerned.[48] His tolerance of Jews, in particular, was gratefully noted. He was the only Gentile to be classified as a messiah (a king divinely appointed) in the Jewish Bible. Even to this day, Iranians refer to Cyrus as 'the Father.'

From Prehistory to History

Some of Solon's reforms opened up trade and raised Athens' commercial position, in part by improving standard weights and measures.[49] The period after Solon is marked by a significant silence about freedom. Evidently Solon's reforms worked so well that, for a time, freedom became a non-issue. But worries about freedom eventually reappeared in the guise of worries about tyranny. Originally, the word *turannos* referred to someone who seized power by force, but not necessarily as a ruthless autocrat. In earlier times, tyrants were often tolerated by all classes. Aristocrats benefited from having someone who would prevent uprisings of the lower classes; lower classes benefited from the tyrants' terminating the political games of the elites.

Democracy

Cleisthenes is usually credited with introducing democracy to Athens after the expulsion of the tyrant Hippias around 508 BC.[50] Athens had traditionally been organized around four founding tribes, but power struggles between these had led to tyranny in the first place. Cleisthenes replaced Athens' demographic organization around four family-tribes with a new one around ten tribes, and in the process he created the *deme* (something similar to a city borough) as an important political unit. He also introduced *isonomia*, 'equality of law' or 'balance of rule' (from *isos*, 'same, equal,' and *nomos*, 'law, rule, custom'). *Isonomia* was a precursor to democracy and brought about some measure of equality before the law. To be sure, Athenian democracy was unlike ours. Most people were excluded from *isonomia*. Women were barred, as were resident aliens and their descendants, even after generations of living in Athens.

Even so, Athens was progressive by the standards of its time. Paul Woodruff suggests that Athenians would have regarded a phrase like 'elected representative' almost as an oxymoron, because the "mere process of election makes its winners represent political parties and action groups more faithfully than they do the citizens who elected them."[51] Athenians, Woodruff continues, understood the problem and aimed to solve it. "In ancient democracy, as now, wealth made a difference to elections; people without money or family connections almost never won elective office in Athens. Because Athenians wanted to curb the power of wealth, they severely restricted the power of those who held elective office."[52]

According to Herodotus, isonomy consisted of three parts:

1   Most city offices were staffed by lottery rather than by class, family affiliation, or wealth.
2   City officials were held accountable for their actions. At the end of their term of service, they had to justify themselves to the people and could be punished for poor performance.
3   The city council was strengthened, with more deliberations taking place in public and with all citizens having a right to speak.[53]

The right to speak was the mark of a free person. Slaves had to hold their tongues; freemen did not. The earliest conception of free speech, developed by the sixth century BC, seems to have been encapsulated by the term *isegoria*, 'equality of speech,' which expressed the idea that every free person's opinion has the same weight as every other free person's. However, by the end of the fifth century, a stronger conception of free speech emerged and was added to *isegoria*: *parrhesia*, 'frankness,' 'outspokenness,' the right to say all. The idea was that a free person not merely had an equal voice, but could express himself fully and frankly, without fear of reprisal.[54]

A further notable advance in the idealization of freedom in Greece seems to have been a result of the Greco-Persian wars between 499 and 449, in which the Persian Empire attempted to conquer the non-unified Greek city–states. The Persian threat required Greek states to put aside their differences and form alliances. This unity was achieved partly by political rhetoric about ethnic differences between the Hellenic race and the Persians. The Greeks regarded the Persians as slavish, deferential, non-autonomous brutes ruled by a super-tyrant (Darius, and later Xerxes). They realized that, by comparison to the Persians, they were relatively free, having more liberties protected by the state and enjoying greater control over their own lives. They regarded this condition of freedom as one of the reasons why they defeated the Persians: there was more at stake for the Greek warriors, since they were free citizens with homes to defend. Athens began to celebrate itself as the 'freest city.'

Athenians increasingly began to seek economic self-sufficiency (*autarkeia*), which, for better or worse, they viewed as making them more free (by minimizing their dependence on international trade). The drive toward autarky led gradually to the formation of an 'Athenian empire,' as Athens gained supremacy over its allies in the Delian League (formed in 478/7 BC against the Persians) and began to gather more resources so as to be 'self-sufficient.'

Pericles

Around 460 BC Pericles became a political leader of Athens. John Danford describes Pericles as the first politician to attribute great importance to philosophy. He promoted Athens as a center of art, philosophy, commerce, and culture. He also promoted democracy. The ancient Greeks conceived of humans as essentially social and political animals, as in Aristotle's famous statement. Nevertheless,

Danford says, for at least the generation of Pericles, there was such a thing as Athenian individualism – where 'individualism' presupposes that people should be understood first as individual organisms, and only secondarily as organisms who need to cooperate if they are to flourish.[55] Patterson claims that Pericles's funeral oration makes the first unequivocal use of freedom in terms recognizable to the modern ear.[56] In this speech Pericles stresses the legacy of those who fought and died for Athens in the Second Peloponnesian War: on account of them, Athens is "a free country." Pericles speaks of *civil* freedom: of our constitution putting the power in the hands of the whole people, of everyone being equal before the law, and of qualification for political office being a matter of merit rather than an accident of birth. He also speaks of *personal* freedom: neighbors mind their own business, and each citizen is the rightful owner of his own person. Finally, Pericles speaks of *sovereign* freedom – the indomitable and aristocratic Athenian soul.

Patterson finds this third part of the triad curious, even out of place, and explains it in terms of Pericles's aristocratic upbringing taking over.[57] Yet the notion of sovereign freedom touches on ideas that retain some resonance today: the feeling of liberation that comes from being true to our natures, from standing up for what we know to be right, from having clean hands and nothing to hide.[58]

Athenian democracy

Plato's *Republic* (probably written around 360 BC, although the chronology of Plato's works is contested) develops in a few remarkable pages the idea of division of labor. Plato does not explain how workers should identify their specialized roles in a commercial society. We are left to infer that the Guardians would know enough to decide who belongs to the working class and what each person's role should be. Two thousand years later, Adam Smith, moral philosopher and Plato scholar, would embellish this story with an explanation of how a price mechanism fosters coordination in a commercial society, with no need for impossibly knowledgeable central planners. Individual workers, deciding for themselves how to try to make a living, are led by self-interest to go where their services command a good price. By gravitating toward well-paying jobs, workers at the same time gravitate toward creating a product that employers or customers truly want, to a point of being willing to pay for it.[59]

Plato's best student, Aristotle, was also a biologist, and thus "brought to the discussion of cities something that Plato lacked: a knowledge of the immense variety of species and an appreciation of the endless creative manifestations of life itself. . . . For Aristotle, the ideal was not a rationally abstract form to be arbitrarily imposed on the community."[60] Instead, Aristotle understood (to some degree) the need to let the species realize its potential by allowing individual organisms to experiment with different ways of adapting to their environment and of learning from, responding to, and building on, each other's ideas. It is a difficult concept: that a beneficial order will always be substantially spontaneous. The imposition of order from the top down, necessary though it may sometimes be, tends to stifle future experiments and innovations. Even into the twentieth century, we find figures such as F. A. Hayek struggling to articulate the point. Indeed Hayek would win a Nobel Prize in Economics for his partial success – the point is that important. Aristotle, without the benefit of insights such as those of Darwin, went a long way toward grasping the unavoidably central place of spontaneous order in a free society.

Aristotle – from Stagira in Chalcidice – was not Athenian and never received Athenian citizenship. He lived in Athens for two long periods but fled after the death of Alexander, fearing anti-Macedonian reprisals. Thus, although he died in the same year (322 BC) as Demosthenes, and at the same age, the two seemingly had little contact. Demosthenes was a believer in individual rights, including property rights, as much as Aristotle was, but more of a believer in democracy.[61] Yet even Demosthenes saw unrestrained democracy as a form of government that would undermine itself. He proposed to curb self-serving legislation through the procedure of legislating "with a noose around one's neck." The basic principle would be: if a proposed law is deemed noble and beneficial, the law passes; otherwise, the noose is tightened and the person proposing it dies.[62]

In his *Politics*, Aristotle stresses that democratic freedom means more than just *isonomia* (equality of participation, political liberty).[63] He says that the ability to live as one pleases is the mark of a free person (probably meaning "free" in both negative and positive senses). Though Athens was not nearly as liberal and tolerant as a modern European or North American country, it was notably liberal for its day. Its citizens and even its slaves had a large degree of freedom in choosing a job, making contracts, choosing which cults to join, and choosing what sort of lifestyle they would lead.

By contrast, Spartans considered themselves free because they were not ruled by other city–states; yet Spartan citizens were expected to submit themselves voluntarily to *nomos*, the 'natural law,' which included many restrictions on ways of life and a subordination of the self to the good of the community. In Athens, too, *nomos* was considered important. Democracy was always seen, both by its detractors and by its supporters, as subject to the politics of special interest, and consequently in danger of dissolving into anarchy. Respect for *nomos* – what we might now call a 'constitutional culture' – played an important part in regulating Athenian democracy. Moreover, Athenians seemed to treat freedom not as something to be sacrificed for the sake of *nomos* when this was necessary, but as a core constituent of *nomos*. Interestingly, Raaflaub claims, contrary to Benjamin Constant (see our Introduction), that, for the Athenian democrats, "sharing in power was essentially a means to an end: their goal was life in freedom and happiness."[64] According to Raaflaub, the "core of the value of freedom guaranteed by democracy" to an average citizen consisted in letting him

> develop a political identity and over time made it so attractive that it became his primary identity. . . . Democracy guaranteed him the integrity of his house and person, put him on a par with all other

citizens in essential areas of life (especially before the law and politics), and made him independent of the power of the mighty. For all these reasons, democracy met an extraordinarily important socio-psychological need: it was the only political system that enabled the freeman to develop and realize his potential to the fullest.[65]

So one value of rights is that they are a badge of honor that make us worthy of respect, giving us the ability to look one another in the eye.

Raaflaub holds that the development of freedom as a personal value was partly the result of applying Athenian ideas of freedom in international relations to personal relations. During the Athenian empire, Athens was free because it was autonomous, not under any other city's control. The Athenian ideal there, in international relations, was 'freedom through power.' This conception of international relations was eventually transfered to relations between citizens. Citizens were free not merely because they were not slaves, but because they were autonomous, having no masters, able to see each other as equals, able to live as they choose, and able to participate in governance. During the fourth century BC Athenian democracy strengthened, and freedom became identified with participation in democratic government. At no point, though, did the Athenians regard democratic participation as *sufficient* for freedom. Freedom meant a host of civil and economic liberties, not just the right to vote or hold office.[66]

Rome and Christianity

Between Aristotle and Cicero, natural law theory emerged. Cicero, famous Roman philosopher, lawyer and orator, observed: "We are all constrained by one and the same law of nature; and . . . we are certainly forbidden by the law of nature from acting violently against another person."[67] Neal Wood considers Cicero "the first important social and political thinker to affirm unequivocally that the basic purpose of the state is the protection of private property,"[68] although arguably a full-blown theoretical defense of private property as natural law would have to wait for Bodin and Grotius.[69]

Cameron and Neal write as follows:

> Rome's greatest contribution to economic development was the *pax romana*, the long period of peace and order in the Mediterranean basin that allowed commerce to develop under the most favorable conditions. Although Roman legions were almost constantly involved in conquering new territory, punishing an upstart neighbor, or suppressing a native rebellion, before the third century these disturbances normally took place on the periphery of the empire and rarely disturbed the most active commercial routes. Piracy and brigandage, which had been serious threats to commerce even in the Hellenistic era, were almost completely eliminated.[70]

Cicero published *De officiis* in 44 BC, a year before he was murdered. (Around this date Julius Caesar became *dictator perpetuo*. Although he cautiously refused the formal title of 'king' or 'emperor' and so did Augustus after Julius was assassinated, the Roman Republic effectively came to an end.)

Church and state

Soon afterwards, Jesus of Nazareth would begin to teach that each individual matters in the eyes of God.[71] Moreover, God is a god of all human beings, not just of one tribe.[72] It was Jesus who said, render unto Caesar what is Caesar's, and unto God what is God's, suggesting the idea of a separation between church and state and stressing that any human ruler's claim to authority and allegiance is limited. Political leaders in particular have no right to decide which deity their subjects should worship.

Ancient Mediterranean religions tended to be 'syncretic,' meaning that people of different religions accepted each other's gods. (Judaism was a notable exception.) The Greek Zeus, the Roman Jupiter, and the Etruscan Tinia were largely the same deity. Still, they were *made* to look as if they were the same deity in part because Greeks and Romans were committed to viewing each others' religions as mutually accommodating, and thus were committed to interpreting each others' gods as different names for, or at least as making room for, their own. So syncretism was in part a self-fulfilling prophecy. The Greeks and Romans had a kind of freedom of religion, but not the kind that citizens of western democracies enjoy today. They lacked a firm concept of freedom of religion partly because their syncretism meant that they lacked a firm concept of heresy.

The reason why early Christians were persecuted in Rome (keeping in mind that the extent of their persecution was exaggerated by Christians) was their refusal to integrate. Christianity was not syncretic. Christians did not see their God as a variation of Zeus. (Their understanding of themselves was not completely accurate, as both Judaism and Christianity grew from, and adopted elements of, pagan religions; see especially Armstrong 1994). The Christians' refusal to be assimilated made them seem a threat.

Tertullian of Carthage (*c.* AD 160–240) believed Christianity to be the one true religion. However, in his *Apologeticus*, he also advocated freedom of religion. Following Apostle Paul (1 Corinthians 10: 20), Tertullian argued that while it was right for Christians to denounce paganism as demon worship and to try to convince pagans of their errors, it was not right to force pagans to change. The idea of freedom of religion thus showed signs of sprouting; but it would not come to fruition before the religious wars of the Reformation and Counterreformation.

Through the conversion of Emperor Constantine in 312, Christianity became the official religion of the Roman Empire. The legacy of Tertullian notwithstanding, an enforced conversion of pagans soon followed. In 385 Emperor Maximus ordered the execution of the Spanish Bishop Priscillian on a charge of heresy, precipitating a stream of executions, torture, and other mistreatments of 'heretics.'

Meanwhile, in the eastern empire, Theodosius I passed edicts depriving 'heretics' of property and of their children's right of inheritance.[73] Mumford comments:

> By the fifth century the life-blood was ebbing from the opened veins of Rome . . . By renouncing all that the pagan world had coveted and striven for, the Christian took the first steps toward building a new fabric out of the wreckage. . . . Many reasons have been assigned for the triumph of Christianity; but the plainest of them is that the Christian expectation of radical evil – sin, pain, illness, weakness, and death – was closer to the realities of this disintegrating civilization than any creed based on the old images of 'Life, Prosperity, and Health.'[74]

By the fifth century AD, Augustine was teaching that we go to heaven or not by the pure, inscrutable grace of God. Augustine coined the phrase 'original sin' and used the idea of it to argue that there is no salvation outside the Catholic church. Peter King comments: "Although Augustine was not the sole author of the Doctrine of Original Sin – bits and pieces of it are found in Tertullian, Cyprian, and above all in his near-contemporaries Ambrose and Ambrosiaster – Augustine was undeniably its principal architect."[75] By contrast, Pelagius, a contemporary of Augustine's, taught that there is such a thing as deserving to go to heaven, and that God would not deny salvation to the deserving. If He did, He would be wrong. Pelagius rejected the doctrine of original sin. (He also rejected the doctrine of divine grace, partly because he saw it as encouraging slackers to be fatalistic.) Pelagius was declared a heretic. Yet his belief in personal responsibility – the belief that God gave each one of us the right and the responsibility to stand or fall by our own merit – did eventually prevail.

The Roman Empire is traditionally held to have come to an end in AD 476, when the last of the western emperors was deposed. Justinian ruled as emperor of the eastern empire until 565, and made the last attempt to reconquer the western part. He also presided over a codification of Roman law, a part of which – the Pandects – would become his most lasting legacy. But this is the beginning of another story.

Acknowledgments

We thank Julia Annas, Nathan Ballantyne, Vaughan Baltzly, Matt Bedke, Ian Carter, Tom Christiano, Stephen Davies, Jerry Gaus, Michael Gill, Rachana Kamtekar, Fred Miller, Shaun Nichols, and Joshua Weinstein for immensely helpful comments. We also thank our copy-editor, Manuela Tecusan, a trained classicist; even more in this chapter than others, Manuela went well beyond the call of duty in supplying suggestions and background information.

Notes

1. Richerson and Boyd (2008, 110) say that *H. sapiens* probably evolved around 200,000 years ago, but the modern form of humans, with their propensity toward trade and progress, appeared later, around 50,000 years ago.
2. Horan, Bulte, and Shogren 2005, 2.
3. On the other hand, the evidence does not conclusively rule out the possibility of mass slaughter. We thank Joshua Weinstein for noting that the arrival of humans in the Americas went hand in hand with the wholesale extinction of American megafauna. There is little direct proof of causation in that case, either, yet archeologists do not doubt that humans played a major role in these extinctions. See Krech 2000.
4. Ovchinnikov, Gotherstrom, Romanova, Kharitonov, Liden, and Goodwin 2000.
5. Trinkaus 2007.
6. As reported in Horan, Bulte, and Shogren 2005, 4.
7. Ibid., 5.
8. Grantham 2008, 8.
9. Horan, Bulte, and Shogren 2008, 3.

10. Grantham 2008, 7. What Adam Smith (1981, 26) says on the matter is this:

> Nobody ever saw a dog make a fair and deliberate exchange of one bone for another with another dog. Nobody ever saw one animal by its gestures and natural cries signify to another, this is mine, that yours; I am willing to give this for that. When an animal wants to obtain something either of a man or of another animal, it has no other means of persuasion but to gain the favour of those whose service it requires. . . . A spaniel endeavours by a thousand attractions to engage the attention of its master who is at dinner, when it wants to be fed by him. Man sometimes uses the same arts with his brethren . . . [But] in civilized society he stands at all times in need of the cooperation and assistance of great multitudes, while his whole life is scarce sufficient to gain the friendship of a few persons. In almost every other race of animals each individual, when it is grown up to maturity, is entirely independent, and in its natural state has occasion for the assistance of no other living creature. But man has almost constant occasion for the help of his brethren, and it is in vain for him to expect it from their benevolence only. He will be more likely to prevail if he can . . . show them that it is for their own advantage to do for him what he requires of them. Whoever offers to another a bargain of any kind, proposes to do this. Give me that which I want, and you shall have this which you want, is the meaning of every such offer; and it is in this manner that we obtain from one another the far greater part of those good offices which we stand in need of.

11. Zak 2008b, 262. Zak tested this hypothesis. The hormone oxytocin facilitates the attachment of mothers to infants and of lovers to each other. High oxytocin levels seem to make us more trusting and trustworthy. Zak conducted experiments in which participants had opportunities to cheat or cooperate with one another. As it turns out, cheaters have low oxytocin levels, cooperators have high levels, and cooperation from others tends to increase one's own oxytocin levels and causes one to reciprocate. See e.g. Zak, Kosfeld, Henrichs, Fischbacher, and Fehr 2005 and Zak 2005. Zak's related research has important implications: Unstable socio-political environments or environments with few shared values inhibit oxytocin release and thus cause people to regard their societies as less trustworthy. This leads to people being more self-oriented, more shortsighted, and tends to reduce growth on account

of high transaction costs. From a liberal point of view, much of this research is reassuring, but not all of it. (In particular, it looks as though, *ceteris paribus*, ethnic homogeneity makes people more trusting and trust-worthy – which counts against the liberal value of diversity.)

12. We thank Daniel Silvermint for this thought.
13. Richerson and Boyd 2008, 127.
14. Muller 1961, 17.
15. Joshua Weinstein (personal communication, 2008) reminds us that gift-giving and the mutual exchange of goods is often depicted in ancient literature as a symbol and a securer of peace. Weinstein mentions Genesis 21 or Herodotus, *Histories*, Book 1. See also Homer – for instance *Iliad* 6.119ff., 21.42, or *Odyssey* 4.79, 19.268ff., 24.284.
16. Jacobs 1970, 7. Historian Stephen Davies tells us in personal communication that Jacobs's view is increasingly supported by archeological evidence.
17. Seabright 2004, 15.
18. Pinker 2002, 57.
19. Presumably there was not so much to raid before hunter–gatherers became herdsmen and then farmers, so agriculture may have made it more attractive to be a raider. We thank Joshua Weinstein for the observation that the ancient biblical story of Cain and Abel implicitly depicts agriculture as morally inferior to nomadic pastoralism, such inferiority being possibly connected to the potential of agricultural society to foster the division of labor and thus the production of sophisticated weapons.
20. Pinker 2002, 57.
21. Muller 1961, 29.
22. Wittfogel 1957 claims that the need for large-scale irrigation led to the need for a bureaucracy capable of overseeing the irrigation system. This is turn led to powerful states with absolute monarchs. Thanks to Joshua Weinstein for bringing this set of facts to our attention.
23. Kramer 1981, 3.
24. Ibid., 45–50.
25. Postgate 1992, 195. We thank Hans Eicholz for describing personal correspondence between Samuel Noah Kramer and Pierre Goodrich regarding the meaning of the *amagi* symbol, which Goodrich went on to develop into the logo of Liberty Fund Inc.

26. Urukagina's kingdom was obliterated by foreign invaders within ten years of these reforms. We do not know whether his philosophy had any influence surviving the invasion.

27. Muller 1961, 33.

28. Patterson 1991, 48.

29. Mumford 1961, 123–4.

30. Grantham 2008, 17.

31. Muller 1961, 94.

32. Wachsmann 1998.

33. Mumford 1961, 124.

34. Ibid., 131.

35. "Smith" is the most common surname in the western world, attesting to the central place once held in western communities by those who worked with metal.

36. Muller 1961, 93–4.

37. Raaflaub 2004, 32.

38. Patterson 1991, 56.

39. Muller 1961, 94.

40. Mumford 1961, 191.

41. See Patterson 1991, 53. Slavery in general is far older than this, and debt serfdom may be older as well. Another reasonable doubt about the story we tell here is that, according to Kramer, there was a currency, shekels, circulating in Sumer in 2350 BC. Muller may not have known about this earlier history of coinage, or perhaps he meant only to refer to events leading to the introduction of coinage into Greek economy.

42. Goolsbee 2007 (on line document) writes:

> The Center for Responsible Lending estimated that in 2005, a majority of home loans to African–Americans and 40 percent of home loans to Hispanics were subprime loans. The existence and spread of subprime lending helps explain the drastic growth of homeownership for these same groups. Since 1995, for example, the number of African–American households has risen by about 20 percent, but the number of African–American homeowners has risen almost twice that rate, by about 35 percent. For Hispanics, the number of households is up about 45 percent and the number of home-owning households is up by almost 70 percent. And do not forget that the vast majority of even subprime borrowers have been making their payments. Indeed, fewer than 15 percent

> of borrowers in this most risky group have even been delinquent on a
> payment, much less defaulted.

Contemporary Peruvian economist Hernando De Soto deems institutions of mortgage lending to mark one of the pivotal differences
between western and developing economies. See our Chapter 4 on
commerce.

43. If the right to equal status as a free citizen is inalienable, then you might
    forfeit it, as you can forfeit the right to vote, but what you can't do is
    sell it.
44. This question vexed natural law theorists of Grotius's time. See Buckle
    1991, 33.
45. Mumford 1961, 126.
46. Patterson 1991, 69.
47. Raaflaub 2004, 268.
48. As reported in a Nobel Prize acceptance speech by Shirin Abadi,
    December 10, 2003.
49. Milne 1943.
50. Raaflaub 2004; Meiggs 2008.
51. Woodruff 2005, 14.
52. Ibid., 15.
53. Robinson 2004.
54. Raaflaub 2004, 222–3.
55. Danford 2000, 2, 8.
56. Patterson 1991, 100.
57. It apparently has some affinity with a conception of freedom emerg-
    ing in fourteenth-century BC Egypt. Amenhotep IV, also known as
    Akhnaton, pursued absolute sovereign freedom for himself, to the
    point of repudiating all gods (other than himself, seen as the living
    personification of the sun-god). Patterson (1991, 41) calls him "the pro-
    totype of the European romantic hero, the man who alone is free and
    in his freedom ensures the glory of others whose freedom exists in mere
    submission. . . . Akhnaton was the first person to identify such total power
    over others as a supreme form of freedom, and to give it intellectual
    expression."
58. See our preceding chapter on alternative conceptions of freedom, and
    our final chapter on psychological freedom.

59. Plato also notes, toward the end of this fanciful yet sophisticated just-so story (*Republic* 372e ff.), that a market society can become "feverish" as consumers become preoccupied with acquiring land and other material goods. The "fever" worry is prominent in Smith too: see below, Chapter 4.

60. Mumford 1961, 184.

61. Fred D. Miller (1996, 31) documents how each thinker had, and repeatedly used, terms corresponding to the Hohfeldian schema of claims, privileges, powers, and immunities.

62. Miller 1996, 36.

63. See Aristotle 1996, 154–5.

64. Raaflaub 2004, 242.

65. Ibid., 276.

66. Raaflaub 2004, 276.

67. Cicero 1991, 110.

68. Wood (1988, 132) has in mind the passage at *De officiis* ii 73. Jack Barlow, in an impressively sympathetic and measured critique, disagrees, saying that, while Cicero is undeniably a defender of private property and sees such defense as an important function of the state, the state's basic purpose nonetheless is different: namely the promotion of the common good, where the good is interpreted in virtue-theoretic terms. Protecting property is a means to this end, an important means, but also a limited one. (Thus Cicero countenances property taxes in extreme conditions, only as a last resort, when it is necessary to avoid catastrophe.) See Barlow 2002, on line document, footnote 2.

69. This is a claim made by Pipes (1999, 10, 12).

70. Cameron and Neal 2003, 39.

71. Danford 2000, 13.

72. Ibid., 16.

73. There is a crucial distinction between heretics and heathens. A *heretic* is a Christian who has heard God's word and turned his back, while a *heathen* is a Jew or pagan who simply has not heard. In political terms, heresy is a form of treason, whereas heathens are enemies of the church, but at least they are not traitors.

74. Mumford 1961, 243.

75. King 2007, 248.

Chapter 2

The Rule of Law: AD 1075

THESIS: *The evolution of the rule of law provided the essential foundation for the explosive economic progress of recent centuries that liberated the west from extreme poverty.*

Feudalism

In the aftermath of the Roman Empire's fall, long-distance trade became more problematic as trade routes became less safe. These were times we once called the 'Dark Ages,' in part because we knew so little about them. However, Grantham says, recent analyses of Merovingian and Carolingian documents

> yield a far less catastrophic narrative of the early medieval transition than the one that scholars have constructed from late Roman and early medieval Christian polemics. In particular, the revisions indicate significant political, administrative, and economic continuity from the fourth through ninth century sustained by a surprisingly literate political and administrative elite. The finding of widespread lay literacy is significant because the supposed illiteracy beyond the confines of ecclesiastical establishments was long taken to be a structural determinant of early medieval autarchy. Intensive culling of that corpus further reveals persisting commercial connections between north and south Europe and between Europe and the near East. While the volume of trade contracted dramatically after 450 AD, the links were never severed.[1]

Grantham concludes that there was no wholesale collapse of civilization. Still, this was hardly a time of notable economic and technological growth. St Benedict (*c.*529) promulgated the self-sufficient monastery as an ideal social organization. The siege mentality was reasonable, given the violence of the times, but giving up on trade meant effectively giving up on economic progress too. Economic historian Carlo Cipolla writes of the ensuing centuries that Europe was poor and primitive, "made up of numberless rural microcosms – the manors, largely self-sufficient, whose autarchy was in part a consequence of the decline of trade and to a large extent its cause as well."[2] Political scientist John Kautsky writes that, from the fall of the Roman Empire until the thirteenth century, Europe was underdeveloped by comparison to the empires of the time – Chinese, Byzantine, or Arab.[3] Archeologist Bryan Ward-Perkins says that, with the fall of the Roman Empire, western material sophistication virtually disappeared. Pottery tells the story:

> In some regions, like the whole of Britain and parts of coastal Spain, all sophistication in the production and trading of pottery seems to have disappeared altogether: only vessels shaped without the use of the wheel are available, without any functional or aesthetic refinement. In Britain, most pottery was not only very basic, but also lamentably friable and impractical.[4]

Meanwhile, conquerors came and went in waves – Attila the Hun, Charles Martel, Charlemagne; Lombards, Muslims, Magyars, Vikings. The Treaty of Verdun in 843 divided the Carolingian Empire – which at the time embraced much of western Europe – among Charlemagne's three grandsons, pitting them against each other. Ordinary farmers needed protection, and protection was hard to come by. It was a seller's market for those who had protection to offer. Farmers gave up just about everything, including their status as freemen, to acquire a measure of security.

Feudalism became well established in continental Europe by 900, and it spread to England with William the Conqueror after 1066.

As Danford describes feudalism, all lands belonged to the king; he granted portions to the barons, who in turn granted smaller portions to lesser nobles; and the process continued down to the serfs, who worked the land as laborers in return for the privilege of living on the land and of keeping some of their produce for themselves.[5] Danford continues:

> Property, under the feudal system, was not really owned, because it could be reclaimed by the holder of a fief with a higher rank. . . . Everything was in principle subordinated to the requirements of survival. It was as if the military leader were also the police chief, and even more: he was also prosecutor, judge, and court of appeals.[6]

Although serf life must have been hard, one might suppose that it was at least simple, predictable, and unstressed. The entry for 'unstressed' in the online version of the *Oxford English Dictionary* actually has a quotation (from P. Bottome) describing peasants as simple and unstressed. On the contrary, according to Marc Bloch, epidemics and constant violence "gave life a quality of perpetual insecurity."[7] Moreover, Bloch documents "an astonishing sensibility" to apparent supernatural manifestations that made people "constantly and almost morbidly attentive to all manner of signs, dreams, or hallucinations."[8] The feeling of helplessness was compounded by the lack of what may appear to us as simple things, such as reliable time-keeping devices.[9]

And yet, however precarious life may have been within the feudal system, the alternative was even worse. According to Vinogradoff says, "[t]he dangers of keeping outside the feudal nexus were self-evident: in a time of fierce struggles for bare existence it was necessary for everyone to look about for support, and the protection of the central authority in the State was, even at its best, not sufficient to provide for the needs of individuals."[10]

Everyone took an oath of allegiance, both to those above and to those below them in the hierarchy. Lords could not simply evict their tenants, and tenants could not simply leave. Feudal society was literally an outcome of contracting. Yet this was a society in which contracting, and in particular the constraints it imposed on the contractors' children, engendered the very opposite of the framework for entrepreneurship that freedom of contract usually creates. As a philosophical ideal, freedom of contract presupposes that bargainers have a right to walk away, to decline to trade. Feudal serfs, though, had no such right; moreover, had any such right been granted to them, they were in no position to exercise it.

Bloch remarks: "It was very rare, during the whole feudal era, for anyone to speak of ownership, either of an estate or an office; much rarer still – never perhaps, except in Italy – for a lawsuit to turn on such ownership."[11] In this society based on status, which for practical purposes had different laws for different ranks, making deals was dangerous, because to advertise that one had something worth buying was to advertise that one had something worth taking. In general, if one had any wealth, one had to hope that the king would not notice.

David Hume (1711–76) wrote in his *History of England* that, as long as the property system was so precarious, there could be little industry. Hume concluded that what he called 'the Dark Ages' were dark because people were unfree. In particular, they were not free to choose how to make a living. Moreover, they lacked a secure entitlement to the products of their labor.[12]

Reform

So, what changed? There are many stories about the events that followed, and the stories do not add up. Here even more than in the rest of the book, we are looking at a jigsaw puzzle. Some pieces fit together nicely, making us fairly confident that they are in the right place. Other parts of the puzzle have gaping holes; we see a certain piece fitting somewhere around here because of its color, but this is all we can say until more pieces are firmly in place. The greatest experts knit known facts together with conjectures that sometimes prove incorrect but this is an inevitable part of doing history, and the risk is worth taking. Hence we offer the following pieces of this fascinating puzzle.

The medieval church was powerful enough to hold European monarchs in check, but not enough to avoid being held in check by monarchs in return. This mutual constraint secured a measure of liberty for the citizens, who otherwise would have been at the mercy of one authority or the other. In Lord Acton's words,

> The nations of the West lay between the competing tyrannies of local magnates and of absolute monarchs, when a force was brought upon the scene which proved for a time superior alike to the vassal and his lord. . . . The only influence capable of resisting the feudal hierarchy was the ecclesiastical hierarchy; and they came into collision, when the process of feudalism threatened the independence of the Church by subjecting the prelates severally to that form of personal dependence on the kings which was peculiar to the Teutonic state. To that conflict of four hundred years we owe the rise of civil liberty. If the Church had continued to buttress the thrones of the king whom it anointed, or if the struggle had terminated speedily in an undivided victory, all Europe would have sunk down under a Byzantine or Muscovite despotism. For the aim of both contending parties was absolute authority.[13]

The monastic order of Cluny, established in 910, would over the course of the tenth century incorporate perhaps a thousand individual monasteries, all ruled by the abbot of Cluny. This hierarchy became a model for Catholicism as a whole, as the church coalesced into a political authority independent of secular kings. Marriage was common among priests, but in the eleventh century the church began to insist on a norm of priestly celibacy. Parish offices that previously would have been inherited by a priest's sons were now left vacant at a priest's retirement or death; thus many more offices came to be available for sale. Kings and popes alike became keenly interested in the question of who had the right to sell such offices.[14] Between 1049 and 1053, Pope Leo IX launched a campaign urging Christians to refuse to take the sacraments from priests who had wives or concubines. Leo also repudiated the authority of clerics who purchased their positions.[15]

Bishops (and, until 1056, the pope himself) were elected by the emperors of what would come to be called the Holy Roman Empire; but Pope Gregory VII declared the independence of the church from the Holy Roman Empire, and in 1075 ruled that appointing bishops was the prerogative of the pope. (After 1056, popes themselves were appointed by the College of Cardinals in Rome.) Gregory's decisions prevailed in 1077, thus establishing the church as an institution endowed with significant power to limit secular authority. Ecclesiastical courts flourished alongside secular courts. Contractual disputes, in particular, were often taken to ecclesiastical courts.[16]

The University of Bologna, which today claims to be the oldest continuously operating university in the world, traces its beginning to 1088, when scholars of rhetoric, logic, grammar, and other subjects began to assemble to study Roman law, with the Holy Roman Emperor's approval and against a backdrop of Pope Gregory's ongoing consolidation of church authority and a general upheaval over the proper respective jurisdictions of church and state.

In 1095 Gregory's successor, Pope Urban II, launched the First Crusade, aiming to wrest Jerusalem from Muslim control. Western military power expanded. International trade was reinvigorated and extended. Innovations such as the water-mill, the three-field crop rotation, the iron plow, the horseshoe, and the plowhorse harness as much as doubled agricultural production. People, even farmers, began to go to market for the full range of agricultural products, and trade relationships began to expand.[17] Kautsky supposes that renewed contact with Byzantium helped to stimulate the commercialization of Western Europe in the eleventh century.[18] In Lord Acton's words,

The opening of the East by the Crusades had imparted a great stimulus to industry. A stream set in from the country to the towns, and there was no room for the government of towns in the feudal machinery. When men found a way of earning a livelihood without depending for it on the good will of the class that owned the land, the landowner lost much of his importance, and it began to pass to the possessors of moveable wealth.[19]

Another pivotal event, possibly triggered by the intellectual explosion in nearby Bologna, was the rediscovery of Justinian's Pandects in Amalfi, Italy, in 1130. David Hume treated this event as singularly important. The Pandects were a digest of Roman civil law, commissioned by Emperor Justinian and produced by the leading legal scholars of his day around AD 530. Within ten years, lectures on this newly discovered civil law were being given at Oxford.

Also coming from Bologna, in 1139, was the first articulation of an ecclesiastical law system known as 'canon law': the *Decretum Gratiani*, a collection of six texts attributed to the jurist Gratian, which became the legal code of the Catholic church. *Usury*, defined as a demand by a lender for repayment in excess of the original principal, was forbidden under Gratian's canon law, although the actual effect of this law was to set out a class of exceptions to the traditional prohibition – exceptions that would facilitate economic expansion. Indeed, as Berman notes, at that time monasteries "were the chief lenders to nobles departing on the Crusades."[20]

Anglo-Saxon law, substantially of Scandinavian origin, had prevailed in England for several centuries, until the Norman conquest of 1066. (The Normans were of Scandinavian origin too, having descended from the Vikings, who conquered Normandy in northern France.) Anglo-Saxon law, especially in England, formed a framework of customs and contract laws, many of which explicitly aimed at keeping the peace. In Icelandic legal traditions, a panel of town elders might find a defendant guilty of the imputed crime and award his ship or cattle to the plaintiff. A defendant who failed to comply with a verdict became an outlaw, effectively placed outside the law and thus not protected by it.

Accusations could culminate in trials by combat or by ordeal; examples of the latter would include being held underwater, or having to retrieve stones from a kettle of boiling water. In effect this was trial by God, since it was up to God to protect the innocent from injury. Those who survived the trial stood to be exiled (perhaps because of a nagging suspicion that a defendant may have been saved by Satan rather than by God), so winning was nearly as terrifying a prospect as losing. It was a legal system with which few wanted close acquaintance.

In 1166, England's Norman king, Henry II, the first Plantagenet, issued the Assize of Clarendon, which began to move English law away from trial by combat and ordeal and toward conceiving of trials as cases to be decided through evidence brought before human judges.

Henry also instituted a system for adjudicating disputes by a jury of twelve local knights. Land disputes had become a serious matter, as crusades and pilgrimages drew people away from their land for years at a time. Sometimes they returned home to find their land occupied by squatters. The Assize of Novel Disseisen, probably passed in 1176 (1166 according to Berman) as part of the Assize of Northampton, streamlined land disputes. The assize directed courts to consider only the conflicting claims of litigants before the court. If a plaintiff disputed the rightfulness of a defendant's possession, the assize directed courts to stick to the question of whether the defendant acquired that possession in a defective manner. Here too, trials were settled by juries of peers. Juries could settle a case by finding that a defendant's method of acquisition was defective, and thus they would award the land to the plaintiff without having to know whether that plaintiff's claim would withstand all possible challenges.[21] Later on someone else might present a better claim than today's winner, but that would be a case for another day.

Henry II also established circuit judges who went from town to town, thereby transferring considerable power (and money) from local barons to royal courts.[22] One effect was to make the scope of this evolving body of judge-made law national rather than local, rendering it the *common law* of England.[23] Among other things, circuit judges would convene juries of locals whose function, like that of grand juries today, was to determine whether there was enough evidence to warrant taking a case to trial.[24] When finished riding their circuit, judges would live in Inns of Court (known records of which go back to the mid-fourteenth century) where they would mix with fellow judges, legal scholars, and students of the law. In the days before long-distance communication and before printing presses or any other easy means of information storage, Inns of Court may have helped to weave the various legal circuits into a coherent nation-wide pattern. Matthew Hale, a prominent member of Lincoln's Inn during the early 1600s, observed that,

> those men who are employed as justices . . . have had a common education in the study of law. . . . [I]n term-time . . . they daily converse and consult with one another; acquaint one another with their judgements, sit near one another in Westminster Hall, whereby their judgements are necessarily communicated to one another . . . [B]y this means their judgements and their administrations of common justice carry a constancy, congruity and uniformity one to another.[25]

An interesting parallel: Sicily was ruled by Muslims between the ninth and the eleventh century, and used Sunni Islam's legal system. Muslim trials could be conducted by a body of twelve jurors chosen from the community and bound to render an impartial and unanimous verdict. Five years before invading England, in 1061, the Normans invaded Sicily; thus Sicily became a gateway for the introduction of Islamic ideas into western Europe.[26] Such ideas may have influenced Henry II's strikingly similar development of trial by jury in England – but, as we write this, no definitive causal link has been established.[27]

Magna Carta[28]

The name 'Magna Carta' refers to a series of agreements, issued in England beginning in 1215, that inspire modern constitutional law. It arose out of disputes between King John and English barons regarding the extent of the rights of kings. The Magna Carta established that the king is bound by a rule of law. The charter was streamlined and reissued by John's successor, Henry III, who ruled for fifty-seven years and whose endorsement helped to solidify the Magna Carta as a touchstone for English legislation. Pope Innocent III declared the Magna Carta void, saying that the king was the pope's subject, and therefore it was the pope's sole prerogative to decide what rules bind kings. The barons and the king ignored the pope. This was a step in the reassertion of secular authority, which, in its ongoing struggle with papal authority, helped to balance and limit the church's power in Europe following the 1200s.

Order for sale

Also in 1215, at the Fourth Lateran Council, Pope Innocent III forbade church-sanctioned trials by ordeal. The demand for secular courts increased. Legal scholar Todd Zywicki states:

> During the era in which the common law evolved, litigants had the ability to choose among many different courts and bodies of law to hear their disputes. Judges were paid by fees paid by the parties, providing judges with an incentive to compete for business and to respond to the needs of litigants through the production of efficient legal rules. Moreover, it provided an ease of exit that reduced the ability of parties to involuntarily redistribute wealth away from parties disfavored by doctrinal developments.[29]

English courts were for-profit operations, aiming to provide systems of adjudication that were faster, more impartial, more transparent, and less expensive than the competition. Litigants could select whichever legal system was easiest to live with, especially in areas of commerce and property where the overlap of competing jurisdictions was pronounced. Zywicki writes:

> Courts ferociously sought to expand their own jurisdictions while protecting themselves from the encroachments of others. The King's Bench, the Exchequer, and the Court of Common Pleas heard many of the same cases and were consistently locked in heated conflicts over allegations that one of these courts was exceeding its jurisdictional limits and invading the proper jurisdiction of a rival.[30]

Thus a breach of contract case between private parties might show up in the Exchequer Court on the pretext that the king had a legitimate interest in the parties' subsequent ability to pay their taxes. Or church courts might seek the case on the grounds that the original contract was ratified by oaths sworn on a Bible. Zywicki comments: "Even the Magna Carta itself arose in large part as a protest by the lords against the King's efforts to infringe upon the jurisdiction of the lords' courts in order to capture those cases for political and financial reasons."[31]

Part of the background for this development was that William the Conqueror in the aftermath of 1066 had no choice but to be an absentee ruler, preoccupied as his army was with defending Normandy. Thus he allowed English law to remain the locally originated set of overlapping and evolving institutions that it was. He respected local English custom and recognized local government by autonomous 'shires,' so that he could maintain control with a skeleton force of Norman knights.

The seeds of efficient local government and of a nimble legal system, responsive to evolving local problems, were in place. Courts competing for business would become a problem, but for a time the dynamic was favorable. People who wanted to resolve their disputes by combat did so anyway, whereas the sort of people who showed up in court were people who actually wanted a resolution – that is, wanted something fair, fast, and final. No one wanted to be in a situation where the losing party would simply shop around for a more favorable court. Instead, litigants sought out courts having a history of issuing verdicts that other courts would not overturn, precisely because litigants wanted the conflict to be over, so that they could get on with their lives. Courts were in the business of offering a product: verdicts that other courts could not reasonably reject. Thus courts competed by trying to supply not only the quickest and least expensive verdict, but also the most robust.

Emerging citizenship

Meanwhile, around 1190 Genghis Khan began to knit together the largest empire in human history: by 1279, during the reign of his grandson Kublai Khan, it stretched from the Mediterranean to the Pacific. The empire was held together by remarkably deep religious and ethnic toleration, a corresponding commitment to decentralized and largely meritocratic authority, and a rudimentary rule of law known as the Yassa Code. Trade and communication routes were open and secure, helping to spread ideas while enabling the core of the Mongol Empire to stay connected to its far-flung periphery. Marco Polo, the Venetian trader, would visit Kublai Khan in 1266, and again in 1271 (at what is now Beijing), the second time staying for seventeen years. Until the Mongol invasion of China, China's Sung dynasty possessed "unquestionably the wealthiest and most advanced economy on the globe."[32] Indeed, Kautsky suggests that Europe's economy decisively surpassed China's only with the invention of the steam engine in 1698.[33]

In Europe, by 1200, as it became more obviously inefficient for laborers to pay higher nobles in agricultural produce, they began to pay rent in cash. The point was to institute a more efficient means of payment; the psychological effect was to put laborers in a position of feeling more connected to the whole produce of the land –

somehow more like its owners. Peasants gained effective economic control over a larger part of their produce: they could bring it to market and sell it at the market price. Since they had no duty to deliver any particular crop to their lord, they had more freedom to experiment with possibly more profitable crops.[34] Later, because leaseholding was seen to encourage industry, laborers were allowed to become leaseholders, thereby securing and stabilizing their connection to the land. At every step, the distinction between serfs and freemen became less important. The economy of feudal Europe, especially in England, was evolving into something else.

At the same time, the rule of law was being reconceived. In earlier centuries, say in parts of western Europe around the year 900, the rule of law was above all a matter of keeping the peace – establishing mutually understood norms that define what counts as doing violence to another person. That is to say, at a minimum, the rule of law enables citizens to develop, and more or less depend on, a mutual understanding of what belongs to oneself and what belongs to someone else, and thus of what is not to be taken without consent. Feudal institutions went some way toward establishing a rule of law in this minimal sense.

By 1200, though, Western societies were progressing to a point where citizens were becoming less concerned about the rule of law as an antidote to anarchy and more concerned about the rule of law as an antidote to tyranny. The need for peace-keeping had evolved into a need to establish limits to the king's power to tax, and to establish that no one (neither kings nor judges, legislators, or police) is above the law. In a sign of things to come, Thomas Beckett, Archbishop of Canterbury and former friend of King Henry II, is credited with the first recorded instance, in 1162, of "determined opposition to the king's arbitrary will in a matter of taxation."[35]

Around 1250, jurist Henry de Bracton famously declared: "The king must not be under man but under God and under the law, because law makes the king."[36] As Debbie Levy describes the evolution of this idea,

In the time of the Magna Carta and half a century later, in Bracton's time, the idea that the king was subject to law was part wishful thinking and part statement of actual fact. Kings of that era did not wish to give up their powers. But times were changing, and Bracton and documents such as the Magna Carta were part of the change. . . . The Magna Carta did not stop the argument. But beginning in 1215, it was a part of the argument.[37]

In the feudal era, peasants and freemen were subject to the arbitrary confiscation of their goods by their lords. In the aftermath of the Magna Carta, English law helped secure property rights (in part by requiring due process) and limit the power of the English king to confiscate and to impose taxes. The result of this and of subsequent reforms was to produce a shift towards stable, predictable taxation schemes, which enabled merchants to form more reliable expectations and to invest with more confidence in long-term projects.[38]

The articles of the Magna Carta underwent a steady process of revision and reinterpretation and thus became part of an ongoing legal and political reflection, slowly coming to permeate English thought and to affect ordinary citizens. Between 1331 and 1368, Parliament enacted six laws that gave substance to such phrases from the Magna Carta as 'lawful judgment of peers,' 'law of the land,' and 'free man.' Thus rights of trial by jury were secured, together with procedural rules governing lawful arrest and the expansion of equal standing before the law so as to include any man, "whatever estate or condition he may be."[39]

The essay *Defensor pacis*, by Marsilius of Padua, appeared in 1324 and was hotly debated for decades thereafter. It denied the pope, indeed the clergy in general, any authority in secular matters. This repudiation of ecclesiastical claims to unlimited authority was a repudiation of tyranny quite generally – and not merely an assertion that unlimited authority should reside in monarchs instead. Certainly Lord Acton saw it this way.[40] Writing around 1877, Acton would describe Marsilius's vision as surpassing that of Locke and

Montesquieu in some respects. In particular, Acton applauded Marsilius's claim that the

> monarch, who is instituted by the legislature to execute its will, ought to be armed with a force sufficient to coerce individuals, but not sufficient to control the majority of the people. He is responsible to the nation, and subject to the law; and the nation that appoints him, and assigns him his duties, has to see that he obeys the Constitution, and has to dismiss him if he breaks it.[41]

John Fortescue, England's Chief Justice from 1442 to 1461, would author *The Difference Between an Absolute and Limited Monarchy*, a plea for limited monarchy that arguably represents the beginning of English political thought.[42]

The Basic Idea: No One Is Above the Law

Hobbes is generally treated as one of the first and greatest social contract thinkers. Typically, he is also described as an advocate of unlimited monarchy. On Hobbes's theory, Leviathan's authority is almost absolute along a particular dimension: namely, Leviathan is authorized to do whatever it takes to keep the peace. This special end justifies almost any means. But note the *end*'s limitations. Leviathan's job is to keep the peace and no more: not to do everything worth doing, but simply to secure the peace.[43] Hobbes, the famed absolutist, in fact developed a model of sharply limited government – limited in this most important way.[44]

Hobbes was a forerunner of liberalism in a further sense. He didn't take for granted that the Leviathan, or any political arrangement, was justified. He asked whether subjects had reason to obey, and treated the question as important. In this way Hobbes sowed the seeds of the liberal view that governments are accountable to those governed. In this way, even if Hobbes was hardly what today we would call a liberal, he was nevertheless among liberalism's inventors.

Due process

Interpreted as an antidote for tyrannical government, perhaps the essence of a maturing rule of law is the principle that citizens are entitled to *due process* of law, which is to say that police, courts, and other agencies are expected to operate according to the written, public laws of the land.[45] Rules of due process are meant to be impartial and impersonal, not to operate in different ways depending on whether the litigants are peasants or aristocrats.

The rule of law is often contrasted with the rule of men. The 'rule of men' is, roughly, a circumstance where some citizens assume the right to decide arbitrarily the fate of others. By contrast, under the rule of law, no one is above the law, not even legislators themselves, indeed not even kings. No person has unopposed authority over others. Or at least no one can claim a *right* to be unopposed in deciding the fate of others.

Judges, too, are in general bound by the law. One implication is that capriciousness on a judge's part is unjust. Judges have a job to do, and, to be doing their job, they must have reasons for their verdicts. "Because I said so" is not good enough. Judges themselves are judged – in terms of how they interpret and apply the more or less settled law.

One implication is that verdicts can be *incorrect*. Liberal societies acknowledge the possibility of error by instituting courts of appeal. On the other hand, when a judge's decision is sufficiently compelling by virtue of its intuitive common sense moral justification, or by virtue of our understanding of why the verdict has to be that way for the sake of our common good, then we go along, and our going along makes that verdict part of our system of law going forward. In this sense, judges have to persuade, not merely decide.[46]

A maturing rule of law is one that is expanding to embrace not only peace-keeping functions but also the stability of expectations in the marketplace, equality before the law, constitutional protections from arbitrary political power, and, more generally, the right to say no to those who otherwise would presume to extend their jurisdiction over us without our consent. The rule of law is not analytically tied to precedent in the way a mature rule of law is tied for example to a repudiation of secret or retroactive laws. On the other hand, what is built into a mature rule of law is that citizens have fair warning about what the law asks of them. This is where respecting precedent can help. Insofar as we achieve a common understanding of what the law requires, we will be able to predict that our rights in a given case will be assigned this way rather than that. This is one reason why we spend as little of our lives in court as we do. An ultimate aspiration of a maturing rule-of-law system is not to provide us with courts as much as to enable us to avoid court altogether, thus helping us to live freer lives, in a practical sense that all but the most litigious of us cherish.

Zywicki says that the first known use of the word 'precedent' occurred in 1557, when a judge said he was ruling in a particular way despite two contrary precedents. That the judge was moved to mention this fact – presumably expecting that other judges would want an explanation – indicates that judges saw a pattern of previous cases as establishing some presumption about how to decide a current case. Zywicki argues that this weak form of precedent fostered the evolution of efficient law.[47]

The Modern West Takes Shape

Jurist and politician Edward Coke successfully insisted, around 1600, that the common law is the supreme law of England. Coke also established that the Magna Carta protected all citizens, not only the nobles, against the king. In his post as Chief Justice (between about 1613 and 1616), Coke ruled that the king had no royal prerogative to grant monopoly privileges, and he created patent protections for innovators. One of Coke's scribes, noted for his meticulous penmanship, was a lad named Roger Williams. Williams would grow up to become one of the true heroes in the history of liberty; but we will save that story for the next chapter.

Coke supported parliamentary over monarchical authority, defying King James I in face-to-face confrontations from 1603 until 1616, when James, at the urging of his Attorney General Francis Bacon, removed Coke from the office of Chief Justice. Meanwhile, in Italy, also in 1616, Galileo Galilei was being summoned by Pope Paul V to explain himself. In Rome, as in England, absolute power was confronting the prospect of a diminished role, and was determined not to go down without a fight.

After being dismissed from his post, Coke returned as an elected member of Parliament. In this position Coke continued to make trouble and was imprisoned for six months in 1620. In 1624, Coke's Statute of Monopolies was passed by Parliament. The statute ruled that "all monopolies, all commissions, grants, licenses, charters [except temporary patents for inventions] . . . are altogether contrary to the laws of the realm, and so are and shall be utterly void and of none [*sic*] effect and in no wise to be put into use or execution."[48]

Coke worked toward a separation of powers in practice, and refused to let Parliament be intimidated by the king. Later on, William Blackstone would claim to be working in Coke's tradition. His *Commentaries on the Laws of England* in 1765 would help to develop the concept of a separation of powers and would influence the writers of the US Constitution. Montesquieu's *Spirit of the Laws* in 1748 was pivotal in the theoretical arena, proposing a separation of government into executive, judicial, and legislative branches, none being subservient to the other two. In this manner, power would be grounded in a system of checks and balances. Its tendency to concentrate into one hand and thus to degenerate into tyranny could be controlled. Leaders of the respective branches would, like the judges, have to persuade, not simply dominate.

Rights to patent, built as they were into Coke's Statute of Monopolies, not only restricted the abuse of royal prerogatives in granting monopolies but also succeeded in grounding claims to intellectual property in the common law.[49] Admittedly, several generations later, we find Adam Smith still looking at a mercantilist world; but in Coke's time the guilds themselves were, with the blessing of the Crown, in charge of deciding who could join, and thus who could practice their trade. Guilds were also in charge of enforcing their regulations. They levied and collected fines, and they kept any fines they imposed. Guilds were, in effect, judges of their own cases, deciding who was competing with them unfairly. The resulting system was a 'rule of men' rather than a rule of law. What Coke accomplished was to reserve to Parliament the right to decide who would have the privileges involved in holding a patent.

North and Thomas write:

> It was Coke who insisted that common law was the supreme law of the land and repeatedly incurred the anger of James I; it was Coke who led the parliamentary opposition in 1620; . . . his leadership of the parliamentary opposition cemented the alliance of parliament with common law.[50]

As a result, "rewards of innovating were no longer subject to royal favor, but were guaranteed by a set of property rights embedded in common law."[51]

Such praise notwithstanding, common law was not an ideal platform for innovative commerce, and this for two related reasons. First, there was a practical barrier to the common law being an evolving form of precedent-guided, judge-made law. As discussed, the idea of judicial precedent could be viewed as a way of making law more transparent and predictable, and society, correspondingly, more orderly. Until Coke's time, though, the point was moot, because any great reliance on legal precedent was impossible. Lawyers lacked easy access to printed matter; the printing press was invented only in 1440. Paper itself, in its modern form, was invented in China, perhaps in the year 200, then made its way to the Islamic world, and finally arrived in Europe only around 1100.[52] Until Coke's time, a judge's opinions were delivered orally and recorded unreliably by lawyers or others present on the occasion. The law was to that extent opaque and unpredictable, which was not good for business.

By 1600, however, greater reliance on legal precedent had become technologically feasible, thanks to Gutenberg's movable-type printing press. The first systematic record of case notes was published by Coke himself in 1609,[53] and Coke used them in his arguments against the Crown, to document the historical continuity of a 'true rule' of common law. (Note that Coke did not treat precedent as *creating* common law rules, but only as *evidence* of what the rules had long been.)[54]

A second problem with common law, though, was that there were too many courts. Thus, by the time there were precedents at all, there were too many; for each court had its own. Even with ready access to the wealth of precedent, the law would *still* be opaque and unpredictable. As Henderson observes,

> There were over seventy law "courts" operating in London in the late eighteenth century, and these were administered by almost 800 judges. Although this plethora of courts gave plaintiffs a wide range of options to find the best venue for their claim, the lack of a centralized or systematic reporting system made the mishmash of courts a nightmare for anyone looking for clear legal rules.[55]

In the words of Lord Mansfield, who was appointed Chief Justice of the King's Bench in 1756, the law of business "ought not to depend on subtleties and niceties, but upon rules easily learned and easily retained because they are dictates of common sense . . ."[56] That was the bottom line. The system of precedent as it had so far developed was not good for business. In philosophical terms, the system of precedent did not foster society as a cooperative venture for mutual advantage. It was supposed to tell people where they stood, but it was not doing that.

The previous chapter discussed trade as the factor that distinguished *Homo sapiens* from *Homo neanderthalensis* and lifted modern humans out of the stone age. Because we came together in communities to engage in mutually advantageous cooperation, life is not the solitary, poor, nasty, brutal, and short experience it had been and would otherwise have remained. The increasing range of capacities that we enjoy today (our positive freedom) is something we owe to our ability to trade. Nevertheless trade, as we also saw, does not by itself guarantee freedom of any kind. *If* the rule of law channels trade in the direction of mutually advantageous commerce, *then* trade will run in that direction, and will to this extent be liberating. But commerce can result, and has resulted, in servitude and even slavery – unless and until the rule of law prohibits it. Trade per se does not solve such problems; on the contrary, in the absence of a rule of law, it can exacerbate them.[57] To reap the potential gains from trade, we have to be able to convey our goods to market in the confident expectation of being able to say no to offers we find unattractive. The rule of law makes it safe to be a full participant in market society – to take the risk of openly displaying valuable goods and of encouraging customers to covet them.[58]

From Law to Commerce

As western merchants came to control eastern trade, they adopted Middle-East mercantile customs, while also mixing in rules common to European fairs.[59] Trade occurred among citizens of different nations, so commercial law developed largely outside governmental control or enforcement. Since there were no governmental courts to bring disputes to, discipline was enforced through reputation. A merchant who reneged on deals or refused to submit to the judgments of privately funded mediators would lose future business. In general, though, a given merchant's reputation would seldom be the only one that mattered. The reputation of the whole system matters too. Being able to count on impartial arbitration – that is, able to count both on arbitration being impartial and on it actually settling the dispute – empowers people to trust each other.

Evolving merchant law did not always fit well with English common law:

> The two distinctive elements in the merchants' law as enforced by their own class were good faith and dispatch. Both were essential to trade, especially in mediaeval times. But to the contemporary English common law the necessities of trade were not regarded as of pressing moment. [An] antipathy . . . existed between the law merchant and the old common law . . . The latter profoundly objected to two principles on which the merchants of all countries set great store – "negotiability" and "grace."[60]

Negotiability concerns, among other things, the trading of debts. For example, your mortgage company can sell your contract to another company. You remain bound by your debt on the same terms, but you are now bound to repay a different company. English common law originally forbade such things. Goetzmann and Rouwenhorst assert that "true negotiability first developed in China and reached its most dramatic expression in the eleventh century in the form of paper money."[61] In other words, the concept of money, especially fiat money, derives from the concept of a loan – in particular a loan that can be transferred.

Grace concerns the degree to which contractual obligations are flexible. English common law required that a party should discharge an obligation (for instance to deliver spice to a certain port) at the time specified, or else it would be in breach of contract. (Dates could be changed only by mutual consent.) Merchant custom, however, allowed 'days of grace' to discharge an obligation. With a period of grace, a merchant ship delayed by bad weather could head for port under no threat of lawsuit, indeed reasonably hoping to be paid for delivering more or less as promised. People were thus enabled to get on with trade and with forging relationships of trust, making allowances for the unforeseen.

Equality Before the Law

Western societies have evolved in the direction of citizens being able to think of themselves as having a right to be treated as *equals before the law*. To a liberal, society does not fall naturally into classes of people who command and people who obey.[62] True, some ways of equalizing people would be inimical to liberty. For example, imagine requiring that everyone should work the same number of hours and be paid the same hourly wage. But other dimensions of equality, particularly treating citizens as equals before the law, can promote liberty or be a precondition for a form of liberty worth having.

Unfortunately, the rule of law in practice is never more than an approximation of this ideal of equality. To be poor and uneducated is, and always will be, a disadvantage. Being young and inexperienced and not having made good connections yet is a disadvantage too, and nothing could ever stop it from being a disadvantage.[63]

Notice that inequality per se is not the problem. If the problem is that *some* defendants have incompetent representation, we cannot solve the problem by making sure that all defendants have equally incompetent representation. If and when we are talking about a zero-sum game – where one litigant wins only if the other loses – liberalism aims to level the playing field. But suppose that, instead of talking about a zero-sum game, we are looking at the trial system in general, where one defendant's success does not entail some other defendant's loss. From this perspective the liberal ideal is not to level the playing field, but to ensure that every defendant has competent representation.

We can hope for a widespread insistence that cases ought to be decided by an impartial weighing of evidence. We can hope for a widespread perception that, when cases are swayed by wealth or status or political influence, there has been a miscarriage of justice. Occasional miscarriages are inevitable, but under the rule of law we are alert to a possibility of miscarriage, and judges have the right and the responsibility to avoid perpetrating miscarriage as best they can.

Gordon Tullock describes the problem of political representation in terms that make the zero-sum aspect of social life seem ubiquitous.

> Conflict is to be expected in all situations in which transfers or redistributions occur and in all situations in which problems of distribution arise. . . . Governments do not, in general, simply go about the world doing either good or evil. Normally, if the government decides to transfer money from A to B, it will be because Mr. B has exerted sufficient political influence to initiate the transfer, and Mr. A's political influence proved insufficient to stop it.[64]

But, here again, political representation is a zero-sum game only insofar as the object is to *distribute* resources to one constituency rather than to another. If the infrastructure is designed not to redistribute what we produce as much as to facilitate productivity in the first place, the game can result in a positive sum. As in the case of legal representation, the idea is to ensure that everyone has a *good* chance to produce – not that no one has a better chance.

Constitutional limits

In western democracies, when we exalt democracy, what we mean is *constitutional* democracy, and the constitutional part is more important than the democracy part. Democracy has to be limited. In a democracy, properly understood, there are things other people do not get to do to us – not even if they are in a majority. For example, Thomas Christiano considers it part of the essence of a democracy that *a simple majority vote is not good enough to legitimize depriving a minority of its right to vote.* The essence of a democracy is not that people vote on whatever they want, but that every adult has a say in how he or she is governed.[65] We are not living in a worthwhile democracy, and on some views are not living in a democracy at all, unless minorities have rights – which is to say, unless we have something like constitutional protections. Individuals must have a standing that cannot be abolished by an opposing majority. As Paul Woodruff observes, "the tyranny of the majority kills freedom as dead as any other form of tyranny. It's not freedom if you have to join the majority in order to feel that you are free."[66]

The dark side of a limited government is that it is, after all, limited. There will always be things we want government to do for us at other people's expense – things that a limited government will be unable to do. The bright side of a limited government is that people with better connections than ours seek power just as we do, and a limited government has a limited capacity to further their aims at our expense.

Conclusion

In abstract terms, the essence of a well-functioning rule of law is that it minimizes the expected payoff of excelling at negative-sum games – that is, of trying to prosper at other people's expense.[67] A well-functioning rule of law also largely stays out of the way of positive-sum games, minimizing obstacles to our inventing ways of becoming rich that are good for neighbors – and for customers too.[68]

Almost by definition, negative- and zero-sum games have little or no role in fostering society as a place of peace and prosperity.[69] The kind of game that fosters rising wealth leads people to spend their creative energy inventing more effective ways of making customers better off. Such a framework marks the difference between a society that makes progress in promoting positive freedom and one that does not.

Where people can rely on markets to be places where people transact only by informed consent, commerce will consist of an expanding web of mutually advantageous exchanges. But the expanding web is not automatic; as Adam Smith well knew, the rule of law can create a framework that encourages community life to evolve in this direction, putting us in a position where the best we can do for ourselves is to run with our natural propensity to truck and barter, and to look for ways of making ourselves more valuable to our fellow citizens.

As with many good things, there is a downside to the rule of law.[70] For example, if the most decisive piece of evidence in a criminal trial is inadmissible in court because of procedural rules, something bad has happened. Judges and juries sometimes reach the wrong answer, and sometimes they *know* it. We cannot expect any set of rules to converge on the right answer in every case. The rule of law has not been perfected, and presumably never will be; but the alternatives have a history of being dismal at best.

Discussion

1 What is the relationship between the rule of law and economic growth?
2 Under what conditions would competing courts be a good thing? When, if ever, were they bad, and why?
3 When, if ever, is the rule of law fair? (What would make it fair?) Is there an alternative?
4 Consider again Tullock's rather dismal suggestion that a law is passed if and only if those who profit from the change are powerful enough to push it through, and those who pay for the change are not powerful enough to stop it. Does this mean that law is simply a tool in an ongoing class war, or are some kinds of law genuinely in everyone's interest?

Acknowledgments

For especially helpful comments on this chapter, we thank students in the Law and Philosophy class of Robin West and Judith Lichtenberg at Georgetown Law School; students and faculty in

Peter Dietsch's reading group at the University of Montreal; students in Dave Schmidtz's graduate seminar in Economics at George Mason University; students in Jerry Gaus's seminar on rights at the University of Arizona; Tom Christiano's Global Society and Justice seminar at the University of Arizona's Rogers College of Law; the Social and Political Theory group at Australian National University; and students in Dave Schmidtz's History of Liberty seminar at Florida State College of Law. We also thank Julia Annas, Nathan Ballantyne, Therese De Vet, John Hasnas, Kate Johnson, Ben Kearns, Jacob Levy, Fred Miller, Christopher Morris, Yaseen Noorani, Madison Powers, Bas van der Vossen, and Leif Wenar.

Notes

1. Grantham 2008, 3.
2. Cipolla 1956, 3.
3. Kautsky 1997, 32.
4. Ward-Perkins 2005, 104.
5. Danford 2000, 26.
6. Ibid., 26–7.
7. Bloch 1961, 73.
8. Ibid.
9. Ibid.
10. Vinogradoff 1924.
11. Bloch 1961, 115.
12. John Kekes (2010, 5) makes the point with admirable simplicity: "The importance of private property is that it enables us to control how we live."
13. Acton 1985, 32–3.
14. Berman 1983, 89.
15. Ibid., 94.
16. Berman 2003, 4–5.
17. Kautsky 1997, 36.
18. Kautsky 1997, 38.
19. Acton 1907, 45.
20. Berman 1983, 249.

21.　The case of *Armory* v. *Delamirie* is instructive (although it took place hundreds of years later). In this case, a chimney sweep found a jewel and asked a goldsmith for an appraisal. The sweep refused to sell the jewel to the goldsmith, and the goldsmith refused to give back the jewel. The sweep sued. The court upheld the sweep's claim. The question before the court was not whether, all things considered, the sweep was the rightful owner, but whether the transfer of possession from sweep to goldsmith was a wrong that should be undone.

22.　There are complex issues here about the relation between customary law, judge-made common law, and Roman law as administered by ecclesiastical courts and as it came to inform legal thinking across much of Europe, but probably less so in England. See Hasnas 2005.

23.　Again, we do not mean to suggest that this counts unequivocally as progress. Glenn (2005, 531) explains that early common law had a certain flexibility. One did not extend a ruling to another jurisdiction without some argument about the reasonableness of applying it to the case at hand. Thus there was a real selection process going on. But if a central authority pronounces on a law's definitive content and application, binding those who otherwise might know more about how to adapt it to local circumstance, then the law has become more bureaucratic – not an altogether bad thing, perhaps, but not an altogether good thing either.

24.　Common law courts would decide cases where monetary rewards would be appropriate. Cases calling for a non-monetary remedy sometimes went to what became known as courts of equity.

25.　Sir Matthew Hale, *The History of the Common Law of England*, 1716, as quoted in A. W. B. Simpson (1973, 96). We thank Bob Goodin for the reference.

26.　Of course, a brief history of liberty cannot be a comprehensive history of western law, let alone of all legal systems. But see Hodgson 1993 for an interesting discussion of why the Islamic world hit its zenith in the sixteenth or seventeenth century, whereas the relatively continuous expansion of technical specialization in the Christian west made for a more continuous economic and scientific progress.

27.　Makdisi 1999.

28.　In this chapter we focus most of our attention on the evolution of English common law and its role in securing the rule of law. We do not mean to suggest that the rule of law depends upon common law or is not well secured by civil law systems. Rather, we simply recognize that we, our publisher, and most of our readers live in common law systems of English origin.

29. Zywicki 2003, 1565.
30. Ibid., 1584.
31. Ibid., 1585.
32. Anderson 1996, 530.
33. Kautsky 1997, 41.
34. See Rasmussen 2008, 144–50.
35. Thurston 1912, 677.
36. De Bracton 1915.
37. Levy 2007, 112.
38. We thank Judith Lichtenberg for the observation that our narrative of the rule of law highlights the rule of law's role in enhancing negative liberty. This privileged place is not a mere appearance created by our way of telling the story. There have in fact been times when the rule of law in free societies evolved in a way that enhanced and secured the right to say no, and those times coincide with dramatic progress along multiple dimensions of human aspiration. In this way the rule of law helps to explain why free societies are as free (positively or negatively) as they are.
39. Holt 1992, 10.
40. In an 1887 letter criticizing Mandell Creighton's deference to the papacy, Lord Acton would pen the famous line, "Power tends to corrupt, and absolute power corrupts absolutely" (quoted in Hill 2000, 300). Needless to say, Acton did not mean to express any greater confidence in kings than in popes.
41. Acton 1907, Chapter II (no page numbers in the on-line version).
42. Lockwood 1997.
43. Christopher Morris (1986, 373) similarly writes that Hobbes's concern is to justify a Leviathan powerful enough to prevent real war of all against all, not to justify a Leviathan powerful enough to prevent voluntary exchange in the market place. In this crucial respect, Hobbes and Adam Smith fall in the same liberal tradition of limited government.
44. Hobbes advocates a number of restrictions on sovereign authority. It is fair to say that he considered the sovereign as being at liberty to

do whatever it may take to preserve the peace. But this does not imply that the *law* is whatever the sovereign says it is, for the law is not merely an expression of sovereign will. Laws must be public, with sufficient signs that they issue from the sovereign (Hobbes 1994, 177–9); they must be written (ibid.), verified by subordinate judges (ibid., 179) in the public registers (ibid.), and interpreted by qualified judges (ibid.). Ignorance of the law sometimes excuses one from punishment (ibid., 192); the punishment for a crime cannot be increased after the crime has been committed (ibid.); there can be no *ex post facto* laws (ibid.); and one cannot be punished unless one has broken a law (ibid., 198). Also, according to Hobbes, I am always free to defend my life, even when the sovereign lawfully tries to take it (ibid., 142–3). Further, I am not obliged (to my fellow citizens or to the sovereign itself) to obey a sovereign who is too weak to protect me (ibid., 144).

45.   As we interpret the concept, a rule of law emerges as an antidote for anarchy, and in this primitive form it does not presuppose the formalities just discussed. Christopher Morris suggests (in conversation) that any group recognizable as a society has established a rule of law in the minimal sense that people can correctly expect that people in general will keep the peace and share an understanding of what counts as keeping the peace.

46.   Yet John Hasnas says in effect that, no matter what the dispute, each side will be able to cite a seemingly favorable precedent. "The fact is that there is no such thing as a government of law and not people. The law is an amalgam of contradictory rules and counter-rules expressed in inherently vague language that can yield a legitimate legal argument for any desired conclusion. For this reason, as long as the law remains a state monopoly, it will always reflect the political ideology of those invested with decision making power" (Hasnas 1995, 233). Obviously, when we spoke above about the virtues of the rule of law, we were talking about an ideal. The mystery is how and why the best legal systems approximate the ideal to any degree at all, given Hasnas's point that, even in the best systems, we are still, after all, talking about being ruled by rulers rather than by rules – politically motivated rulers to boot. Perhaps the secret of such systems is that not even the rulers themselves are really in charge. (In the mid-1990s, President Bill Clinton was asked by a reporter what surprised him most about his first two

years in office. Without hesitation, Clinton answered: "My biggest surprise was learning how little power a President has.") If judges find themselves having to persuade rather than merely to decide, they will feel constrained to judge in ways that they can justify to peers, and to this extent they will be constrained (in the process creating a semblance of the reality) to create the appearance of a rule of law.

47. Zywicki 2003, 1568.

48. Sandefur 2005.

49. North and Thomas 1976, 148.

50. Ibid., 147.

51. Ibid., 154.

52. Hodgson 1993, 18.

53. Henderson 2008, 293.

54. Zywicki 2003, 1569. The doctrine of *stare decisis* ('abiding by what has been decided') did treat precedent as a source of law binding upon future courts, and not as mere evidence. So there are many scholars (Zywicki included) who take a dim view of *stare decisis*, even while they appreciate the role that precedent can and should play in a rule-of-law system.

55. Henderson 2008, 297.

56. Quoted in Henderson 2008, 299.

57. To be accurate, there is *some* tendency for trade spontaneously to evolve in mutually advantageous directions, quite apart from the rule of law, because, even if one does not regard the right to say no as sacred, there are relationships where one prizes the *willing* cooperation of another – in which case one wants something that intrinsically cannot be taken by force.

58. The rule of law can also make it rational to deliver goods now in return for a mere piece of paper that blithely announces to the world that rule of law can also make it rational to deliver goods now in return for a mere piece of paper that blithely announces to the world that one is entitled to buy comparably priced goods at a future date.

59. Bewes 1986.

60. Maccassay 1924, 180.

61. Goetzmann and Rouwenhorst 2005, 7.

62. This is how Gerald Gaus (2000, 143) characterizes the essence of liberalism.

63. As Holmes and Sunstein say of the adversarial legal system,

> To level the playing field so that all criminal defendants received roughly the same quality of legal counsel, for example, regardless of their personal assets, would require an unacceptable degree of governmental supervision and discretionary coercive control. A government capable of entirely neutralizing the influence of private resources on the value of individual rights would have to be so immensely powerful, in fact, that even the trivial misuses of its powers that would be bound to occur would probably be worse for most citizens (including the poor) than the inequalities it was ostensibly established to abolish. (Holmes and Sunstein 1999, 202)

64. Tullock 2006, 9–10. Cory Booker, elected Mayor of Newark in 2006, characterized politics in similar but more earthy terms, saying there are six themes to political life in Newark:

> First . . . by every means necessary, protect your turf. Second, resist change. Third, expand one's sphere of control, always hoping to control more and more resources and authority. Fourth, enlarge the number of subordinates underneath you because having subordinates means having power, having election workers, and keeping yourself in office. Next, protect programs and projects regardless of whether they are effective or not. Finally, maintain the ability to distribute the greatest amounts of wealth from taxpayers to people and organizations of your own choosing. (Booker 2001, 4)

65. Christiano 2008.
66. Woodruff 2005, 12.
67. James Buchanan (2003, 17) says: "If the government is empowered to grant monopoly rights or tariff protection to one group, at the expense of the general public or designated losers, it follows that potential beneficiaries will compete for the prize."
68. One reason why the rule of law would be designed mainly to stay out of the way, rather than to actively manage the life plans of its citizens, is that at any given time some citizens will know more, and care more, than any government official knows about what they can contribute to society. Societies where central planners make the decisions have always been societies that stagnate, then implode. Societies that leave

their entrepreneurs alone, working mainly to limit the rewards of predatory entrepreneurship, are societies where upheaval – and progress – lie around every corner.

69. In a world where other people's talents are a cost, or a threat, we get different and more egalitarian principles of justice. At the very least we get the idea of leveling the playing field, as opposed to maximally liberating talents.

70. We thank Matt Zwolinski for this idea.

Chapter 3

Religious Freedom: 1517

THESIS: *The Reformation sowed the field for liberty, but it would take time for much to grow.*

Early Religious Freedom

Throughout the early Christian era, the church and the Latin tongue were the major unifiers of Europe. Though the church had a *de jure* monopoly on religious authority in Europe, heresies kept coming and needed to be crushed. As the church's political power waned with the rise of nation–states, the church's stance on heretics became harsher. The Third Lateran Council of 1179 anathematized all heretics and offered spiritual rewards to those who killed them, enslaved them, or took their property.[1]

Though Europe became less tolerant of heretics as it grew out of the Middle Ages, tides that would lead to religious freedom were already rising. The eleventh and twelfth centuries brought a commercial revolution and the growth of towns.[2] Agricultural surpluses, better coinage, the crusades, better ship-building technologies, and other changes brought about increased trade. With trade came wealth, and with wealth came leisure. With leisure came time to think for oneself about religious matters. Moreover, the commercial revolution led to an increase in literacy, partly because it made more people rich enough to afford rudimentary education, and partly because international trade, with its reliance on contracts, required literacy.

Joel Mokyr writes, "Whenever religious and intellectual intolerance spread through Europe, as they did in the fourteenth century, their advent coincided with a temporary slowdown in technological development."[3] Regarding the changing fortunes of Christianity in relation to Islam, Mokyr observes that "Europe adopted many inventions from Islam, from the lateen sail to Arabic numerals. [By contrast,] the Moslems allowed European inventions to filter in only slowly and selectively. The first book printed in Arabic script appeared in Istanbul in 1729, almost three centuries after the invention of movable type"[4] – despite the fact that western Europe first acquired paper from China *via the Islamic world*. How could this happen? To Mokyr, the answer lies in religious culture. For example, "A saying attributed to the prophet Muhammed has it that 'whoever imitates a people becomes one of them,' which was interpreted in the Ottoman Empire as a stricture against western technology."[5]

The Eve of Revolution

The Hundred Years War (1337–1453) was a conflict between France and England that left France a country in name only by 1422, when Charles VI died after having agreed to acknowledge England's king as his heir. Charles VI's son Charles, uncrowned and disinherited, set about trying to regain the kingdom. The turning point occurred in 1428. Joan of Arc, a seventeen-year-old farm-girl, talked her way into being given command over the French troops. She led them into a battle against the English and the Burgundians (against the wishes of her more cautious immediate superiors) that broke the siege of Orléans and reversed the tide of the war.[6]

By the 1430s, Charles VII, now the acknowledged king of France, achieved a monopoly over protection services.[7] His control over taxing power became complete in 1439, after the Assembly at Orléans. Charles established a professional army to replace mercenaries. By 1453, the year of the official ending of the Hundred Years War, the English were gone from France. Charles centralized and institutionalized the practice of selling public offices. He instituted internal tariffs that prevented French market areas from expanding.[8] He established monopolies and guilds, and required various kinds of sellers to have a government license. The centralized bureaucracy of the modern nation–state was beginning to take shape.

Purgatory

As Europe's culture became more commercial and more bureaucratic, so did its religion. By the twelfth century, the doctrine of purgatory was established, indeed quantified: one would spend a particular amount of time there, atoning for one's sins, until one was purified enough to enter heaven. This spawned the idea that one could shorten one's stay in purgatory by saying masses, performing good works, and so on. The idea gave birth to spiritual trading: I give the beggar a coin and he prays for me to spend less time in purgatory. Indulgences – paying the church to reduce one's sentence in purgatory – were partly an outgrowth of this mentality.[9]

The concept of religious trading was natural, given common understandings of Heaven. The faithful saw Heaven as being stratified and hierarchical, like an earthly kingdom.[10] Rather than approaching God directly, they asked a saint closer to them to intercede – one with whom they had something in common, say a vocation or a birthplace. Perhaps one's patron saint would talk to Virgin Mary, who would talk to God.

The concept of purgatory was more important in the North than South. Going back to pagan traditions, gift-giving was more common in the North, as was exchange, and there was a greater concern with death and penance. Italian religious thinking focused on obedience to ritual, whereas eastern Christianity tended to regard salvation as a matter of right thinking rather than of right action. Accordingly, much of the sale of indulgences took place in the Northwest, and it is not surprising that the Reformation would occur in northwestern

Europe. Yet Italy was, in its own way, no less of a scene of revolutionary change. The court of Lorenzo de Medici would witness an explosion of patronage that sustained Ghirlandaio, Botticelli, da Vinci, and Michelangelo. Lorenzo himself died in 1492, six months before the voyages of the Italian navigator Christopher Columbus and two years before a young Florentine named Niccolò Machiavelli entered public service.

Whereas in the Middle Ages the average European was content with the idea that personal salvation could be reached through the obedient performance of rituals, by the dawn of the Renaissance more people believed that they needed a thorough religious understanding. As trade made Europeans richer, they had more time to pursue religious knowledge. However, this pursuit would lead to an increase in religious dissent. Laypeople thought for themselves and were seeking ways to come closer to God without the mediation of the church. Some were pondering the implications of the voyages of Columbus, which established the existence a previously unknown continent. Within a few decades ordinary citizens would be grappling with the scientific advances of the Enlightenment, beginning with the Copernican Revolution, which was arguably catalyzed by the heresies of Martin Luther.

The Dutch theologian Erasmus published new editions of the New Testament and encouraged readers to study the texts themselves.[11] His *Praise of Folly* (1509) emphasized Christian living and thinking for oneself. Martin Luther was indeed thinking for himself, and the result would be apocalyptic. Luther was not the first priest to challenge the pope; but, unlike previous challengers, Luther would win.

Luther and Liberalism

Martin Luther was a professor of theology at the University of Wittenberg and a preacher at Castle Church. His scholarly study of the Bible led him to conclude that many prevailing Catholic practices went against Christ's teachings. In particular, he thought that the sale of indulgences had become a way for Christians to avoid receiving the sacraments properly. Rather than confessing and repenting, or seeking God's forgiveness through faith, Christians thought they could simply buy salvation. The sale of indulgences, Luther worried, deceived many into thinking they were saved.

Initially, Luther did not deny the pope's authority to grant indulgences per se. Rather he thought that indulgences were overdone, and was asking for sound theological debate over their legitimacy. On October 31, 1517, Luther nailed his 95 Theses to the door of Castle Church. (This is the date according to legend; not all scholars accept it.) Among other things, the 95 Theses disputed the legitimacy of the sale of indulgences, finding no scriptural basis for thinking that salvation could be gained through such means.

Though Luther did not know it at the time, his challenge would break the Catholic monopoly on faith. In 1523 Luther wrote that "worldly government has laws which extend no farther than to life and property and what is external upon earth. For over the soul God can and will let no one rule but Himself."[12] Luther was not the first to say this, but his message was the first to reach those who needed to hear it.

Within months, Luther's challenge had been printed and spread throughout Germany, and could not be ignored. This revolutionary event in the history of religious freedom was also a seminal one in the emergence of a popular press, and a non-trivial instance of technological innovation. Johannes Gutenberg invented a movable-type printing press in 1450.[13] Luther's 95 Theses of 1517 became perhaps the first document to be widely circulated via the Gutenberg press, which helps to explain why it was Luther's rebellion (and not those of his many forerunners) that sparked the Protestant Reformation.[14] The Gutenberg press dramatically lowered the cost of producing books and newspapers. Previously, much of a scholar's time was spent copying manuscripts by hand, on parchment. Now, by contrast, as print editions of important books appeared, scholars could spend more time reading and thinking, which spurred creativity. More-over, upper middle-class people could afford their own Bibles – in particular Martin Luther's vernacular German translation. For printers, Protestantism was good business.[15]

Danford remarks:

> The Reformation is perhaps the single most important development that separates the experience of the peoples of northwestern Europe from the experience of the other European peoples with whom in other respects they share a heritage . . . The Reformation could be described as a crisis to which the institutions of liberal society were a response and a solution.[16]

Danford also notes that the Reformation was both a religious and a political movement. The Reformation was, most fundamentally, "a reaction against central authority, especially distant authority, in the name of individual judgment (Luther) or local rule (Henry VIII of England)."[17] This is obvious in the case of England, where Henry VIII split with the Catholic church in 1534 because it refused to annul his marriage to Catherine of Aragon. The Anglican church continued (and still continues) to retain many doctrines and practices of the Roman church. The most significant break consisted in locating the seat of ecclesiastical power in England. The English monarch is the supreme governor of the church, while the Archbishop of Canterbury is its primate and spiritual leader.

While in our day we worry about religion intruding into, and corrupting, politics, Luther worried about how political intrigues corrupted the church. Dan Philpott writes:

> [Luther's] theology of the Reformation advocated stripping the Catholic Church of its many powers, not only its ecclesiastical powers, but powers that are, by any modern definition, temporal. Luther held that the Church should no longer be thought of as a visible, hierarchical institution, but was rather the invisibly united aggregate of local churches that adhered to right doctrine. Thus, the Catholic Church no longer legitimately held vast tracts of land that

it taxed and defended, and whose justice it administered; it was no longer legitimate for its bishops to hold temporal offices under princes and kings; nor would the Pope be able to depose secular rulers through his power of excommunication; most importantly, the Holy Roman Emperor would no longer legitimately enforce Catholic uniformity. No longer would the Church and those who acted in its name exercise political or economic authority.[18]

Aside from killing heretics, the church's other main weapon was excommunication. The church taught (and most people believed) that there was no salvation outside of the church. Excommunication meant that, unless one repented and was re-admitted into the church, one was damned. Luther protested that the church could not speak for God; in particular, it had no license to decide who was to be saved or damned.

Luther taught that there was no hierarchy before God. Protestant sects emphasized the need for personal engagement with Scripture. Luther taught that the government of a church is legitimated only by consent, rather than by natural authority.[19] Luther himself was by no means a liberal, yet it is no accident that Protestant culture gave birth to liberal political philosophy.

The Reformation would lead to the Enlightenment: in other words, to the view that reason, not faith, should be a person's guide. Yet Luther himself was no champion of reason:

> Faith must trample underfoot all reason, sense, and understanding, and whatever it sees must be put out of sight and . . . know nothing but the word of God.[20]

Also,

> There is on earth among all dangers no more dangerous thing than a richly endowed reason, especially if she enters into spiritual matters which concern the soul and God. For it is more possible to teach an ass to read than to blind such a reason and lead it right; for reason must deluded, blinded, and destroyed.[21]

Luther's Protestant Reformation helped to open the way for the Enlightenment; but, to do so, it had to get out of the way, for early Protestants were far from being advocates of freedom of religion. Just like the Catholic church, which they sought to reform, they persecuted dissenters. Luther himself was no exception. He expected the Jews to convert to his new form of Christianity. When they declined, he reacted viciously.

Neither were the Protestants kind to Catholics in their midst. A century later, puritan totalitarianism and religious civil wars in England would lead to the reactions of Hobbes and Locke, two of the most seminal thinkers in the liberal tradition.[22] Catholics, in turn, were cruel to Protestants. In the 1530s, the Spanish Inquisition, originally launched (in 1478) to detect covert Judaism among converts, began persecuting Protestants. Catholics were cruel to Catholics too, for that matter. In 1542, a new Roman Inquisition began punishing dissenting Catholics. In 1559 the church published an Index of Prohibited Books; in 1600 the astronomer and philosopher Giodorno Bruno was burned at the stake for publishing views that contradicted Catholic dogma – for instance the view that the stars are moving rather than fixed, and made of the same elements as the Earth.

So the Reformation's immediate effect was not to increase freedom, but to limit it in new and unpredictable ways. In 1200, one could count on not being persecuted if one stuck to Catholic orthodoxy; in 1550, one was at risk of persecution no matter what one professed. However, the Reformation's long-term result is that, in the twenty-first-century western world, one is at little risk of persecution regardless of what one believes. (But there are no guarantees. We realize that our confidence may some day seem ironic in retrospect.)

Wars of religion

In 1541, the French philosopher Sebastian Castellio of Basel wrote the treatise *On Heretics*. Castellio attacked religious persecution on the grounds that Christ wanted people to live together in peace, not to kill each other over disputes. He said that the killing of heretics comes from a lust for power and is repugnant to Christ.

Castellio argued that doctrinal disputes arose because the Scriptures are obscure. Theologian John Calvin was infuriated. How could the Word of God be obscure? Castellio retorted that Calvin himself must believe the Bible to be obscure, since Calvin thought it necessary to write so many commentaries explaining it, and his interpretations were unlike those of his rivals. Castellio challenged Calvin and others: a good physician can defend his opinions without the use of the magistrate's force. Why can't a good theologian do the same? In a later work, Castellio insisted that the right to punish heresy belongs to Jesus, not to secular authority. God alone has the right to punish thoughts; secular authorities are to punish physical actions only.

Another major pro-toleration writer was the Dutch philosopher Dirck Volckertszoon Coornhert. In 1581 he drew up a petition for the town of Haarlem to advocate freedom of worship, saying that no religion should ever be imposed by force and that civil peace and unity required religious freedom. One of his most important works was the *Synod of Freedom of Conscience* (1582). He noted that every sect claims to be the sole possessor of the truth. The only solution to conflict is freedom of religion for all.

When it comes to religious freedom, the march of history has not been a steady one. Progress remained sporadic and tenuous. Calvin maintained that heretics should be coerced and killed, if need be: he bore significant responsibility for the burning of the heretic Michael Servetus in 1553 in Geneva, and his *Defense of the Orthodox Faith*, published one year later, defended such acts.[23] Yet Calvinism laid some of the groundwork for religious liberty, in part because it held that individual churches belonged to particular villages of worshippers, so that their officials had to be elected from within.

The century following Calvin was bloody. German princes tended to force their subjects to adopt whatever religion, Catholic or Lutheran, they themselves adopted. Between 1592 and 1598, hundreds of thousands died in the French Wars of Religion between

Huguenots (Calvinists) and Catholics. During the Thirty Years War – which started as a religious war – the population of what is now Germany may have dropped from 21 million to 13.5 million.[24] As much as a third of the German towns and villages were destroyed. Casualties were not only from combat, rape, looting, and economic devastation, but also from bubonic plague and other epidemics. The Peace of Westphalia in 1648 more or less ended the war. Religious conflict and persecution continued, but on a smaller scale.

Historian Herbert Butterfield suggests that western freedom of religion sprouted from mutual exhaustion.[25] After decades of bloody wars between Protestants and Catholics, it was clear that no stable hegemony of either religion was possible. There comes a time, in wars over religious matters, when warriors realize that our best hope for peace lies not in agreeing on which religion is the correct one, but in agreeing to let people (or at least 'peoples') decide for themselves what religion to practice. Among intellectuals, permissive attitudes toward religion spread, which in turn led to increased indifference toward religion.

Contrary to Butterfield, Perez Zagorin claims that, although intellectual indifference and public exhaustion were reinforcing factors, they were not enough to explain the growth of tolerance.[26] In Germany and France, laws were passed on the basis of expediency to allow Catholics and Protestants to live side by side. But peace built on expediency does not last. As soon as one side came to believe that it could get away with persecution, it began persecuting. Instead, Zagorin stresses that people came to see toleration as an end in itself.

John Knox and the Scottish Enlightenment

John Knox was Scotland's Martin Luther, launching a Calvinist reformation in 1559. Calvinism's rules were harsh. "Gambling, card playing, and the theater were banned. No one could move out of a parish without written permission of the minister."[27] The penalty for adultery was death. On Sundays, working, dancing, and music were forbidden.[28]

However, as historian Arthur Herman notes, Knox's fanaticism opposed not only individual freedom but also public tyranny. Thus Knox and his followers opposed monarchy, favored democracy, and more generally favored governance by the will of the people.[29] In 1638 Scottish nobles, ministers, and ordinary citizens signed a National Covenant denying the king's right to make law without the consent of a free General Assembly and Parliament.[30]

There is also another respect in which Knox's legacy was to be far more liberating than he could have imagined, or approved of. Part of the point of all the repression Knox imposed was that he wanted the Scots to become God's chosen people. To be that, in the mind of a Protestant such as Knox, people could not simply buy indulgences or otherwise lean on the church to intercede with God on their behalf. They had to confront God individually – which meant that they had to study God's Word individually; this meant that they had to study the Bible; and this meant that they had to learn to read. Thus "Knox's original 1560 Book of Discipline called for a national system of education. Eighty years later Parliament passed the first statute to this effect."[31]

Finally, in 1696 Parliament reaffirmed its mandate by establishing a school in every parish. Each parish was to provide a building and the salary for a teacher. In the same year, a nineteen-year-old theology student at the College of Edinburgh named Thomas Aikenhead was arrested and ultimately executed for questioning the Scriptures. It was the second of many years of weather-related crop failures, which resulted in thousands dying from hunger. Nevertheless, the 1700s would be a century of explosive progress.

Herman says that "[i]n 1700 Scotland was Europe's poorest independent country. [Yet this] culturally backward nation rose to become the driving wheel of modern progress."[32] "Before the eighteenth century was over, Scotland would generate the basic institutions, ideas, attitudes, and habits of mind that characterize the modern age."[33]

Scotland would give birth to Adam Smith (who founded economics as an academic discipline), Adam Ferguson (who founded sociology), and James Hutton (who founded geology) – to name just a few of the intellectual leaders of the time. It would also produce the writers James Boswell, Robert Burns, and Walter Scott; the philosophers Francis Hutcheson, David Hume, and Thomas Reid; the physicist James Clerk Maxwell; and the inventors Alexander Graham Bell (inventor of the telephone), James Watt (inventor of the steam engine), James Small (inventor of the iron plough) and James Young (inventor of the method of oil refining).

Much of the inventing was in effect collaborative, with particular instances made possible by the torrent of creativity occurring all around any given inventor. For example, in 1712 Thomas Newcomen had devised a type of steam engine that, unlike its predecessors, was efficient enough to have some commercial uses. In 1769 the Scottish engineer James Watt invented a better form of condenser, which made the engine more efficient and powerful. Yet it was not until seven years later, when Watt partnered with an entrepreneur, Matthew Boulton, that the engine began playing a significant role in industry.[34] Boulton's innovation consisted in pioneering the use of interchangeable parts and a better integrated factory model. (He also developed a form of disability insurance for his workers.)[35]

In Scotland, according to Herman,

> By one estimate male literacy stood around 55 percent in 1720; by 1750 it may have stood as high as 75 percent, compared with only 53 percent in England. . . . Even a person of relatively modest means had his own collection of books, and what he couldn't afford he could get at the local lending library, which by 1750 virtually every town of any size enjoyed. A good example is Innerpeffray, near Crieff in Perthshire. Its library's records of borrowing run from 1747 to 1800. They show books loaned out to the local baker, the blacksmith, the cooper, the dyer and the dyer's apprentice and to farmers, stonemasons, quarriers, tailors, and household servants. Religious books predominated, but more than half of the books borrowed were on secular themes, and included works by John Locke.[36]

By the end of the 1700s, Scotland's literacy rate would be the highest to be found anywhere.[37] Freedom of thought was real, even if unintended and not officially endorsed. Perhaps even more importantly, Scotland became a society in which intellectual accomplishment was revered. Children were growing up with parents who read and admired books and debated fine points over dinner with similarly literate neighbors. No wonder that it was, intellectually, such an explosive time and place.

Hodgson remarks on how ideas of progress and technological efficiency were capturing imaginations across eighteenth-century Europe in a way they never had before:

> The new economic order depended on a large and mobile supply of skilled labor, and particularly on a mass market of persons living above subsistence levels to absorb the steadily increasing product of what was becoming mass production. With mass production and mass consumption, the lower classes, even the peasantry, had to share in the refinements associated with urban living at levels previously reserved to an elite: eventually it became clear that mass literacy was required if a technical society were to function well. . . . Finally, technicalization carried with it an important moral discipline of its own, which merged with and reinforced the gentling of manners we have noted. It presupposed not only a mass society but, as its complement, an individual at once privately isolated and yet highly cultivated and cooperative. Only an independent self-reliant individual, not tied to guild rules or tribal loyalties or communal religious conventions, could innovate with the freedom required or even cultivate secondhand the ever-new specializations demanded for technical efficiency. This made for an increasingly high valuation of individual freedom from controls by other individuals.[38]

The society of feudal Europe, stratified as it had been according to status, was giving way to a modern contract economy. Cities arose, mobility increased, and feudal culture died away, along with the feudal economic system. Meanwhile Protestantism was reconceiving (in some ways retrieving) the individual's relationship to God.

The old hierarchy, in which requests for mercy worked their way up the chain through priests, popes, or angels, was no longer in place. With Protestantism's conception of individual souls as having an unmediated relationship with God, much status hierarchy had to disappear in that realm too.

What lesson should we take from this bit of history? Sometimes it is easier to see that the lesson is important than to see exactly what the lesson is. Many historical events are double-edged swords in terms of how they change history. Thousands of years ago, the invention of coinage freed poor people, enabling them to participate in the marketplace: an enormously liberating development, yet one that also helped to spawn debt servitude. Thousands of years ago, the expansion of markets spurred a Mediterranean renaissance, but also encouraged plantation slavery. In the 1500s, Knox's attempted imposition of authoritarian religion helped to launch the Scottish Enlightenment. Likewise, the industrial revolution would bring astounding increases in living standards. But even the revolution's supporters wondered whether the phenomenon was not also, if accidentally, creating an intellectually slothful working class and an envy-driven, materialistic upper class: bored, petty, guilt-ridden about unearned privileges, and unhappy even though rich.

Many of the most important consequences of people's actions have been unintended. Often one sees in retrospect why events unfolded as they did; yet no one would have *predicted* that events would unfold as they did. What Knox intended and what he actually accomplished are two different matters. There is a lesson here for would-be reformers; but the lesson is neither obvious nor easy to implement. The history of connections between intention and actual outcome is complex.

Natural Law

Europe was reaching a stage where ideas would increasingly drive events. The history of liberty would be a history of evolving ideas at least as much as one of evolving technology. Hugo Grotius held that liberty is inalienable property. "Inalienable rights are things which belong so essentially to one man that they could not belong to another, as a man's life, body, freedom, honor." The distinction between ordinary and inalienable rights allowed Grotius to deny people the right to give up their liberty by placing themselves in bondage. Grotius wrote these words between 1618 and 1621, while he was in prison, serving a life sentence for having repudiated Calvinist doctrines (doctrines that had gripped a Dutch Republic originally founded on principles of religious freedom). Such passages may represent the earliest articulation in intellectual history of the idea that liberty is an inalienable property; they lay the foundation for the concept of inalienable rights, while also planting the seeds of liberalism – the political philosophy that would shape and reshape European society for centuries to come.[39] In 1621, after three years of imprisonment, Grotius escaped with the help of his wife.[40] From exile he published *The Law of War and Peace* in 1625.

Grotius also played a primary role in explicitly reconceiving rights as *alienable* possessions.[41] Aquinas and other medieval figures used the term 'right' to signify accordance with natural law. Francisco Suarez spoke of 'right' as signifying "a certain moral power which every man has, either over his own property or with respect to that which is due to him."[42] Yet according to Haakonssen it is Grotius, not Suarez, who shifted the discourse, such that people came to treat rights as personal possessions rather than as relations or properties.[43]

Of course, trade had been going on for millennia, so people had some concept of the alienability of rightful possession, but Grotius built the philosophical foundation of liberalism by arguing that the legal idea of a right was also an infrastructure of moral thinking about how a person ought to be treated – what kind of treatment a person could command – and not merely hope for – by virtue of having the status of a person. The idea was that of *natural* law: that is, a moral law by which even legislators were bound.[44]

Although Grotius himself was a theologian of note, who argued for the truth of Christianity even as he was arguing against its

Calvinist interpretation, his work also had the effect of secularizing natural law theory – taking it from the province of theologians to that of lawyers and philosophers. (This is another aspect of what makes Grotius one of the inventors of what we now call liberalism).[45] Grotius himself notoriously remarked that his theory would have a degree of validity even if we were to grant what we cannot grant without the greatest wickedness, namely that there is no God, or that human affairs are of no concern to Him.[46] Like Suarez and Aquinas, Grotius held that the dictates of natural law can be discerned by reason because they are not arbitrary.[47] Indeed natural laws are so far from arbitrary that God Himself could not have willed them to be otherwise (short of willing human nature to be something else). Like Suarez again, Grotius repudiated 'the Divine Right of Kings,' treating sovereign authority as deriving instead from the consent of individual citizens. This made Grotius a seminal thinker both in natural law and in contractarian traditions. Grotius argued that rights and duties of natural law are universal, binding us with respect to all humans (and in particular, he stressed, to aboriginal peoples) – not just to Christians.

To Grotius and all subsequent natural law theorists – and to western systems of law and conceptions of morality, influenced as they are by natural law theory – a notion of property lies at the heart of morality, or at least at the heart of respecting the separateness of persons. Specifically, to be respecting persons at all, we must treat them as entitled to life, limb, and liberty. Moreover, for such entitlements to mean what they are supposed to mean, they must enable a person rightfully to live a life fit for a human being. This implies that they must extend far enough to imply a right to work. That is, they must imply a right to work in and on parts of the world that are not already the exclusive possession of anyone else. A person must be at liberty to gather food, for example. (We wonder what Grotius would have made of a society like ours. Today there is virtually no public space for gathering food, so hardly anyone is at liberty in that sense. Yet no one needs to be at liberty in that sense, for anyone with normal abilities earns enough to buy food with just a few hours' labor per day.)

Grotius's story of the original acquisition of private property begins with the supposition that at least some of the earth was given to all humans in common, but the substance of this common right was in fact a right of individuals everywhere to appropriate what they could use, so long as they were using it to support human life. This 'common' right was in fact a primitive form of private property, namely what we now call a *usufructuary* right. To Grotius, there had to be such rights because human beings need to exercise them to survive, and doing what one needs to do to survive is a person's natural right.[48] Grotius further supposes that people are not content merely to survive. They naturally aspire to a more refined life. Such aspirations gave rise initially to trade and then to a division of labor, as people sought ways to use their time more productively, the better to secure a more commodious life. To achieve these more productive ways of life, people had to establish enduring title to land and tools so that they could physically vacate their property (say, to go to the market) without being treated as having abandoned their property.[49]

Therefore the emergence of usufructuary and full-blown private property rights are conceptually (and, to Grotius, historically) distinct events.[50] As people began to lay claims to territory, and to mark by signs what they regarded as their territory, neighbors started, in some cases at least, to accommodate themselves to these claims. To do this, though, it had to be true that neighbors could discern and *could afford to respect* the boundaries of territorial claims.[51]

Toward Religious Freedom

The Jewish ancestors of Baruch Spinoza, the Dutch Enlightenment philosopher, left Spain for Portugal to escape the Spanish Inquisition, then fled to Amsterdam when the Inquisition came to Portugal. In 1619, Amsterdam granted Jews the right to practice their religion. The

Dutch Republic had been founded as a secular state in 1581, but had come under the sway of Calvinism. Amsterdam was relatively permissive, but religious orthodoxy was weighty nonetheless. In 1624 Dutch forces defeated Portugal and captured portions of Brazil. Thousands of Jewish settlers sailed off, hoping for Brazil to be a land of even greater opportunity and freedom. They re-enter our story shortly.

Spinoza was born in 1632. He would be excommunicated in 1656. Formal charges were never made specific, although presumably this punishment was for such heresies as questioning the immortality of the soul and rejecting the idea of a providential God.[52] Neither side ever attempted a reconciliation. In his *Theological–Political Treatise* (1670), Spinoza argued that peace and prosperity depend on the "liberty of philosophizing." He claimed that the reason why Amsterdam was doing so well economically was its liberty. He also argued for democratic republican forms of government. On his view, democracy and liberty enable people to live together despite conflicts of opinion. People who want to impose one opinion on all, by force, may say that they seek truth, unity, or justice, but in reality they seek power. Spinoza's *Treatise* argued against a literal reading of the Bible. Spinoza held that the Scriptures and the writings of the Jewish prophets were acts of imagination and of faith. These texts could teach people faith and benevolence, but they were not instruments of truth. Truth could be found through reason alone. Critical reactions to Spinoza's writing at the time were mostly negative.

American children are often taught that the Puritans who founded the Massachusetts Bay and Plymouth Bay colonies did so in pursuit of freedom of religion. Yet, although the Puritans indeed wanted the freedom to practice their religion, this is not to say that freedom of religion was their *ideal*. On the contrary, they did not permit other religious practices, and they persecuted dissenters. In general, as Zagorin says, "There is no reason to think that the heretics were more tolerant than their persecutors; had the followers of popular heresies possessed the power, they would surely have abolished the Catholic Church and imposed a religious order of their own."[53]

Roger Williams, though, truly believed in freedom of religion. As a teenager, he transcribed sermons and speeches for Edward Coke. Under Coke's patronage, Williams was educated at Cambridge, and he turned out to have a gift for languages. (Williams gave John Milton lessons in Dutch in exchange for lessons in Hebrew. Milton later wrote *Paradise Lost*, but before that he published *Areopagitica*, a denunciation of censorship.) Later on, as a chaplain, Williams found himself in an untenable position of dissent from religious authorities, especially with regard to his intransigent insistence that there be a "wall of separation" between church and state. Williams left England for Boston in 1630. His insistence on the separation between church and state would one day inspire the US Constitution's first amendment, which for the first time explicitly made religion a matter of private conscience and not the rightful business of government. Cyclone Covey writes:

> He was the first American to advocate and activate complete freedom of conscience, dissociation of church and state, and genuine political democracy. From his first few weeks in America he openly raised the banner of "rigid Separatism." In one year in Salem he converted the town into a stronghold of radical Separatism and threw the entire Bay Colony into an uproar. Banished for his views, after being declared guilty of "a frontal assault on the foundations of the Bay system," he escaped just as he was to be deported to England.[54]

Williams also preached that Native Americans, not the king of England, were North America's rightful owners. The parishioners were not amused. Williams was banished from Salem in 1634 and

> settled in Providence with thirteen other householders and in one year formed the first genuine democracy, as well as the first church-divorced and conscience-free community in modern history. Williams felt that government is the natural way provided by God to cope

with the corrupt nature of man. But since government could not be trusted to know which religion is true, he considered the best hope for true religion the protection of the freedom of all religion, including *non-religion*, from the state.[55]

Williams obtained land for the Providence colony from the Narragansett tribe by purchase, not by theft. He tried to persuade other European settlers to purchase land from the natives rather than to seize it or homestead on it. Williams sailed to London to obtain a charter establishing Providence as an independent colony in 1643. He wrote *A Key into the Languages of America* while en route. Published in London, the book established him at the time, and still today, as a respected authority on aboriginal language and culture.

Williams intended Providence to be a sanctuary for all religions. His *Bloody Tenent of Persecution* (1644) argued for a complete separation of church and state. In 1647, Providence united with the colony on Rhode Island. In 1654, Williams returned from a second trip to London to ask the government of Oliver Cromwell to ratify the colony charter, and officially became Governor of Rhode Island.

Brazil's Jewish settlers re-enter the picture in the same year, 1654, when Portugal recaptured Brazil. Once again fearing the Inquisition, Brazilian Jews set sail to return to Amsterdam. They never made it. Attacked by Spanish pirates, their ship plundered and crippled, themselves destitute, they limped into the Dutch settlement of New Amsterdam. After a series of threats of eviction and desperate appeals to Amsterdam, the Dutch West India Company in 1665 (against the wishes of the colony's director-general, Peter Stuyvesant) granted the Jews permission to settle in New Amsterdam.[56] (New Amsterdam would be captured by the English in 1664, and renamed New York.)

Freedom of religion in North America was a fragile thing at best, yet the contrast with Europe remained significant. In 1685, under Louis XIV, France outlawed Protestantism and revoked the Edict of Nantes (originally passed for reasons of exhaustion and expediency), which had protected Protestants in the Catholic country for ninety years.

Louis XIV's government went so far as to seize Protestant children from their parents in order to rear them in the Catholic faith. Revoking the Edict of Nantes hurt the country: many Protestants fled, depriving France of many educated and skilled workers.

Ireland's Penal Laws, especially following 1695, fostered a similar oppression, going the other way. It is not unusual for North Americans of Irish heritage to describe themselves as having descended from horse thieves. But it might have been hard for an Irish Catholic in 1700 to avoid being a horse thief, since Catholics were required by law (on pain of being a 'horse thief,' a crime punishable by death) to turn over any horse they owned to any Protestant who offered five pounds and five shillings for it (a small sum for a horse, even at the time). The actual law ran as follows:

> No papist shall be capable of having or keeping for his use, any horse, gelding or mare of five pounds value. Any protestant who shall make discovery under oath of such horse, shall be authorized with the assistance of a constable, to search for and secure such horse and in case of resistance to break down any door. And any protestant making such discovery and offering five pounds five shillings to the owner of such horse, in the presence of a justice of the peace or chief magistrate, shall receive ownership of such horse as though such horse were bought in the market overt.[57]

By the eighteenth century, English colonies in North America enjoyed unprecedented, if not perfect, freedom of religion. Why? Zagorin explains:

> The de facto limitations on formal authority in America due to the great distances and spread of settlement; the weakness of ecclesiastical authority and organization; the ability of dissident religious communities to move to other parts of the country where they were free of control; and the continual arrival of growing numbers of immigrants of different religious affiliations – all these factors created a fluid situation favorable to the emergence of new religious bodies and popular movements and caused the United States to become a "free market of religion."[58]

Conclusion

There is something pragmatic, yet also heroic, about being willing to live and let live, letting one's fellow citizens be as different, and even as disturbingly heretical, as they please. Critics tend to think that liberalism's 'live and let live' attitude is too undemanding a maxim to be inspiring; but, as Gerald Gaus (among others) has pointed out, people find this maxim extraordinarily hard to live by. "The virtue of minding one's own business is a terribly difficult one."[59] It took most of human history to develop societies where people could conceive of 'minding one's own business' as undemanding. Often, for those who acquire a measure of power, the first option is to assert that power as brutally as possible, lest others have the chance to do unto one what one is doing unto them. Most of the readers of this book live in countries where we no longer treat being of a different religion as a reason for people to kill each other. This is progress in the history of liberty. It has been a long time coming, and there is no guarantee that it will last. Arguably, the things we might contemplate doing in order to try to guarantee that freedom from religious persecution will endure – such as to wipe out illiberal religions – would be self-defeating. Perhaps freedom of religion requires faith, at least faith in the rudimentary good will of other human beings.

Discussion

1   Liberals advocate diversity of viewpoints, philosophies, and lifestyles. Can liberalism survive among people with fundamentally illiberal commitments? Must liberalism be forced upon them? Should the liberal state try to ensure that liberal opinion predominates?

2   Philosopher Michael Walzer sees "spheres of justice" demarcated by types of goods, including money, health, education, office,

recognition, and political power. Different societies demarcate the goods differently and attach different meanings to them. On Walzer's view, oppression is always mediated by the misuse of social goods. He describes injustice as one sphere invading another. An example of such an invasion: Priests in theocracies claim a right to greater political power and wealth on account of their divine grace. Walzer asserts that in just societies the spheres, whatever they are, are kept separate. Is the history of the freedom of religion sometimes a counterexample? For example, did the market sphere's invasions of religion's sphere undercut religion's invasions of the spheres of family, politics, and so on, resulting in a society that is (on Walzer's understanding of justice) more rather than less just?

Notes

1. St Thomas Aquinas advocated a stronger stance toward heretics than Augustine's. In his view, heretics threaten the souls of others, tempting others to reject the Word of God. In Aquinas's view, this permitted the execution of heretics, much as John Stuart Mill would later endorse the use of force to prevent people from harming others even while he rejected the use of force to prevent people from harming themselves. (Contemporary scholars debate whether a line between harm to self and harm to others can easily be drawn. In any case, one historical lesson is that a sufficiently expansive notion of harm to others can become a license to kill heretics.)
2. See Lopez 1976 for a comprehensive account of commercial activities at this time.
3. Mokyr 1990, 183.
4. Ibid., 187.
5. Ibid.
6. North and Thomas 1976, 121. In nine days, she broke a siege that for nearly seven months had been grinding toward an expected English victory, which would have culminated in France becoming part of England.

7.   Ibid.

8.   Ibid., 122.

9.   MacCulloch 2004, 12.

10. Ibid., 20.

11. Erasmus would be accused by fellow Catholics of being as responsible as anyone else for starting the Reformation, while he was also accused by Lutherans of cowardice in refusing to follow his anti-Catholic arguments to their logical conclusion. He was caught in the middle, perhaps, because he did not anticipate Luther's cataclysmic departure. However, although he remained a Catholic, Erasmus was poised to learn from the emergence of Protestantism. In 1533, his *On Repairing the Unity of the Church* advocated a less doctrinally rigid form of Catholicism, which allowed for compromise and for honest doctrinal disputes.

12. Luther 1958, 382–3.

13. The first printed newspaper rolled off the presses in 1605, a fact which, political theorist David Johnston surmises, was a major influence on Thomas Hobbes, leading him to switch from Latin to English prose and to pitch his arguments at an altogether new audience. See Johnston 1989.

14. Of course, many other factors also contributed to Luther's success. The Electors of Saxony and of Brandenburg were powerful lay elites, whose struggles with Holy Roman Emperor Charles V and with Rome itself enabled Luther to fall between the cracks of divided and contested authority. We thank Stephen Davies for the thought.

15. MacCulloch 2004, 72.

16. Danford 2000, 35–6.

17. Ibid., 39.

18. Philpott 2003.

19. Danford 2000, 44. See Luther 1958, 392.

20. Quoted in Kaufman 1979, 305–6.

21. Quoted in Kaufman 1979, 306.

22. Locke's *Letter Concerning Toleration* argues that a peaceful society has to tolerate all Protestant sects (although not Catholics or atheists) that affirm the need for such toleration. His argument was based in part on skepticism about the possibility of ever identifying conclusively the one true religion. In any event, Locke held that "the business of

law is not to provide for the truth of opinions, but for the safety and security of the commonwealth" (Locke 2005, 168).

23. Zagorin 2003, 77.
24. McFarlane 1997, 51.
25. Butterfield 1980, 4–8.
26. Zagorin 2003, 9.
27. Herman 2001, 16.
28. Herman writes that people could be arrested for plucking a chicken on the Sabbath (ibid., 15).
29. Ibid., 18–21.
30. Ibid., 20.
31. Ibid., 23.
32. Ibid., viii.
33. Ibid., 11.
34. Cameron and Neal 2003, 194. Watt may also have been delayed by difficulties in obtaining a patent. See Uglow 2002, 294.
35. Robinson 1953, 376.
36. Herman 2001, 23.
37. Ibid., 23.
38. Hodgson 1993, 64–5.
39. Pipes 1999, 31.
40. His wife petitioned repeatedly to be confined along with her husband and to share his sentence, and her plea was eventually granted. She was allowed to leave for brief periods, such as to fetch Grotius his library. Eventually she staged a spat with Grotius, and seemingly in a vindictive fury shipped several trunks of his books home again, so as to deprive him of them. Grotius himself, of course, was in one of those trunks.
41. Miller 2005.
42. Ibid.
43. Haakonssen 1985, 240.
44. We thank Jacob Levy for confirming this thought.
45. If there is a general, secular account of natural law theory, it is roughly this. First, natural law commands us to arrange institutions in general and positive laws in particular so that they are conducive to the betterment of human beings, or at least to that of fellow citizens, without working to the detriment of non-citizens. Second, the answer to the question

of what institutions promote human flourishing depends on human nature. In particular, if human beings are naturally self-interested, yet have a propensity for benevolence under some circumstances and a propensity for self-destructive envy under other circumstances, that has a bearing on the question of what institutions work.

Does failing to maximally benefit non-citizens count as working to their detriment? A sophisticated natural law theory treats this question as answerable within the framework of the theory itself. That is, we settle on how to interpret the moral significance of national borders by asking what would be conducive to the betterment of human beings in general. Borders prevent, or at least limit, the damage caused by uncontrolled overuse – that is, commons tragedies. At some point, inevitably, if the question is how to promote the flourishing of human beings in general, avoiding or limiting commons tragedies becomes primary. For further discussion, see Buckle 1991, chapter 1. For background on the significance of boundaries in empowering people to avoid 'tragedies of the commons,' see Schmidtz's essay on "The Institution of Property," reprinted in Schmidtz 2008.

46. Grotius 2005, 89. There are many translations of this remark. We have not followed any of them to the letter.

47. Buckle 1991, 24.

48. Intuitively, a fairness issue arises here. What about those who arrive too late to have a shot at privately appropriating a share of that common land? Some people say that the first appropriators are extraordinarily lucky, and therefore the rich (presumably descendants of the first appropriators) should give money to the poor. See Schmidtz 2008 ("The Institution of Property") for a discussion of how much better off we are in virtue of arriving centuries too late to be first appropriators. In response, it has been suggested in conversation that, if the first appropriators' being *better* off does not provide grounds for transferring wealth from rich to poor, perhaps the first appropriators' being *worse* off is – that is, a fitting way of commemorating their sacrifices would be for the rich to acknowledge that they did not deserve to be so lucky, and for that reason to transfer their wealth to the poor. The second argument has the advantage of starting with something closer to a true premise.

49. Grotius 2005, 426. See also Buckle 1991, 41.

50. Buckle 1991, 42.

51. Carol Rose (1985) says that, when one takes possession of a patch of land, one takes on two obligations. One is to do something useful with the land. The second and more subtle obligation is to provide the world with continuous and clear notice of the borders of one's claim, lest a would-be settler accidentally try to settle apparently unoccupied but in fact already claimed land.

52. In his *Ethics* of 1677, Spinoza conceived of God and nature as being the same. God has no personality. God's orders are the laws of nature, which are themselves part of God's nature. There are no miracles. See Spinoza 2005, 1–30.

53. Zagorin 2003, 36.

54. Covey 1966, 3.

55. Ibid.

56. By 1654, eighteen languages were in use on the streets of New Amsterdam. The Dutch had become a minority. Stuyvesant saw the colony becoming a "babble of confusion," and asked Dutch East India's board of directors to endorse his effort to ensure that "none of the Jewish nation be permitted to infest the colony." To Stuyvesant's astonishment, the board responded by reminding him

> that he was running a business colony, not a religious establishment, and for the sake of that business, no one should be turned away. The consciences of men ought to be free and unshackled, so long as they continue moderate, peaceable, inoffensive and not hostile to government. Such have been the maxims of toleration by which this city has been governed, and the result has been that the oppressed and persecuted from every country have found among us an asylum from distress. Follow in the same steps, and you shall be blessed. (Burns, Sanders, and Ades 1999, 15)

We thank Cathleen Johnson for this information.

57. Schaffer 2000. From the Statutes of the Penal Laws, 7 Will III c.5 (1695) sec. 10.

58. Zagorin 2003, 302.

59. Gaus 1997, 28.

Chapter 4

Freedom of Commerce: 1776

THESIS: *As trade emerges, there emerges with it a new way of being self-sufficient: in a market society, people can produce enough to meet their own needs by producing enough to meet other people's needs. Freedom of commerce under the rule of law empowers people to cooperate on a massive scale, liberating each other from poverty.*

Freedom from Poverty

It was a complete surprise to nearly everyone when, on July 24, 1959, Vice President Richard Nixon showed Soviet Premier Nikita Krushchev a model of a six-room American house. Krushchev and the Soviet press scoffed, saying the model was no more representative of typical American living standards than the Taj Majal was of life in India. Western journalists, stunned, realized that Krushchev was not kidding. Kruschev was the *leader*, not some naïve pawn, of a Soviet machine that, until then, had been assumed to be mapping the furthest frontiers of productivity and prosperity.[1] Yet he had no clue that an economy could be as productive as America's.

The model house that Krushchev believed impossible was selling for $14,000, which made it affordable to typical steelworkers at the time.[2] Later that day, Nixon remarked that America's 44 million families owned 56 million cars, 50 million television sets, and 143 million radios. 31 million families owned their own homes. Nixon concluded: "What these statistics demonstrate is this: the United States, the world's largest capitalist country, has from the standpoint of the distribution of wealth come closest to the ideal of prosperity for all in a classless society."[3]

In a command economy, a central planner cannot know whether to order a factory to produce plastic or metal shovels, gold or aluminum wire, leather or canvas shoes. Planners must guess what to produce and where to send it. People line up for hours to receive whatever is being doled out that day, and perhaps they go home with a plastic shovel. If it is useful, they may be able to exchange it (illegally) for canvas shoes, doled out to someone else on some other day; but a factory producing plastic shovels won't know and won't have reason to care whether they are producing anything useful, since there are no customers (except perhaps on the black market) to buy the factory's product anyway.[4] The Soviet GDP per man-hour in 1987 was less than a third of that of the United States.[5]

Many countries could not feed all of their citizens in 1800, when 95 percent of their workers were farmers. Today, some of those same countries, employing under 2 percent of their workforce in agriculture, produce excess food.[6] Most people now living in these countries are liberated so completely from the shackles of material deprivation that they need not concern themselves with food production at all. Some aim to make lasting contributions in literature, art, or technology. The result is that the most commercially advanced societies of any given age produce not only the widgets and the food, but also the artists, poets, and inventors. It is no accident that, historically, cultural hubs have also been commercial hubs: Athens in ancient Greece, Venice and Florence in Renaissance Italy, or New York today.

Greg Easterbrook observes that, "[f]our generations ago, the poor were lean as fence posts, their arms bony and faces gaunt. To our recent ancestors, the idea that *even the poor* eat too much might be harder to fathom than a jetliner rising from the runway."[7] The wealth we enjoy at the dawn of the twenty-first century did not exist any-where in the world a thousand years ago – or even fifty, for that matter. In constant dollars, the United States today has, by itself, an economic output that is (even by conservative estimates) about 50 percent greater than the *entire world*'s output in 1950.[8]

We have come a long way. This chapter is the story of how it happened.

Freedom from War

Francis Bacon foresaw science's potential to foster material progress. In Bacon's mind, the knowledge of his day was nothing compared to what people could and would learn over the coming centuries. Thus Bacon repudiated medieval scholasticism's reverence for antiquity. He tried to cultivate dissatisfaction with the current state of human knowledge and to replace complacency and deference to the past with a spirit of adventure.

Bacon was a philosophical expositor of scientific methods, as was Bacon's towering contemporary, Galileo. We remember Bacon as a champion of the modern scientific method.[9] Less often remembered is the fact that Bacon was preoccupied by the topic of ambition; he distinguished three kinds. In Bacon's words,

> The first is the ambition of those who are greedy to increase their personal power in their own country; which is common and base. The second is the ambition of those who strive to extend the power and empire of their country among the human race; this surely has more dignity, but no less greed. But if anyone attempts to renew and extend the power and empire of the human race itself over the uni-verse of things, his ambition (if it should so be called) is without a doubt more sensible and more majestic than the others'. And the empire of man over things lies solely in the arts and sciences. For one does not have empire over nature except by obeying her.[10]

This was part of Bacon's attraction to science. As he saw it, ambition could concern not the dominion of self over others, or even the dominion of one's nation over others, but instead the dominion of humanity over nature.[11] In Bacon's mind, channeling one's ambition into science, on behalf of humanity, was a move toward peace, in contrast with the constant wars plaguing Bacon's time.[12] Vanity is dangerous even under favorable circumstances, and it makes for abject misery when it drives people to try to outdo each other in war: far better when vanity drives people to outdo others in commercial or scientific achievement. In the words of political theorist John Danford, "modern science, as the visionary Bacon taught, would contribute greatly to 'the relief of man's estate' and thus to the increase of an important kind of freedom, freedom from want, from anxiety, and from bondage to our most basic bodily needs."[13]

So, when we speak of the rule of law as a framework for commerce, we do not simply mean garden-variety trucking and bartering. We also mean the most far-reaching consequence of our trucking and bartering, namely the rising tide of innovation.[14] In other words, when the rule of law is working, it constitutes a two-fold liberation of human ingenuity and of human society. It frees us both to *form* expectations (about what people around us are likely to want and need) and to *exceed* expectations (by inventing new ways to make our neighbors better off). We will return to the topic of expectations.

Somehow we have accomplished what Bacon (and his one-time secretary Thomas Hobbes) said we needed to accomplish in order to avoid the prospect of vanity degenerating into a war of all against all. Western powers figured out how to turn people away from war and toward trucking and bartering. The West turned other people's talents into a boon rather than a threat.

In a nutshell, society's most liberating achievement lies in how, under favorable circumstances, it turns human energy and ingenuity away from war (away from zero-sum and negative-sum games in general) and toward peaceful, voluntary, mutually advantageous cooperation. To be sure, we still live in a world plagued by war. The peace of which

Bacon dreamt still eludes much of the developing world. However, western powers are no longer embroiled in century-long wars with each other. Bacon's vision of what science could achieve turned out to be right.

Freedom from absolute poverty

We spoke in Chapter 3 of the torrent of intellectual and scientific achievements pouring out of the Scottish Enlightenment in the 1700s. The work of a scientist such as Marie Curie is one paradigm of Bacon's noblest ambition for humanity. Adam Smith, in a less obvious way, was another paradigm. Indeed Smith followed in Bacon's footsteps, insofar as both, like Hobbes, pondered the prospects for channeling natural human propensities in the direction of mutual advantage rather than of mutual destruction. Thus Smith studied how natural propensities (to truck and barter, and to be more or less insatiably acquisitive) could be channeled toward pursuits that would make the rest of humanity better off rather than worse off. A third kind of exemplar of Bacon's noblest ambition would be technological innovators. For the 1700s, consider Smith's fellow Scots, the steam engine pioneers James Watt and Matthew Boulton. For the 1800s, consider the American steamship operator Cornelius Vanderbilt and the steam-powered locomotives of the Canadian railroad builder James J. Hill. Meanwhile, the "Suez Canal, completed in 1869, and the Panama Canal, completed in 1914, dramatically cut international shipping times, as did the progressive development of faster and larger steamships from the 1840s."[15]

By the 1840s, we find sentiments such as this:

> The bourgeoisie, during its rule of scarce one hundred years, has created more massive and more colossal productive forces than have all preceding generations together. Subjection of Nature's forces to man, machinery, application of chemistry to industry and agriculture,

steam-navigation, railways, electric telegraphs, clearing of whole continents for cultivation, canalisation of rivers, whole populations conjured out of the ground – what earlier century had even a presentiment that such productive forces slumbered in the lap of social labour?[16]

As Marx and Engels were recording this thought, the technological revolution we see all around us today was just picking up steam (so to speak).[17] Automobiles would replace horses – and cities would be much cleaner because of it: imagine walking through the manure of a hundred thousand horses in London in the mid-1800s. The Scrantons would pioneer innovations in heavy industry, and would be superseded by Charles Schwab and Andrew Carnegie. (Schwab would develop the H-beam steel girder. A refinement of the concept, the I-beam, was light enough, strong enough, and flexible enough to permit the building of skyscrapers.) Abraham Gesner invented kerosene in 1854. By the 1870s John D. Rockefeller pushed oil drilling and refining technology to a point where the price of oil would fall from fifty-eight to eight cents per gallon. People could light their homes with kerosene for about one cent per hour, reducing the demand for whale oil.

Friendly societies would spring up in America, England, Australia and all over the world to provide health insurance and other social services to immigrants, migrant workers, and urban populations in general. In France, Louis Pasteur and Claude Bernard invented a technique called pasteurization, which slowed microbial growth. Pasteur also continued Edward Jenner's work on developing a vaccine for smallpox, rabies, and many other diseases. In England, James Tyndall and (in the twentieth century) Alexander Fleming were discovering antibiotics. (Precursors to both vaccines and antibiotics were known in China at least 2500 years ago.) Technology was driving heavy industry, which was driving urbanization, and the need for better epidemiology and better sanitation was being met at the same time. Alexander Graham Bell patented the telephone in 1876, and the

Hungarian engineer Tivadar Puskas, with help from his collaborator Thomas Edison, invented the telephone exchange and, later on, the multiple switchboard. The cost of transportation and the cost of communication were falling drastically, driving a new age of commercial and technological progress.

As recently as two hundred years ago, an average person lived on about a dollar a day – a state of extreme poverty, as the World Bank defines it today. On one estimate, worldwide gross domestic product per capita between 5000 BC and AD 1800 did not even double.[18] Since then, it has risen more than thirty-fold.[19] Wealth was created, not merely captured.[20]

Many of us think that life was simpler for our ancestors, and in one way this has to be true: our ancestors had a smaller and thus less intimidating menu of life choices. Be that as it may; average life expectancies in the West rose several decades over the past century, translating directly into staggering gains in terms of what average people can do with their lives. (Our chapter on psychological freedom notes that these gains can be staggering in a less metaphorical sense. It turns out that there are limits to our ability to cope with expanding sets of unfamiliar options.) We are not saying that this explosion of wealth increased positive liberty *by definition*. Indeed, we all know people whose rising wealth did not set them free. Still, as a matter of fact, average people can and generally do live far richer, freer, and longer lives than average people led in 1800. What average workers can buy with a day's earnings has risen explosively, and rising wealth tends to translate into being in able to accomplish more. For example, buying a bicycle in 1895 would cost an average American 36 times as many hours of labor as a vastly more useful bicycle would cost by 1997. Buying *Encyclopedia Britannica* would have cost 35 times as many hours in 1895.[21] Today about two thirds of Americans attend some college after high school; about a third end up with college degrees. A hundred years ago, the question would have been what percentage finish high school.[22] Hundreds of years ago, most families could afford few books, if any. Today, most families can access millions of books for free, without leaving their homes, if (as most do) they have a computer with internet access.

Freedom to criticize

Jean-Jacques Rousseau criticized commercial society for teaching people to be vain, stupid, manipulative, and preoccupied by trinkets.[23] Economist of culture Tyler Cowen would say: yes, the market produces Britney Spears – but also Mozart, Beethoven, and your ten favorite artists, whoever these may be.[24] Unquestionably, our economy is more commercial than Rousseau's was. Yet a child born to working-class parents is more likely to read Rousseau in our day than in Rousseau's.[25]

We observed earlier that a civilization's commercial hubs will also be its cultural hubs. Suppose you find market society repulsive, and you are seeking the most devastating *critique* of markets you can find. Where would you go? The places for top-quality criticism are London, New York, or Boston – not Pyongyang, Havana, or even Moscow. Only in commercial society were critics such as Marx and Rousseau free to speak their minds. Critics, needless to say, come from the right as well as from the left. Conservatives, fundamentalists, and evangelicals today, who lament the moral decay of commercial society, never dream of leaving it, because there was a good reason why their ancestors risked their lives in order to migrate to commercial societies. Only in commercial society were they secure in the right to choose their faith. This is to say that alternatives to materialistic lifestyles tend to be secure in commercial societies and less so elsewhere, since commercial societies tend also to be tolerant societies.

Ingredients of Commercial Progress

Our daily dealings with each other are a vast, intricate, evolving web of mutual understandings: these come into play every time we stop at a traffic light, leave a tip at a restaurant, leave our weapons at home, or enter a voting booth. We know roughly what to expect from each other, and knowing roughly what to expect enables us to live well together. This is why we can live as close together as we do, while at the same time having as much room to breathe as we do. Knowing what to expect enables us to adapt to each other.

Not being obliged to conform to expectations is, likewise, an enormous benefit. The two benefits seem mutually exclusive, yet freedom of contract lets us reap both at once. We can rely on being able to go to market and find someone selling cauliflower at an affordable price. We can also rely on being able to go to market and find someone rendering obsolete what a few years ago had been cutting-edge technology. We make progress by testing what has not previously been tested. We experiment.

There is, however, a problem with experiments: many of them *don't work*.[26] Rather, the ideas they test turn out to be bad ideas.[27] Thus a long-term successful society encourages people not only to experiment, but also to shut down experiments when the ideas behind them prove unsound.[28]

What kind of framework encourages experimentation without at same time perpetuating *bad* ideas? Here is one hypothesis that holds true in a wide range of cases, yet has enough substance to be interesting: in societies that work and sustain progress over long periods, people are free *from* the burden of paying for other people's experiments and free *to* derive substantial benefits from their own experiments.

We have considered one of the most crucial ingredients of commercial progress: intellectuals must be free to invent and to push the frontier of technological progress. If some intellectuals choose to become social critics or philosophers instead of inventors, so be it. Critics and philosophers serve us well in their own way. They make us pause to reflect on the point of technological progress – and occasionally remind us that there has, after all, been progress. Society was not always the way it is today, nor will it remain as it is today.

The right to say no

Rosenberg and Birdzell discuss just price and compulsory exchange laws in medieval Europe. These laws denied craftsmen and farmers the right to get the best price they could for their services. The church set prices. The laws had a noble purpose: to prevent exploitation, to increase fairness, and to serve the needs of the poor. But the laws did not deliver the intended result. Instead, they reinforced the medieval guilds – which had monopolies on the trade of certain goods and services – and prevented goods from being produced at a level that might have reflected the relative scarcity of, and demand for, those goods. The laws kept Europe economically stagnant and made sure that the poor stayed poor. Eliminating price controls helped Europe and its poor classes to become rich.[29]

Philosophers have written much about the idea that the consent of the governed is a prerequisite of legitimate government, but little about the parallel idea that consent is a prerequisite of legitimate trade. In a free society, you can vote. But in a really free society, you can vote with your feet. The fundamental thing about commerce in a market is that you have a right to walk away from any proposed terms of trade, in search of something better.

This was a right that farmers in the French province of Limoges lacked when Adam Smith was composing his *Wealth of Nations*. So, in 1774, when Anne Robert Jacques Turgot became controller-general of France, he tried to do something about it. Turgot had been a tax collector for the province of Limoges since 1761. There he found half a million peasants living in mud huts and using plows that were no better than those of ancient Rome. Between taxes and church tithes, the peasants managed to keep about a fifth of their meager incomes. Turgot saw that, as long as peasants were not allowed to sell their products to the highest bidder but were legally required instead to sell their produce to a particular aristocrat at prices of that aristocrat's choosing, they would live on the edge of starvation.

In 1776, as controller-general, Turgot issued the *Six Edicts*, which included removing controls on grain production, reducing tariffs, and ending the *corvée*.[30] (The *corvée*, defended by Rousseau, was a vestige of feudalism, requiring peasants to spend up to fourteen days per year without pay, building and maintaining the king's roads.) Turgot also eliminated the craft guilds' monopoly privileges on grounds that people should not need permission to choose an occupation.[31] Turgot sought and temporarily won for his constituents the right to choose their own occupation – a right the denial of which was another vestige of feudalism. He also increased taxes on higher estates, which made him unpopular with the nobility and landed gentry. He was dismissed after refusing to grant favors to friends of Marie-Antoinette. His reforms were reversed. The *corvée* continued until the French Revolution in 1789.

In sum, Turgot found rural France in tatters, with peasants lacking the most rudimentary freedoms: the freedom to choose an occupation, to choose their customers, to choose their prices, and so on. Under such circumstances, it was inevitable that peasants would be impoverished. Turgot knew what the workers needed. He knew that the rudimentary ingredients of negative liberty were the key to releasing that ingenuity and perseverance by which they could liberate themselves from material deprivation, thereby parlaying their negative liberty into positive liberty. Turgot did everything he could to give the peasants the freedom they needed. The debauched monarchy that thwarted him thereby sealed its own fate.

Turgot was a force in intellectual as well as political circles. He was an influential acquaintance of Condorcet, Montesquieu, Benjamin Franklin, and Voltaire.[32] He met Adam Smith in 1765 and gave him several books pertaining to Smith's research on the wealth of nations. In 1750 Turgot predicted the American Revolution, and foresaw that this new country, America, would suffer from the legacy of slavery and from civil war far more than it would ever suffer at the hands of a foreign invader. He also predicted a bloody revolution in France that would culminate in the king's execution.

He warned that switching to paper currency could and would result in hyper-inflation.[33]

In his essay *Reflections on the Formation and Distribution of Wealth*, written in 1766, Turgot helped to polish the theory of Quesnay, a representative of the physiocratic school, according to which land is the only source of wealth. This physiocratic view prompts the following skeptical thought. Even today, people speak of the value of land in commercial society as if land itself, rather than human ingenuity and toil, were the ultimate producer of the explosion of wealth we see all around us.[34] Yet no one stays home nowadays hoping to inherit the family farm: a person's fortune is constituted mainly by her job skills, as long as people are free to move where their job skills are most valued. The price of land *within* cities rises relatively quickly, in part because so many people have been willing to pay a premium to live in close proximity to increasingly productive concentrations of job skills.

The price mechanism

We can expect a rule of law to evolve into a framework that brings people together, fosters the kind of trade that is the essence of a community, and begins to generate information in the form of prices.[35] Reliable information about prices, when people have it, tells them how to be of greatest service to others and to prosper in the process. Yet prices must be flexible, not just knowable; because, to reflect facts about what buyers and sellers need and want, prices must continuously respond to *changing* facts about what buyers and sellers need and want. So, as Hayek taught us, prices can't be fixed, or even planned. For prices to be able to teach us – *in timely fashion* – anything about what people want right now, how much they are willing to do in exchange for getting what they want, what they can produce, and how much we would have to give to make it worth their time to give us what we want, prices must rise and fall with supply and demand.

Lowering transaction cost

Chapter 1 noted that the invention of coinage was liberating, allowing people to move beyond bartering. George Selgin observes that
westerners today rarely have to worry about a shortage of coinage,
or of currency in general; but this was not always the case. In the
early modern era, British economy faced the crisis of not having enough
coinage to do business.[36] Precious metals were scarce; the debasement of coins was rampant. China, the birthplace of paper, invented
paper money in the eleventh century,[37] but Spiegel notes that, in Europe,
"paper money did not emerge until the end of the seventeenth
century, and its rise reflected the perpetual troubles that arose from
the debasement of metallic currencies."[38] Copernicus, a Prussian
administrator who would revolutionize astronomy by producing the
first scientifically grounded heliocentric theory, observed in 1522 that
"money usually depreciates when it becomes too abundant."[39]

Selgin remarks:

> The Irish coin shortage quickly spread to Great Britain, becoming
> especially serious there during the critical first stages of the Industrial
> Revolution. That revolution . . . generated a huge demand for coins
> suitable for paying the wages of miners, factory workers, and journey-
> men. . . . Whether the Industrial Revolution was liberating or not,
> the fact remains that, thanks to it, large numbers of families that had
> once pastured animals on the waste while obtaining gleanings, brush-
> wood, and turf from common fields now had to purchase their but-
> ter, flour, and fuel, and had to purchase them with money. Having
> lost their cows, the new "waged proletariat" found themselves utterly
> dependent on their coppers. But while landless workers multiplied,
> the supply of good money, and of good small money especially,
> dwindled.[40]

Selgin tells us that, because of a shortage of coinage needed to make
transactions, the British industrial revolution came close to not

happening. (Imagine how well our economy would function if there were no credit or debit cards and the smallest unit of currency were a fifty dollar bill.) For various reasons, the Royal Mint failed, for a long time, to provide enough small coin for workers, and small bank notes were illegal. The mint focused on gold coins, but these were too large for daily transactions, and there were problems with silver coinage. Selgin reports that button makers solved the problem by issuing high quality private coinage. Private 'tradesmen's tokens' were heavily used for small transactions until 1821.[41]

Today transaction costs are plunging. Suppose we want to query a scholar who lives in Australia. Twenty years ago, such an exchange would have taken weeks, at non-trivial cost. Now, with the emergence of the internet, it can be done in minutes, at virtually no charge. Monetary transactions are made electronically. Average people (not only tycoons and presidents) can initiate a moving of goods around the world with a few strokes at a keyboard.[42]

Property rights

Consider, then, the point of property rights. In a way, such rights are like fences:[43] their whole point is to *get in the way*. Or, if putting up fences does not sound liberating, consider a different metaphor: rights are like traffic lights. Traffic lights facilitate movement not so much by turning green as by turning red. Without traffic lights, we would all have, in effect, a green light, and the result would be grid-lock. By contrast, a system where we face, in turn, red and green lights helps to keep us moving. The system constrains us, but we all gain in terms of our ability to get where we want to go; for we develop mutual expectations that enable us to do so uneventfully. Red lights can be frustrating, but the game they create for us is a positive-sum one. We all reach our destination more quickly, more safely, and more predictably, because we know what to expect from each other.

We don't want *lots* of rights for the same reason why we wouldn't want to face red lights every fifty feet. Getting our traffic management system right is a matter of getting the most compact set of lights that does the job of enabling motorists to know what to expect, and thereby to move from point A to point B with minimal delay.

Commerce is a kind of traffic. The point of commercial traffic management is to enable people not only to stay out of each other's way, but to come together to execute plans that seem, upon reflection, almost impossibly elaborate. (Consider how much cooperation is involved in being able to exchange a few minutes of your labor for a slice of pizza. Implicitly, you cooperate with those who produce the pepperoni, with those who build vehicles that transport the pepperoni, with those who manufacture tires for these vehicles, with those who produce rubber for tire manufacturers, and so on. You have no idea who these people are, where they live, or what language they speak, yet you are cooperating with untold thousands of them in stunningly intricate and successful ways.)

What about pedestrians?[44] The question is important, since everyone enters the world as a 'pedestrian,' too young to drive the community's commercial traffic. The question, we admit, reveals a crucial flaw in our traffic light metaphor, a way in which the metaphor radically understates the scope and magnitude of the benefits that derive from a successful property regime. Literal traffic lights are working well when people manage simply to stay out of each other's way, but *commercial* traffic management aims not merely to be accident-free but to generate synergy, bringing people together and launching the process by which twenty-year-old have-nots become forty-year-old haves. Commercial traffic – the trucking and bartering of multitudes – is a community's lifeblood, enabling children to grow up to become *drivers*, not a permanent underclass of spectators.[45]

As David Hume joked, property conventions would seem magical to an outside observer.[46] Somehow they help us to form expectations, and thereby to live in peace and prosperity. Analogously, traffic lights hardly do anything. They just sit there, blinking. Without them, however, we are not as good at figuring out what to expect, and consequently we are not as good at getting where we need to go while staying out of each other's way.

What counts as a properly defined property right is itself an evolving puzzle. For example, in *Hinman* v. *Pacific Air Transport* (1936) a landowner sues an airline for trespass, asserting a right to stop airlines from crossing over his property. The court's predicament was this: on the one hand, the right to say no is the backbone of a system of property, which in turn is the backbone of cooperation among self-owners. On the other hand, much of the point of property is to facilitate commercial traffic; and, when it comes to that, the skies were becoming the scene of one of the most important developments in human history. For a judge to rule that landowners can effectively veto the air traffic industry would be the equivalent of interpreting property rights as a license to gridlock traffic; landowners would profit by threatening to *stop* commercial traffic, not by helping to *facilitate* it. As the case turned out, the judge ruled that the right to say no extends only as high as a landowner's actual use. Higher altitudes were subject to navigation easements, which were held by the public and administered by the federal government.

The *Hinman* verdict is explainable in terms of transaction costs. (Transaction costs are costs incurred in concluding a transaction: commissions, time and money spent on transportation to and from the market, equipment and space rentals, time spent waiting in line, and so on.) Forcing airlines to transact with untold thousands of landowners for permission to pass over each owner's land would be prohibitively costly. The ruling could also be explained in terms of an imperative to curb *rent-seeking*. The transactions that are increasing wealth in society are between airlines and their customers. Permitting landowners thousands of feet below to try to grab a piece of the action would add nothing to the value of the commerce and would reduce the rewards of commercial air traffic for those whose trading creates the rewards. This economic argument is relevant not as a justification for trespassing, but because it bears on whether commercial air traffic should count as trespassing in the first place.

From Grotius to Locke – and indeed to Hume and Adam Smith – private property's justification was predicated on the massive contribution it was thought to make to productivity, hence to trade, and hence to the prosperity of everyone involved. Property rights can be seen as a set of conventions, in the same way stopping for red lights or driving on the right side of the road are conventions. Some conventions are the products of deliberate design, but many of them, including the ones just mentioned, emerge spontaneously. We could imagine legislators passing laws that require everyone to conform to a particular pattern of behavior, but this is not the story of how most conventions emerge. Rather, people simply observe how others are doing things, and then follow suit. Language and money are prime examples. Our evolving understandings (for instance, of what people are referring to when they say 'aubergine' or of whether people around us accept American dollars as a medium of exchange) are not precipitates of philosophical principles or of legislation in any straightforward sense. Our changing conventions are an *alternative* to society by top-down design, not a form of it.[47]

Such institutions emerge spontaneously, as people search for safer, more productive ways to interact. Theory, the law, and even religion must catch up with evolving practice.

Division of labor, economies of scale, and specialization

As trade emerges (and begins to produce patterns that add up to what we call a community), there emerges with it an opportunity for people to be self-sufficient in a new sense, not by producing to directly meet their own needs, as much as by producing to meet *other people's* needs. We all have met people whom we think of as more or less self-sufficient; but such people are nothing like Robinson Crusoe. Most of them come nowhere near to producing enough to meet their own needs, in the way a hermit would need to do. They do not even try to be self-sufficient in that sense. Instead, plumbers (for instance) go to the market to offer their plumbing skills to other people, and after a series of trades they go home with plenty of food for their families, without ever growing a grain of food. They are self-sufficient not in the sense of sustaining themselves in a vacuum, but rather in a sense of having *earned* the goods they need to sustain themselves. They obtain goods by offering something in exchange – something their trading partners consider more valuable under the circumstances than what they are giving up. (Needless to say, not everyone impresses us as self-sufficient in this way, and children hardly ever do.)

The division of labor creates opportunities to serve and be served by vast multitudes. In an advanced commercial society, one produces for customers whom one may never meet. One may be only dimly aware of their purposes, or of their very existence. One knows only that sales are good; someone deems the product to be worth its price, which is all that an ordinary producer needs to know. This is the ground on which modern society and modern prosperity are built.[48]

When Adam Smith wrote *The Wealth of Nations* in 1776, European governments were seeing themselves as having a direct role in promoting commerce by protecting domestic industry from foreign competition. Smith is remembered as a defender of free trade, but his practical goal was to repudiate mercantilism's way of protecting domestic industry.

The guiding thesis of mercantilism is that a country prospers by exporting more than it imports, thus maintaining a positive cash flow. In practice, this involves the imposition of tariffs and other restrictions designed to limit imports so as to protect politically influential domestic producers from foreign competition. Smith commented: "It is the industry which is carried on for the benefit of the rich and the powerful, that is principally encouraged by our mercantile system. That which is carried on for the benefit of the poor and the indigent, is too often, either neglected, or repressed."[49] Ordinary consumers pay more for protected goods than if there were foreign competition to discipline those who otherwise monopolize domestic markets.

Smith's main point was that, in the long run, nations get rich by being productive and by making goods cheaper, not by subsidizing unproductive enterprises and making goods more expensive. Stated so simply, the principle seems obvious; and yet, as Smith says, most economic policy in his day did the opposite. So he concludes:

> By means of glasses, hotbeds, and hotwalls, very good grapes can be raised in Scotland, and very good wine too can be made of them at about thirty times the expence for which at least equally good wine can be bought from foreign countries. Would it be a reasonable law to prohibit the importation of all foreign wines, merely to encourage the making of claret and burgundy in Scotland?[50]

Smith's own answer is:

> The taylor does not attempt to make his own shoes, but buys them of the shoemaker. The shoemaker does not attempt to make his own cloaths, but employs a taylor . . . All of them find it for their interest to employ their whole industry in a way in which they have some advantage over their neighbours, and to purchase with a part of its produce . . . whatever else they have occasion for . . . What is the prudence in the conduct of every private family, can scarce be folly in that of a great kingdom.[51]

Smith claims that the typical result of providing monopoly rights or tariff protection to any industry is to divert capital from more to less productive work (such as tending vineyards in Scotland).[52]

What sort of foreign policy goes with mercantilism? A feverish one, Plato might have said; and 2000 years later Adam Smith, moral philosopher and Plato scholar would have agreed.[53] If one believes that to buy foreign products is to be a loser in a zero-sum game, then one will want to acquire foreign products by some means other than paying for them. By the same token, if one believes in self-sufficiency as an economic ideal, then merely avoiding trade with neighboring countries will not be enough. One will want to acquire their land and their working populations, thereby moving closer to the ideal of national self-sufficiency. If one is a mercantilist, one begins to think of military might as a first resort, and of voluntary trade as a last resort. Mercantilists do not treat either game as *mutually* advantageous. They see trade – *paying* to import wanted goods – as a way of losing, and the military alternative as a way of making the *other side* lose. So, partly in the name of protecting domestic industry and promoting self-sufficiency as an alternative to international trade, and partly out of a desire for glory, mercantilist European states began building empires.[54]

Smith wanted to dismantle the mercantilist system. According to him, nations become wealthy by expanding their markets, thereby expanding the opportunities for people to become more specialized producers of sophisticated products for millions of Europeans rather than for dozens of fellow villagers. The opening pages of *Wealth of Nations* explain how the division of labor in a market economy makes workers thousands of times more productive than they would be otherwise; and Smith was not exaggerating. (Returning to an earlier example, if you want pizza today, you can acquire a slice of it in exchange for a few minutes of work. But if you tried to make a pizza all by yourself, eschewing all reliance upon the division of labor, you would not live long enough. On your own, you would not even be able to smelt the iron to make the oven and other basic tools that you would need to get started.) Smith notes that the occupation of porter could not exist in a village. There are no porters except where there is enough commerce to support hotels. There may be a carpenter in a village, specializing in anything involving wood. A carpenter in London, though, might specialize in cabinets. Or, a factory might specialize in making nails, thereby enabling thousands of people around the world to earn a living as carpenters, by making the tools of their trade affordable; it might be able to make millions of nails per year and to profit by selling them for a penny each. But there is no point in being so specialized, employing economies of scale to drive down production costs as low as this, unless one has access to a huge customer base. Thus, Smith notes, specialization is limited by the extent of the market.[55] A system of extended trade allows for goods to become progressively cheaper, and thus it allows people to become wealthier.

Smith thought that part of what made specialization work was the fact that people would specialize at what they, compared to others, were best at. Forty-one years after the publication of the *Wealth of Nations*, David Ricardo argued that successful specialization and mutually beneficial trade do not require one to be the best at what one does. Company presidents hire teenagers to mow the lawn not because teenagers are better at lawn mowing, but because company presidents have better things to do. Therefore teenagers will always compete successfully for entry-level jobs, not because teenagers are the best but because the best are busy running the company. Because teenagers have a lower *opportunity* cost, they have what economists call a *comparative advantage*: no matter how much more skilled the president may be at manual labor, teenagers still outcompete presidents for manual labor jobs: presidents would have to give up too much to compete for such jobs. Similarly, even if France could produce better wool than Britain, France might buy English wool rather than produce its own, because France has better things to do with its own farmland – for instance to grow grapes. If France mistakenly considered it important to be self-sufficient in wool and devoted land to raising sheep – land that could be producing the world's best grapes – an opportunity would be lost both for France and for those who would otherwise have been France's eager trading partners.

Smith had some success in rolling back the tide of mercantilism and in fostering a reduction of trade barriers. The result? Maddison notes that, since 1820, the "volume of exports per head of population rose 103-fold in the UK, 114-fold in the US. [Trade] eliminated the handicap of countries with limited natural resources. It was also important in diffusing new products and new technology."[56] John Nye gives the following figures: Between 1820 and 1910, exports as a percentage of the GDP in the UK and France went from just under 10 percent and 5 percent respectively to about 20 percent. Imports as a percentage of the GDP went from 5 percent to 20 percent in France and from 15 percent to about 35 percent in the UK.[57] In summary, in a ninety-year period, the UK went from having 25 percent to having 55 percent of its economy based on international trade, while France went from having 10 percent to having 30 percent of its economy based on international trade.

The early years of the industrial revolution are often presumed to work as a counterexample to the thesis that increasing economic liberty is liberating in the sense of enabling people to do more with their lives. This sense of liberty is not easy to measure; it would be denominated in terms of life expectancy, literacy, per capita real income, and the like. But whether the industrial revolution is in fact such a counterexample is controversial, and the controversy seems to be resolving itself in favor of the thesis that the industrial revolution made people more free in the positive sense even in its early years.[58] Economist Clark Nardinelli says:

> The most influential recent contribution to the optimist position (and the center of much of the subsequent standard-of-living debate) is a 1983 paper by Peter Lindert and Jeffrey Williamson that produced new estimates of real wages in England for the years 1755 to 1851. . . . Lindert's and Williamson's analyses produced two striking results. First, they showed that real wages grew slowly between 1781 and 1819. Second, after 1819, real wages grew rapidly for all groups of workers. For all blue-collar workers – a good stand-in for the working classes – the Lindert–Williamson index number for real wages rose from 50 in 1819 to 100 in 1851. That is, real wages doubled in just thirty-two years.[59]

Adam Smith was a champion of free trade, but not of 'big business.' He correctly saw big business as favoring subsidies and protections, not free trade. Seldom do businessmen assemble – Smith observed

– without someone raising the topic of how to fix prices. He thought that tradesmen are also constantly trying to form unions, to petition for government monopoly licensing, or otherwise to collude so as to raise their wages above competitive levels.[60] Yet Smith judged that it rarely did much good to create government power in order to prevent collusion, because that very power tends to become the prize that would-be monopolists are seeking. So, above all, Smith warned, government should avoid making it *easier* for would-be monopolists to collude, as governments were aggressively doing in his time.

Externalities

Any given transaction has costs and benefits. I sell you a widget for $1.50. The benefit of the transaction to me is $1.50, minus what it cost me to bring that widget to market. Presumably we're both better off, because we traded by consent. I manufactured the widget for, let's say, 79 cents, so I'm better off. You use your new widget to manufacture a gizmo that you can sell for a profit of $3.14, so you too are better off.

What can go wrong? Suppose you use your new widget at 4 a.m. in a way that makes an ear-splitting noise, and your neighbors lose sleep. In this case your neighbors are, in a way, paying for your purchase: they are giving up their sleep. It turns out that your acquiring the widget was costly to the neighbors, not only to you. The cost to your neighbors is an *external* cost. When you make that horrible noise with the widget I sold you, neighbors are worse off. You and I are better off, but bystanders are worse off, which raises a question regarding whether society as a whole is gaining or losing.

But now consider a different case. Suppose you don't make noise with the widget, but you do make lots of gizmos and offer them for sale at $1.99 rather than at their going rate of $3.14. As a result, people who had been selling gizmos for $3.14 are worse off. In this second case, competitors are worse off; yet this worsening is legitimate. Being awoken in the middle of the night by an ear-splitting widget noise is, arguably, a form of trespass; but, in the second case, my customers are not my property and your 'stealing' customers from me is not stealing at all, but simply outperforming me and thus taking from me business that never belonged to me by right. From a social perspective, the falling price of gizmos reflects the fact that supply has risen, and thus, from the community's perspective, there is less reason for me to be making gizmos. Externalities that affect people's welfare only by affecting the price of goods they are buying or selling are called *pecuniary* externalities, and from a social perspective they are good because changing prices induce buyers and sellers to adjust their behavior in ways that benefit customers.

In 1707 the case of *Keeble* v. *Hickeringill* came before the Queen's Bench of England. Keeble was a farmer who had set up a system of decoys to lure waterfowl into traps. He would then sell the captured birds. His neighbor, Hickeringill, began to fire guns into the air so as to frighten the birds away and interfere with Keeble's business. Keeble filed suit. Judge Holt ruled in favor of Keeble. Holt reasoned that Keeble was minding his own legitimate business and Hickeringill had no right to interfere. Judge Holt referred to another case, where a defendant interfered with a neighbor's school *by starting a better school*. The defendant won in that case because the students were not the plaintiff's property. In consequence, the plaintiff had no right to be protected against the defendant 'stealing' the students by offering a better alternative. Then Judge Holt considered a hypothetical case, where a defendant interferes with a neighbor's school by firing guns into the air and frightening the students away. That would be an intentional trespass, because the defendant would be aiming to sabotage the plaintiff's product, not to enhance the defendant's own product. Thus Judge Holt drew a distinction between genuine and merely pecuniary externalities centuries before the concepts were developed in formal theory. He refined the property system so as to limit genuine externalities while leaving intact the liberty to compete in the marketplace.

Thereby he made it easier for neighbors to live, and to make a living, together.

Sometimes externalities are not worth eliminating. When people live miles apart, we don't bother to develop laws regulating the shooting of guns into air. As population density rises, a cost becomes worth internalizing at some point.[61] Likewise, there is an external cost to driving, but we don't want people to stop driving; we simply want to limit the cost to reasonable levels. *Eliminating* external costs is not the aim. It will always be part of the idea of being a good neighbor that it is worth living among neighbors despite minor irritations, and good neighbors take reasonable steps to tread lightly on their neighbors' normal sensibilities. There is no perfect substitute for being considerate. No system of law will enable us to be good neighbors just by obeying the law.[62]

As mentioned in our introduction, T. H. Green said that we consider true freedom to be the greatest of blessings because it enables "citizens as a body to make the most and best of themselves. Thus, though of course there can be no freedom among men who act not willingly but under compulsion, the mere enabling a man to do as he likes, is in itself no contribution to true freedom."[63] Moreover, freedom, rightly understood, cannot "be enjoyed by one man at a cost of a loss of freedom to others."[64] We can find a partial realizing of Green's vision of positive freedom in a system of free trade constrained by a rule of law that, above all, internalizes externalities. If law, custom, and appropriate caution limit the opportunities to enrich oneself at other people's expense, and if commerce within the rule of law enhances the opportunities to enrich oneself in ways that contribute to the prosperity of the community in general, then the community will be a mutually advantageous and increasingly prosperous cooperative venture. Whether free trade within the rule of law actually approximates this greatest of blessings is a big question, depending in part on whether people are free to pursue their opportunities in ways that avoid imposing external costs, and whether they do so willingly rather than under compulsion.

Historian Paul Seabright notes:

> division of labor can create great benefits for those societies that can
> make it work. These benefits come mainly from specialization, the
> sharing of risk, and the accumulation of knowledge. But advantages
> to society as a whole cannot explain why a division of labor evolved.
> We also need to understand why individuals have an interest in par-
> ticipating. A division of labor needs to be robust against opportunism
> – the behavior of those who seek to benefit from the efforts of others
> without contributing anything themselves.[65]

This is to say that, in order to make specialization and division of
labor work as engines of rising productivity, a society has to do an
adequate job of internalizing externalities.

Smith's Nineteenth-Century Legacy[66]

Adam Smith's impact on nineteenth-century France was particularly
deep, which was part of the reason why Thomas Jefferson felt so much
at home there. In 1817, Jefferson arranged the publication of an English
translation of the philosopher Destutt de Tracy, who coined the term
idéologie ('ideology'):

> Society is purely and solely a continual series of exchanges. It is never
> anything else, in any epoch of its duration, from its commencement
> the most unformed, to its greatest perfection. And this is the greatest
> eulogy we can give to it, for exchange is an admirable transaction,
> in which the two contracting parties always both gain; consequently,
> society is an uninterrupted succession of advantages, unceasingly
> renewed for all its members.[67]

To de Tracy, the emergence of community and the emergence of
trade are the same thing. People do not begin to constitute a community until they begin to interact in mutually beneficial ways. It is

an arresting idea. However, in 1837 Jérôme-Adolphe Blanqui would suggest that de Tracy was ignoring a second possibility. "In all the revolutions, there have always been but two parties opposing each other; that of the people who wish to live by their own labor, and that of those who would live by the labor of others."[68] Blanqui's observation, of course, concerns society per se, not only society in times of revolution. His observation would prepare the way for theories of class struggle later in the nineteenth century. Jean-Baptiste Say, for example, was well aware, as was Adam Smith, that individual interests do not *automatically* translate into social benefits "as if by an invisible hand." Smith's theory and those of his nineteenth century followers were rather more sophisticated. In fact, Smith held that a stable, predictable, liberal system of property rights and contract laws – in other words, the right system of traffic management – would channel individual interests in directions that were mutually beneficial rather than mutually destructive. However, in Say's words,

> personal interest is no longer a safe criterion, if individual interests are not left to counteract and control each other. If one individual, or one class, can call in the aid of authority to ward off the effects of competition, it acquires a privilege and at the cost of the whole community; it can then make sure of profits not altogether due to the productive services rendered, but composed in part of an actual tax upon consumers for its private profit; which tax it commonly shares with the authority that thus unjustly lends its support.[69]

Charles Comte, writing in 1817, saw government power as producing "a kind of subordination that subjected the laboring men to the idle and devouring men, and which gave to the latter the means of existing without producing anything, or of living nobly."[70] Karl Marx, speaking about something that we might today call the 'military–industrial complex,' lamented: "All revolutions perfected this machine instead of smashing it. The parties that contended in turn for domination regarded the possession of this huge state edifice as the principal spoils of the victor."[71] In a later work, *The Civil War in France*, Marx writes of "the State parasite feeding upon, and clogging, the free movement of society."[72]

Bastiat

The cost of government is widely dispersed among taxpayers and largely hidden from view. It consists, as the French philosopher and politician Frédéric Bastiat noted in the 1840s, in all the progress that otherwise would have been catalyzed by consumer and investment choices, had the money been left in the taxpayers' hands.[73] Bastiat asks the following sort of questions: Why doesn't breaking windows make us rich? It creates jobs. Why didn't Hurricane Katrina make New Orleans rich? It too created a lot of work. However, there is a reason why work makes a country richer. Work makes a country richer because it adds to the stock of wealth. *Destroying* wealth creates work, to be sure, but that misses the point of work. If you seek liberation, meaning the kind of work that makes us more free to do what we want, we have to think of ways not to create work per se, but to add to the stock of wealth, *taking the unseen into account*. The country and the world will get over Hurricane Katrina, undoubtedly. But we won't be as rich a country as we would have been if Katrina hadn't happened.

Bastiat refers to the "third person," the unseen, unknown, or 'hidden' worker who would have been employed in place of the glazier, were it not for the broken window – and that worker may have been the same person as the glazier.[74] Imagine turning the broken window into a widespread social policy – for example, imagine a neighborhood of one hundred homes. Now imagine going to each house in the neighborhood and breaking a window. The neighborhood glazier is now happy, having plenty of work for the foreseeable future. But the glazier is not the only person who needs work; so we go around the neighborhood again, this time slashing a hundred tires. By the end of the day, we went around a hundred times, reduced the neighborhood to rubble, and made a hundred plumbers, mechanics, painters, bricklayers, and landscapers happy. Or have we? Everyone has plenty of work, yet everyone is poorer than they would have been. They are poorer not just because they have to pay for all the ruined windows, tires, and so on, but because of all the productive things everyone would otherwise have done with their time.

Part of Bastiat's point is that the whole idea of creating work by taking money out of the economy and then putting it back in is ludicrous. But to make 'make-work' less ludicrous, we could tell the glaziers to break the windows themselves, tell the mechanics to slash the tires, and so on. Taking the initiative sounds criminal, but remains an improvement over the government vandalizing the neighborhood on their behalf.

Here is a further improvement. Instead of going to all the trouble of breaking windows and slashing tires, let the neighborhood just pretend that the windows are broken and the tires are slashed, and pay glaziers and other workers anyway, as if their services were needed. This operation reduces the cost of the full employment scheme enormously. What is the remaining cost? Bastiat would say that the remaining cost is still high, for we have a hundred workers collecting money as if they were working when they are actually not. All the money that pays them for pretending to work could have been spent paying them for real work.

Further improvements to this system are there for the taking. So, if the glazier is just sitting around doing nothing but collecting checks, he may as well do something useful with his time. Suppose he offers to do some actual work for his customers. This would reduce the cost of the employment scheme still further. What do his prospective customers say? Some will say, I'd like to hire you, but my money was taken to pay the broken window tax, the slashed tire tax, and so on. Thus some glaziers who want work won't find work that otherwise would have been readily available. So the neighborhood has unemployment – the real thing. Officially it looks as if the glazier had a job, but in fact the whole system is faking it. Bastiat's point is not only that consumption patterns shift in directions subsidized by government so as to create jobs in favored industries; real wealth disappears too, being spent on pretend work instead of being spent employing workers who actually make their customers better off.[75]

The age of robber barons

In 1846 England finally repealed its Corn Laws, which had protected English landowners by limiting the importation of corn since 1689. An era of relatively free trade ensued. Meanwhile, every transcontinental railroad subsidized in the nineteenth century by the United States government went bankrupt, while the only unsubsidized transcontinental railroad prospered. Subsidies divert effort into what generates them rather than into what attracts customers. In this case, subsidized railroads were subsidized by the mile, and responded by maximizing the number of miles of track laid, with no overriding concern about offering their customers the shortest or the safest route between two points. This is how some of them came to deserve the nickname of 'robber barons.' Ill-served customers turned to the unsubsidized Great Northern Railroad – the one transcontinental railroad that labored to keep transportation costs to a minimum, the one transcontinental whose mission was to provide valuable service at an affordable price, and thus the one transcontinental railroad that never went bankrupt.[76]

Each of the railroads was run by people who were in some sense entrepreneurs, but whether entrepreneurs are productive or destructive depends on circumstances.[77] William J. Baumol concludes that there are more entrepreneurs in some societies than in others, but that the number of entrepreneurs does not explain why some societies grow rich while others stay poor. The key variable is whether a society's entrepreneurs are productive, unproductive, or downright destructive. Citing evidence from ancient Rome, early China, and Middle Age and Renaissance Europe, Baumol finds enormous variation between societies in term of how entrepreneurs allocate their time and resources. Simply put, entrepreneurs are entrepreneurial. They go where the opportunities are. If there is money to be made at other people's expense – organized crime, rent-seeking (including campaigning for subsidies), and so on – then we'll find entrepreneurs in those roles, doing what entrepreneurs do. If there are fortunes to be made by inventing new ways of making willing customers better off, then there, too, we will find entrepreneurs.[78] And when philosophers and moral leaders are careful to distinguish between the two – honoring entrepreneurs who create wealth while damning entrepreneurs who merely capture it – they can help to tip entrepreneurial energy in a positive direction.[79]

Smith's Twentieth-Century Legacy

We have discussed the institutional background that encourages technological innovation, division of labor, and expanding markets. A society's infrastructure must also secure people in their possessions, so that people feel comfortable showing up at the market with goods for sale, feel secure enough to invest in the future, and so on. Some ways of allocating property rights are conducive to the creation of wealth; others are not. Property rights are allocated in one way in Zimbabwe (President Mugabe took whatever he wanted, whenever he wanted it), and the result is devastating poverty. By contrast, stable, private ownership of the means of production robustly translates into nearly all of us being wealthier than our grandparents were.[80] Therefore the wealth-creation game that relatively well-conceived property rights enabled citizens of the West to play over the past two centuries is not a zero-sum one.[81] And with that wealth goes freedom, in the sense of acquiring more options and expanding capacities.

Prosperous countries take formal property rights seriously.[82] They also, as a rule, make it safer to lend money, thereby making it cheaper to borrow money. Adam Smith saw the value of cheap credit. In Smith's day, interest rates as high as 60 percent were both a sign and cause of why some countries do poorly.[83] By contrast, cheap credit is a sign that people generally trust each other and generally are trustworthy. They believe that investing in each other is a good bet.[84]

Critics of capitalism express concern about the worth of mere negative liberty. Classical liberals wanted to guarantee everyone, rich and poor, certain rights. However, as Marx in particular could see, poverty could make those rights worthless. To the average person, the right to own a yacht is worthless because she lacks the material means to acquire a yacht.

We might place ourselves in Marx's shoes. Looking around nineteenth-century Paris or London, Marx would see a stark material contrast between the rich, the middle class, and the poor. England had made significant progress in implementing liberal property laws. But many poor proletarians – laborers who worked for wages and did not own the means of production – owned little of anything. Both the rich gentleman and the poor laborer had a right to own property, but the laborer did not *enjoy* the right. Marx concluded that what the poor need is a substantive right to property: that is, a guarantee that they would actually acquire property. This sounds right. Could it be wrong?

Contemporary Peruvian economist Hernando De Soto claims just that. De Soto aimed to find out why there is such a contrast between the West, where we find pockets of poverty, and the rest of world, where we find pockets of wealth. People in developing countries are smart, hard-working, and willing to take risks. Why do they not prosper as their counterparts do in the West?

To Marx, the problem is that the poor have formal rights but no actual property. De Soto says that the opposite is true in developing countries: the poor possess real assets but lack formal rights. He estimates that the poorest of the poor in the developing world possess $9.3 trillion worth of land, which is roughly the size of US GDP, and perhaps a thousand times the size of the entire world's non-military foreign aid budget. But there is a difference between *possessing* land and *owning* land, as western citizens do. A person who would be starting up a chain of Mexican restaurants in Tucson puts that same energy into a sidewalk vending business in Mexico City. He has no deed to his land and perhaps no official address. As far as the government is concerned, his business does not exist. Having no legal property, he has no access to police protection for his business, or to government courts for settling disputes. He lacks the legal means to sell franchises or to post share offerings on a stock exchange; indeed, he cannot even raise capital for a proper building, with a kitchen and a flush toilet.

On De Soto's analysis, western entrepreneurs operate within an infrastructure of formal law that enables them to expand their businesses. It is relatively easy for them to get a business license, and thus relatively easy for them to access lines of low-cost credit. Western legal institutions also make it relatively easy to secure formal property titles, and with the same effect: such titles enable people to use their property as collateral and thereby to access low-cost credit. De Soto argues that low-cost credit has liberated human ingenuity in the West, and may one day do so around the world.[85]

De Soto is right about this much. Imagine a country, in other respects like yours, but in which there were no institutions of mortgage lending, and the only people who could buy a house would be those who could afford to pay cash up front. Would you be able to buy a house? Probably not. Would anyone you know be able to buy a house? Perhaps a few could, perhaps not. So what would you do? Rent an apartment? Probably not: there would be a lot more people who needed to rent an apartment, and hardly anyone who could afford to pay cash up front to *build* apartment buildings. What would such a country be like, a country otherwise like yours but with no mortgage financing? It would not be very much like what we call the West. It would be a developing country.

So it is in Peru, says De Soto. In rural Peru, how do you know when you cross from one owner's land to another's? Answer: a different dog starts barking. De Soto's point: you can't take that to the bank. So, De Soto's answer to why capitalism works in the West and not elsewhere is that capitalism depends on the availability of credit. To obtain credit, one must establish a stable title to collateral, so that lenders can afford the risk of low-rate lending.

Suppose that Lauren, an American, owns her own house. If she wants to open a business, she can get a loan, using her house as collateral. The bank issuing the loan has a registry through which it can determine her house's market value and verify that her title to the house is uncontested. Since Lauren participates in the legal credit system, she can be held responsible. If she defaults on her loan, the government may allow the bank to seize some of her assets, garnish her wages, or take her house. Moreover, her creditworthiness can be checked through credit bureaus. Even more incredibly, her reputation follows her worldwide. Thus, because she has a good enough credit rating, she can show up at a counter in Hong Kong, a city she has never seen, flash a credit card, and be supplied with a rental car from strangers she has never met and will never see again. All of this operates on her promise to pay for the car, should she damage it. The miracle of formal property is that it makes such a promise mean something. It allows strangers to trust her. This process is so natural to citizens of advanced industrial nations that they hardly notice it. Imagine a country in which you could only make contracts with people you know well. It would not be a rich country.

De Soto concludes that globalization per se is not failing, but particular countries are failing to 'globalize' their capital.[86] Successful globalization won't be just about linking up elites. De Soto says that capital is the source of productivity, and consequently of the wealth of nations, but he adds that foreign capital investment in the long run is not good enough.[87] The benefits of capitalism will not spread to remote parts of developing countries until the firm foundations of formal property are in place domestically. (And even that, we presume De Soto would admit, is no panacea. It would, at most, be a great and perhaps indispensable start.)

When Formal Freedom Is Enough

Rosenberg and Birdzell claim (as do North and Thomas) that the West grew rich because it got its legal institutions right. Getting the legal institutions right fostered an explosion of trade and investment, which resulted in the radical increase in material standards of living that we enjoy today. The West grew rich because it combined new technology and science with organizational innovations and with a massive division of labor, made possible by extended trade. To give a small but important example of organizational innovation, traders in Amsterdam invented calls and puts in the early seventeenth century. A call is an option to buy, and a put is an option to sell, a stock or commodity at a specified price, should it come to be traded at that price. Calls and puts give traders tools for managing investment risk in general and market volatility in particular.[88] To give another example, the concept of interest on loans was a Mesopotamian invention of around 3000 BC, enabling movement and investment of capital ever since, despite the historically ubiquitous hostility to the concept of usury.[89] To be sure, scientific progress need not translate into economic growth; Rosenberg and Birdzell note that China and the Islamic nations were far ahead of the West in the sciences until the early modern period, and yet their science did not drive technological and economic growth.[90] People explore new technological frontiers only when they can expect to benefit from what they discover or invent in the process. Increasingly secure property institutions steer people into games where exchange occurs only by consent, and thus only on terms that leave the parties better off in their own eyes. Otherwise they decline the offer. This implies that people can go to the market reasonably expecting to get what they want if, but only if, they show up with the means to make their trading partners better off in return. The point in this case is that people can go to market with complicated proposals for translating new science into new technology – proposals requiring investments of time and venture capital, which make sense only if the background legal and political framework is stable, yet flexible enough to permit and indeed to encourage innovation. Charles Darwin might have said that a similar point holds in the realm of biological evolution: that is, natural selection can produce beneficial adaptation only if an ecological niche is stable enough for selection over generations to have time to produce a population better adapted to that niche.

Critics of market society, following Marx, say the formal freedom that liberal society aims to provide – freedom from interference – is not enough. Real freedom, they say, is a matter of what workers can *do*. Yet this 'real' freedom is found in commercial society and almost nowhere else. In fact, as a matter of historical record, the formal freedom that liberal society provides *is* enough to put workers in a position to have many other freedoms, and thus to do far more with their lives than workers have ever done in any non-liberal society. So of course formal freedom by itself is not enough; but what matters is that, wherever there is formal freedom, there will also be more than purely formal freedom. There will be a world of substantive opportunity, created by generations of gamblers, inventors, and hard workers – people who made their formal freedom count. Market societies have evolved to become more free (more free than they were, and more free than any alternative is or ever was) in precisely the way that really matters according to market critics: that is, they make people of all classes wealthy enough to do more with their lives than would otherwise have been possible. Market society does not offer official *guarantees* of prosperity. What it offers is the real possibility.

Marx saw early capitalism in zero-sum terms. He was wrong, but still he had a point. On his view, early capitalism, with its sweaty 16-hour workdays, was justified only insofar as it was better than what had preceded it, and only insofar as it was leading to something better. We cannot disagree. There was indeed something deplorable about the nascent capitalism of the decades between Adam Smith and Karl Marx, at least by comparison to what was to follow. After all, the very fact that the working conditions of 1840 seem appalling today tells us how much things have improved. Neither Adam Smith in 1776 nor even Karl Marx in 1848 could have foreseen that life expectancy among the working class would some day exceed fifty years.

Some contemporary political theorists talk about a static economy (a 'stationary state') being desirable, as if we had reached the apex of technological innovation and the only thing left to discover were how best to distribute it.[91] People in Bacon's time talked as if everything worth knowing were already known by the time of Aristotle. As Bacon would have predicted, there has not yet been a time when such ways of talking did not look foolish in retrospect.[92] With each passing century, such statements become even more patently foolish than they were in Bacon's time – but people still make such statements today.

Discussion

1   If farmland is so valuable, why do subsidies flow from those who do not own farms to those who do?

2   In market economies, the people (engineers, entrepreneurs, money-lenders, inventors, salesmen) who figure out how to make unskilled labor more productive get paid more than do the unskilled laborers themselves. Why?

3   Where do people have the most access to the world's greatest art, music, and literature? Why?

4   How virtuous are people in market societies? Whatever your answer to this question is, what evidence (if any) would make you change your mind?

5   North and Thomas, as mentioned, say that the secret of western prosperity is the extent to which the West got its institutions right. So suppose we find, say, a certain banking system clearly working well – promoting peaceful commerce – in the USA and in Canada. Does it follow that the International Monetary Fund or the World Bank should be cajoling African and Eastern

European countries to adopt the North American system? What are some of the pitfalls of exporting institutions that seem to work well in a given context?

6 How much economic freedom do we want? The question has many dimensions. Should we be free to buy and sell alcohol? Heroin? Abortions? Instruction manuals for building chemical or nuclear weapons? Should we be free to trade with people from other countries? Should employees be free to look for employers who pay more? Should employers be free to look for employees who cost less? Should manufacturers be free to market new and possibly dangerous products, and, if so, under what conditions – what counts as fair warning?

7 A monopoly is a market where there is a single seller, while a monopsony is a market where there is a single buyer. A group that becomes the sole supplier of labor in a given industry has achieved a monopoly. An employer that becomes the sole buyer of labor in a given industry has achieved a monopsony. Are trade unions liberating? Under what conditions?

8 Can a person be less free by virtue of having the option to take a low-paying job?

Notes

1. Once critics of capitalism began to realize that capitalism's material productivity dwarfs that of communism, critics of capitalism began to say that money isn't everything, and began to criticize capitalism more for its crass materialism than for its economic inefficiency. This criticism, too convenient though it was, is worth pondering. On the one hand, capitalism provides people with the material freedom to carve out enclaves within which they and like-minded people can pursue their non-materialistic dreams in reasonable health and material comfort. But, even given that capitalism liberates people to form their own thick communities, a further question remains: do people actually use their material wealth in this way, or does capitalism tend to seduce people into being less spiritual, more envious, or simply more frivolous than

they otherwise would be? Surely it can, and surely it does at some level. But how pervasive and how lamentable this phenomenon is would be hard to settle.

2. Lindsey 2007, 16.

3. Nixon 1962, 252–63, as quoted in Lindsey 2007, 17.

4. Socialism was supposed to bring about production for use rather than for profit, but much of the USSR's growth in the 1960s came from production for *image* rather than for *use*. The trouble was that the Soviets produced not in response to consumer demand for particular goods – their system ruled that out – but simply with the aim to outcompete the United States in official figures. Meanwhile, the proletariat waited in breadlines and shopped in empty markets. See Bergson 1961, Brainard 2006, and Maddison 1998, 319. DeLong (2002, 147) cites, as an example of growth-retarding policy, the tendency of governments to embark "on 'prestige' industrialization programs that keep resources from shifting to activities in which the country had a long-run comparative advantage."

5. The USSR's GDP in some ways overstates how well its economy did. The USSR tried to outproduce the US in terms of heavy industry. But it did so without worrying whether that was what the people of the USSR needed. The US economy wasn't planned with the goal of beating the USSR in some statistical race. The US had the level and type of industry it had because (in its comparatively freer market) customers, via prices, signaled that the product was worth that much. See Maddison 1998, 319.

6. http://www.epa.gov/oecaagct/ag101/demographics.html.

7. Easterbrook 2004, xiv.

8. Maddison 2007, 70. Current US GDP is taken from https://www.cia.gov/library/publications/the-world-factbook/print/us.html, last accessed 3/6/08.

9. Stephen Davies sees modern methods of empirical history as originating in the Renaissance and in the Reformation, along with the modern scientific method. William of Ockham's 'razor,' the idea that one should take the simplest hypothesis that fits the facts (where 'simplest' is not itself simple by any means, but includes the rough notion of positing the existence of unobserved entities only when that is the most elegant or illuminating way to explain the observed phenomena), was

a crucial fourteenth-century contribution, which would not have an impact until later. Davies reports that one of the early events in the ascendance of empirical history was Lorenzo Valla's demonstration, in 1440, that "the *Donation of Constantine*, a document that purported to record the granting by the Roman Emperor Constantine the Great of temporal powers over a large part of Italy to the Pope, was a forgery from the early Middle Ages. Valla's motives were not scholarly but polemical, as his aim was to embarrass the papacy. The significance of his demonstration lay in the way it was done, by applying critical techniques and particularly linguistic analysis to the text of the *Donation* to demonstrate that it could not possibly have been a product of the fourth century" (Davies 2003, 12).

10. Bacon 2000, 100.

11. Ironically, Bacon is remembered as a calculating opportunist in his personal and political life. Yet there is a sincere and very modern sound to Bacon's remark that nature, to be commanded, must be obeyed. Taking an attitude of domination toward nature is no longer assumed to be healthy. As people get richer and don't see nature as a threat, they often find they'd rather look at nature not as something to conquer, but as something to appreciate. We are all too aware today that our rule over nature is precarious to the extent that it is capricious. See Brennan 2007a.

12. Danford 2000, 63.

13. Ibid., 67.

14. A social contract is a gradient-seeking, locally optimizing product of negotiation, while a utilitarian framework is, by comparison, globally optimizing in theory but downward-seeking in practice, because it licenses people to experiment *at other people's expense.* Internalization is only one factor here. Role models make a difference to people's propensity to innovate. Education makes a difference. The nuclear family no doubt wastes a lot of potential, but every selection mechanism is wasteful. Selection mechanisms generate new possibilities, though, and, probabilistically, they select the ones fit to survive. What the nuclear family does is to provide a framework within which role models and education come together. Parents internalize the prospects and progress of their children, and to that extent they can internalize the externalities of their success in providing education and role models.

15. Sachs and Warner 1995, 7.
16. Marx and Engels 2002, 11.
17. The scientific revolution, likewise, was building on its own success. Stephen J. Gould remarks: "I believe that the theory of natural selection should be viewed as an extended analogy – whether conscious or unconscious on Darwin's part I do not know – to the laissez faire economics of Adam Smith" (Gould 1982, 66).
18. According to DeLong (2002, 120), it would have gone from $130 in 5000 BC to $250 in AD 1800 (each figure is calculated in US dollars at the value they had in 2000). Angus Maddison (2007, 70) gives different figures: $467 world GDP/capita in AD 1 (calculated in 1990 US dollars) up to $6,516 world GDP/capita in AD 2003. We were curious about why Maddison would normalize GDP figures for 2003 to the year 1990. Why not leave the 2003 number in 2003 dollars, and then render the GDP figure for the year AD 1 in 2003 dollars? It turns out that there is such a thing as a 'Geary-Khamis' dollar, a hypothetical unit of currency which renders values in terms of the purchasing power of a 1990 US dollar. It is used occasionally as a 'lingua franca' for translating figures from different data sets.
19. GDP per capita worldwide as of 2006 is about $8,175. Americans now live on $120 a day, on average (DeLong 2002, 120). Deirdre McCloskey (1992, 1) comments that a very brief history of economic liberty would go like this: "Once upon a time we were poor, then capitalism flourished, and now as a result we're rich."
20. *Colonialism* involves moving settlers into an area so as to establish a territorial claim, for the ultimate purpose of transferring resources to the mother country at less than the market price. Robin Grier concludes that colonies held for longer periods perform better after independence. We would conjecture that (a) colonial wealth transfers account for little of the liberation of human capital that accompanies growth; (b) port cities such as London and New York, the preeminent scenes of progress in commerce, arts, sciences, and technology, also sustain intellectual circles within which colonialism is morally repudiated; and (c) among nations that abandon colonialism in favor of relatively free trade, economic growth tends to accelerate rather than to decelerate. See Grier 1999.
21. DeLong 2002, 127.

22. While discussing the causes of the explosion in wealth of the past two hundred years, Angus Maddison (2007, 74) says that, since 1820, the "average number of years of education per person employed . . . rose by a factor of 12 in the US, 11 in Japan, and 9 in the UK." Increased human capital no doubt leads to increased productivity. At the same time, this factor is not completely exogenous. Education is also a superior good (i.e. a good that people pursue more as they become wealthier), and so, just as increasing education tends to lead to increased wealth, increasing wealth tends to lead in return to increasing education. The authors of this book would not have become professional philosophers had they been born 100 years ago into families like their own; Brennan would have been a factory worker in the American northeast, Schmidtz a farmer in Canada.

23. Smith was hardly a giddy apostle of the free market, even if, all things considered, he defended it. Jean-Jacques Rousseau criticized commercial society for making people overly concerned with trinkets, for pushing people into vanity and manipulativeness, and for stupefying them. Adam Smith shared many of these concerns. However, unlike Rousseau, Smith thought that the market was better than what came before it. Rousseau had a romantic, unrealistic view of pre-commercial society. Smith saw commercial society, for all its ills, as curing the most severe economic insecurities. For comparisons between Rousseau and Smith, see Rasmussen 2006 and 2008.

24. Cowen has written several important books on this topic, beginning with Cowen 1998.

25. In light of claims like this, one hears thinkers like Rousseau or Marx asserting that markets make people vicious, selfish, and indifferent to others. Adam Smith and others tell opposite sorts of stories. Who is right? We'd have to be careful about deciding from the armchair, just on the basis of whose story we find the most congenial. Paul Zak remarks: "market exchange itself may lead to a society where individuals have stronger character values. The clearest evidence for this is the studies of fairness in small-scale societies conducted by Henrich and his colleagues. They showed that the likelihood of making fair offers to a stranger in one's society is more strongly predicted by the extent of trade in markets than any other factor they have found. Exchange is inherently other-regarding – both you and I must benefit if exchange

is to occur" (Zak 2008a, xv). Economists like to conduct games in which participants have the opportunity to cheat and swindle each other or to play fairly. As it turns out, the strongest predictor that participants will play fairly with strangers is how market-oriented their society is. People from market societies characteristically know how to put themselves in their trading partner's shoes. People from non-market societies do not.

26. What does it mean to speak of an experiment as failing? We have in mind such things as the reputed fact that eighty percent of restaurants close their doors within two years of opening. Some go bankrupt, but eighty percent of the restaurants that close were not losing money at the time they closed. Mainly, owners were learning that they did not want to spend as much time as it takes to make a restaurant succeed, that they wanted to be in a different location, or that they wanted to try a different kind of restaurant. And so on. We thank Chris Griffin for helping us to clarify this point.

27. We thank Kate Johnson for noticing the relevance of this to the discussion at hand.

28. Think of graduate school. If as a graduate student, you don't fail fairly often, and walk out of a seminar embarrassed by something you said that turned out to be naïve, then you aren't trying hard enough. You also need to forget your failures for the most part. Learning from mistakes is essential, but letting them go and getting on with the next experiment is likewise essential.

29. Rosenberg and Birdzell 1986, 38–9, 51, 77.

30. Ibid. (on the general impact on Europe of price controls and their elimination).

31. Powell 2000, 240.

32. Ben Franklin would, among other things, invent the lightning rod (without which tall buildings would have been impractical), bifocal glasses, and the metal-lined fireplace now known as the Franklin stove.

33. Powell 2000, 237.

34. The early history of economic thought shows a variety of attempts to demonstrate that all economic value ultimately is a function of some single objectively valuable good, x. The physiocrats thought that x was land. Marx, and many others, thought that x was a certain kind of labor. These kinds of views have fallen out of favor with economists.

35. After the 1986 explosion of the space shuttle *Challenger*, it took a presidential commission five months to determine that the problem involved an O-ring produced by Morton Thiokol. Within three *hours* of the explosion, though, while all of the major contractors refused to comment, Morton Thiokol's stock had fallen by 12 percent, while others' stock had fallen only 2.5 percent. A few people knew something, and, within minutes, many other people were learning fast. See Maloney and Mulherin 2003.

36. During a visit in May of 2009, Schmidtz found Argentina to be suffering from a shortage of coins, which made small transactions more difficult. See www.globalpost.com/dispatch/argentina/090428/argentina-cash-problems, accessed July 23, 2009.

37. Von Glahn 2005, 66.

38. Spiegel 1983, 70.

39. Quoted by Spiegel 1983, 88. The English banker Thomas Gresham reformulated the idea seventy years later, and it is now referred to as Gresham's Law: bad (debased) money drives out good money (that is, money the face value of which is an honest reflection of its actual bullion content).

40. Selgin 2008, 5–7.

41. Selgin (2008, 25) says that company stores originally developed not to take advantage of workers, but to economize on coinage during the shortage. Without enough small coins to make wage payments, employers had to provide retail outlets that accepted company-issued credit notes.

42. See Robert Wright 2000, 197–202.

43. But in another way they are not like fences: fences are partly for show. There is a reason to put up a more costly, prettier fence when a cheaper one would keep out the neighbor's dog just as well. But there is little reason to put up a more costly or prettier legal system for show.

44. We thank Daniel Bell for this question.

45. Not every would-be driver gets a car at the same age or on the same day, but the point here is to meet demand, not to guarantee that all demands will be met at the same time. Markets don't do everything for us any more than traffic lights or plumbers do. The most that people can get at the market is whatever their trading partners bring to it. Traffic lights don't cure cancer; neither do markets (at least not

necessarily). Markets do bring together people who are willing and able to finance cancer research, and oncologists who are willing and able to conduct it; but on any given day there will be, literally and figuratively, numerous cancers that markets are not yet curing. Intellectual property temporarily gives an inventor the only green light to sell his or her invention, which is a troublesome tradeoff. On the one hand, we want inventors to be eager to invent. On the other hand, we want free competition. So, eventually, we want an inventor's patent to expire, turning the light green for everyone, leaving everyone free to produce better, cheaper versions of the invention without having to pay the original inventor. In sum, we want to maximize the rate at which inventions are brought to market where they can begin to benefit customers, and we want to maximize customer access to the invention in the long run.

46. Hume 2000, 198.

47. What we mean by a top-down design is this: Joe Theorist imagines what an ideal society would be like, then he or his converts try to make actual society conform to the ideal. By contrast, a bottom-up approach would be like this: Jane Pragmatist studies how a given actual society operates, looks for defects, speculates about what might suffice to patch the defect, and then makes a suggestion. She believes there is no such thing as an action that has only one effect, and no such thing as an action that has only the intended effect. Thus her first concern is to avoid suggesting a patch that will take the whole society in a different and unknown direction. She does not claim to know what an ideal society would be like. See generally Hayek 1945.

48. Think of an operator at a microchip manufacturer in northern Massachusetts who is paid $16 an hour to push buttons. (Earning this wage at such a company for two thirds of a year allowed Brennan to stay in college when he did not qualify for financial aid and the scholarship money had run out.) In a state of nature, that button pushing motion is worthless. Yet some people figured out how to make that motion result in microchips. And still other people figured out how to get microchips into the hands of people who could use them. The value of button pushing is predicated upon the cooperation of multitudes and on a few innovators who could see, or guess, how to make the labor more productive than it had ever been before.

49. Smith 1981, 644.

50. Smith 1981, 458.

51. Ibid., 456.

52. When trade barriers are lowered, consumers get better value for their money; but what happens to the workers? Some sellers profit from protection in the short run – those who produce inferior goods at high prices would not be able to remain in business otherwise. But, in the long run, workers are similarly well-served by relaxing trade restrictions, for two reasons. First, they are better off as consumers of less expensive, higher quality imported goods. Second, they are better off (because everyone is better off) when domestic companies redirect their previously wasted labor into producing the kind of goods that they, along with other domestic and foreign customers, want to buy and can afford to buy.

53. Plato 2004, 51.

54. Adam Smith argued that the tax revenue needed to support empires was usually more than the total benefit of the goods received from them. (Of course, the costs of the empire were spread, whereas the benefit of those goods was concentrated.) Lance Davis and Robert Huttenback (1988) have written a book-length study on whether Smith was right.

55. Smith 1981, Book 1, chapter 3.

56. Maddison 2007, 74.

57. Nye 2007, 8–9.

58. The events of the seventh century BC in Lydia make a clearer counter-example. See Chapter 1.

59. Nardinelli acknowledges a variety of legitimate, if not decisive, critical responses to Lindert and Williamson. Some of the responses indicate other ways of calculating the costs and benefits, by employing a different price index or different ways of discounting the part of the rising wage that can be explained as compensation for rising risks and deteriorating living conditions. Nardinelli also cites economists who corroborate Lindert and Williamson's data, such as N. F. R. Crafts. See Nardinelli 2005, on-line. See also Lindert and Williamson 1983.

60. Smith 1981, 145.

61. To explain the jargon: choices have costs and benefits. An *external* cost is a cost paid by someone other than the chooser. An external cost is

internalized when the person making the choice becomes the one who pays the cost, or rather, when people not involved in making the decision are not involved in paying the cost either. (For example, the external cost to neighbors of starting a garage band is internalized by soundproofing the garage.)

62. As population rises, externalities proliferate. Likewise, as trade becomes increasingly global, externalities proliferate along with opportunities for mutually advantageous commerce. The rule of law will always face new challenges in defining the fences that make good neighbors. When new problems emerge that make it imperative to be clearer about where one person's right ends and another person's right begins, law has to rise to the challenge without becoming so bureaucratic that it costs more than it is worth.

63. Green 1986, 199.

64. Ibid., 199.

65. Seabright 2004, 5.

66. We are greatly indebted here to Raico 2006.

67. De Tracy 1970, p. 6.

68. Blanqui 1837, x.

69. Say 1964, 146–7.

70. Comte 1817, 22.

71. Marx and Engels 1983, Vol. 1, 477.

72. Ibid., Vol. 2, 222.

73. Bastiat 1995.

74. Ibid.

75. Ibid., 1225.

76. Folsom 1987.

77. Baumol 1990.

78. Ibid., 893.

79. Folsom 1987 develops the distinction between economic and political entrepreneurs.

80. Schmidtz 2008, chapter 32. Marxist philosopher G. A. Cohen observes that money is like a ticket, and there are things we can do if we have a ticket but not otherwise. Thus to have money is to have an important kind of freedom.

81. Some Marxists would prefer to regard this as controversial. G. A. Cohen (1995, 57) claims that state-backed property rights do not increase

freedom. Enforced property rights are a zero-sum game. They allocate a given resource to one party at the expense of other parties, whom the state could just as easily have favored instead. Cohen has a point: if the resource that concerns us is in fixed supply, then the only question is how to slice the pie, and the only way to make one slice bigger is to make some other slice smaller. If the resources that concern us can be *produced*, though (such as food and shelter), then the zero-sum assumption does not hold, and the question of distribution is not the first question, however important it may eventually turn out to be. See also Brian Barry 2008, who describes social mobility as contingently positive-sum in an absolute sense (that is, if the stock of middle-class jobs is increasing, then the poor can move into them and improve their lot without displacing anyone else) and necessarily zero-sum in a relative sense (that is, there is no way to get ahead of the Joneses except by making the Joneses fall behind).

82. A student of Brennan's said, in conversation, that this may be true of all currently prosperous countries, but that doesn't make it true as a matter of logic. There could be other paths to prosperity. As a matter of logic, she is certainly right. What's the upshot?

83. Rothschild and Sen 2006, 325.

84. Credit markets are (at best) viewed with suspicion as we write this, as recent events are only now revealing what a disastrous combination of corruption and incompetence have been corroding our financial system over the past several years, with no end in sight. Many hundreds of billions of dollars continue to be redistributed from taxpayers to the very people who created the mess, in a seemingly calculated strategy aimed at triggering and then capturing this historically unprecedented wealth transfer. Nevertheless, current events notwithstanding, credit markets have been a massive liberator of human capital.

85. We have no doubts that cheap credit can sometimes reduce freedom rather than expand it, when people make bad choices. There's a difference between the credit De Soto is talking about, which is used to fund production, and the credit James Scurlock complains about in *Maxed Out*, which is used to fund current consumption. Scurlock wants to be entertaining and to sell his view, which makes him overstate his case. But the one grain of truth in his complaints is that people have not yet learned to deal with low-cost credit. As we write this book, we

see over and over again that liberating elements often cause an initial crisis, as people learn to deal with them.

86. De Soto 2000, 207.

87. Ibid., 209.

88. Gelderblom and Jonker 2005, 191.

89. Van de Mieroop 2005, 17.

90. Rosenberg and Birdzell 1986, 9.

91. In his recently published correspondence with Van Parijs, Rawls says that he favors a stationary economy, such as the one Mill describes (Rawls and Van Parijs 2003, 15). Would Rawls rather see us rendering stationary the economy of Mill's time, with its average life expectancy of around forty years? Or, if he would not want to give up the progress made in the ensuing century, what makes him think that a century from now he would regret any progress made – including, perhaps, another doubling of life expectancy? Suffice it to say that a stationary economy is hard to imagine, but it is no fluke that the world's poorest societies are also our closest approximation to stationary economies. Needless to say, we do not view progress as something to accept with reluctance. Had we succeeded in rendering stationary the economy of Mill's time, we would have no idea now how tragic that would have been, but tragic it nevertheless would have been.

92. Even small rates of growth lead to huge gains over time. Suppose that the poor make 50 percent more in society A than in society B, but also that society A has no growth. If the income of the poor in society B grows at 2 percent a year, they will catch up with the poor of A in 21 years; in 56 years they will double what the poor of A make; and in 76 years they will triple it. For a criticism of Rawls based on the issues of income growth, see Brennan 2007b.

Chapter 5

Civil Liberty: 1954

THESIS: *The security of civil rights, and ultimately liberal society within the rule of law, depend both on a culture of freedom and individualism, and on individual heroic catalysts.*

Must Liberty and Equality Come Apart?

When people speak about civil liberties or call themselves civil libertarians, they usually have particular rights in mind: rights of privacy, of free speech, of assembly, of lifestyle choice, of control over sexual conduct, voting rights, or legal rights such as the right to a fair trial.

Some elements of the rule of law are preconditions of civil liberty, and there will never be a once and for all victory for the rule of law. Even today, civil liberties remain precarious for many. We still have a long way to go; perhaps we always will. Honestly determining where we are and where we still need to go requires not only that we recognize real problems, but also that we acknowledge real solutions and real progress already made.

It was once a revolutionary idea: kings don't own their subjects. Subjects own themselves. It took further revolutionary moments to establish that men cannot own other men, and that men cannot own their wives. It takes even further moments for people to realize that, among fellow citizens, owning *oneself* means being treated as an equal before the law.

Citizenship is a topic where ideals of liberty and equality meet. Thus Martin Luther King Jr, in his "Letter from Birmingham Jail," mentions 'freedom' sixteen times and 'rights' eight times, while evoking, once each, the idea of equal rights and the idea of all people being created equal. He identifies in his community a longing for freedom, of which equality is a part. The fight for black civil liberties in 1960s America was a fight to end oppression, to lessen violence, to increase opportunities, and to improve the quality of life. Equality is a part, if only a part, of this American dream of a culture in which people see one another as partners, acknowledging and indeed celebrating their success in building a society they can each revere.[1]

Our thesis is that civil rights do not emerge, and do not last, except where there is a general reverence for (negative) liberty and individualism. And, it must be said, even such a culture is no guarantee. Culture sets the stage. Ultimately, though, progress in lifting a given society to the next level of civil liberty – especially in extending civil liberties to previously disenfranchised groups – seems so often to require, even in otherwise liberal societies, heroic individual catalysts such as Martin Luther King. Society may be tinder, poised to acknowledge and correct the hypocrisy involved in treating some groups but not others as equals before the law; yet, at least on the surface, heroic individuals often seem to be the match needed to light it. (Chapter 6, on psychological freedom, reflects on why this would be so.)

Today most of us are committed to equality in civil rights. Why? Our commitment cannot be predicated on the vain hope (if this were something to hope for) that people would be descriptively equal, if only all discrimination were ended. Whatever qualities one offers as bases for thinking that humans command reverence as ends-in-themselves (for instance the fact that they are endowed with free will, or with the power of reason), we do not possess that quality equally. So here is an odd situation. We have capacities that define the core dimensions of our worth as human beings. Whatever capacities we identify as the ones that matter most, we are not equal along these dimensions. Yet, somehow, we don't think that inequality along these most important dimensions is itself important. How can this be?

Suppose it turned out that what we call *H. sapiens* really fell into two biological species, one species being distinctly superior to the other along every dimension we care about. So what? Would there be grounds for constructing two tiers of citizenship, and giving superior rights to the superior species? In a recent book on democracy, David Estlund considers a similar question and responds that, even if you are smarter, "Who made you boss?"[2]

Estlund's question nicely frames one of political philosophy's perennial issues. Estlund is implicitly questioning the nature and historical source of political legitimacy, and is asserting something like what we would call the right of self-ownership (though he would not call it that). At the very least, Estlund's question implies that authority rather than equality is what has to be justified. Knowing better, or even *being* better, is not enough to justify taking over.

Common sense morality today presupposes that everyone who is above some threshold of competence should have full and equal rights. Children are below the threshold. They have rights, but they are not equal citizens. Women, minorities, and landless white males have been treated historically like children – below the threshold of competence. Aristotle supposes that some people are natural slaves, who cannot be responsible for themselves.[3] And there are, after all, thresholds. Some people are too young to have a driver's license. Despite this, or perhaps because of this, the greater danger to liberty has always been the idea of some classes being below the threshold, and not the bare fact that people are not descriptively equal.

Freedom of Conscience

The ideas of free speech and freedom of the press grew in part out of concerns for freedom of religion. As people came to accept that each person's view of religion is her own to judge, they came to expand the ideals of freedom of conscience and freedom of the press.

The polemical writer François-Marie Arouet, better known as Voltaire, was an early advocate of freedom of conscience. He needed to be; his writing tended to get him into trouble. (He was imprisoned once in the notorious Bastille for criticizing the duke of Orléans.) In his 1763 *Treatise on Toleration*, Voltaire argued for freedom of thought in general. One of the principal reasons why people advocated censorship and intolerance was their worry about civil war and strife. Voltaire challenged this reasoning, pointing out that there were no known instances of tolerance leading to war, but many instances of *in*tolerance leading to war. He thought that killing over words was barbaric. He quipped that animals kill each other over food or turf, but only humans kill each other over contrary opinions.

Until 1694, nothing could be published in England without being licensed by the king. Criticizing the government in print was illegal. Seditious libel had been established by English common law in 1606. However, the 1689 English Bill of Rights, established by Parliament as a restriction on the power of the monarch after the Glorious Revolution, granted members of Parliament freedom of speech within Parliament.

In 1735 John Peter Zenger, publisher of the *New York Weekly Journal*, was arrested for seditious libel against the British Royal Governor of New York William Cosby. Given the definition of seditious libel operating at the time, Zenger had indeed committed a crime. His lawyer, Andrew Hamilton, defended him not by claiming that Zenger was innocent, but by arguing that seditious libel *should not be a crime* when the criticisms of the government are true. In an instance of jury nullification, the jury found Zenger not guilty. William Penn, one of Pennsylvania's founders, and the Earl of Shaftesbury, a former pupil of John Locke, were saved by jurors who refused to convict, although the actions of both men were clear instances of seditious libel. The 1798 Alien Enemies and Sedition Act, signed into law by President John Adams and contributing to his subsequent electoral defeat by Thomas Jefferson, made "false, scandalous, and malicious writing" against the government illegal in the United States; but, by the same token, it also made *truthful* criticism legal. The law was allowed to expire in 1801, under Jefferson's presidency. Jefferson pardoned everyone convicted of crimes under the act.

In 1786, the Virginia General Assembly enacted the Virginia Statute for Religious Freedom. This law, now part of the Virginia constitution, runs as follows:

> WE the General Assembly of Virginia do enact that no man shall be compelled to frequent or support any religious worship, place, or ministry whatsoever, nor shall be enforced, restrained, molested, or burthened [*sic*] in his body or goods, nor shall otherwise suffer, on account of his religious opinions or belief; but that all men shall be free to profess, and by argument to maintain, their opinions in matters of religion, and that the same shall in no wise diminish, enlarge, or affect their civil capacities.

Other states followed in enacting their own laws guaranteeing freedom of religion, of speech, and of the press. The 1791 United States Bill of Rights reads:

> Congress shall make no law respecting an establishment of religion, or prohibiting the free exercise thereof; or abridging the freedom of speech, or of the press; or of the people peaceably to assemble, and to petition the Government for a redress of grievances.

By the time the US Constitution was being ratified, rights to free speech, free assembly, and a free press were becoming uncontroversial. In Federalist Paper 10, James Madison argues that federalism is the best way to protect such freedoms, as a larger republic was less conducive to building abusive majorities than smaller, loosely confederated states. Interestingly, in Federalist Paper 84 we see Alexander Hamilton arguing against a bill of rights, because he thought that such a bill would *limit* rather than protect liberty: he worried that it might establish, even if fallaciously, a presumption that citizens have only those rights that are specifically enumerated.

At the time of the American founding, the idea was taking hold that representative democracy was the best form of government, but few were fervent democrats. The founders did not believe that people became angels upon entering politics; James Madison once remarked that, if men were angels, no government would be necessary. The founders were well aware that government power attracts people who would abuse such power. Many thinkers hoped that a press free to criticize the government would keep the public vigilant against potential abuse. In addition, only a free press could keep voters informed. When governments control or fund the press, the press will be biased toward the government.

However, despite protections guaranteed by the first amendment, freedom of speech as we think of it today was not firmly in place until late in the twentieth century. Historian Eric Foner notes that a right to free speech generally was not enforced until after the 1920s. The right to own 'obscene' material such as pornography did not appear until much later. Foner writes that, before the 1920s, "[f]ree speech claims rarely came to court, and when they did, judges generally allowed authorities wide latitude in determining which speech had a 'bad tendency' and could be suppressed."[4]

Since the passing of the first amendment, these banned 'bad influences' tended to include: workers' rights pamphlets; articles on birth control and sexual autonomy for women; abolitionist newspapers; and pamphlets advocating radical political views.

Self-Ownership and Universal Suffrage

Marx was not the first to claim that wage labor is a kind of slavery or dependency. Proto-liberals had argued that wage earning is essentially servile and second-class (and there have been classical and modern liberals who argued the same thing ever since). In 1760s England, the influential legal theorist and jurist Sir William Blackstone wrote that allowing wage earners to vote would threaten the "general liberty," because wage earners were under the dominion of other men.[5] Foner comments that freedom in eighteenth-century England was defined in terms of economic independence, and economic independence was defined in terms of property ownership.[6] People believed that landless laborers would simply vote as their masters directed; thus, they should not be allowed to vote.

One reason why British subjects in American colonies saw themselves as being more free than their counterparts in England was that land ownership was more widespread in the colonies. By the mid 1700s, most white males in the colonies were independent farmers.

Anglo-American eighteenth-century society was stratified. As was true of the democratic Athens in the days of Plato and Aristotle, a great variety existed among the kinds of legal status. Chattel slaves – usually blacks – could be bought, sold, and disposed of as property. They were not *simply* property – they could for example be charged with crimes – but the respects in which they were deemed to be human entitled them to none of citizenship's benefits. Above chattel slaves were apprentices, indentured servants, household servants, wage earners, and married women. Above these were the free men: merchants, shop owners, independent farmers, petty bourgeoisie, and gentlemen. Finally, above these was, in Europe, the nobility: knights, barons, dukes, and the royals. (The American Constitution specifies that no titles of nobility shall be granted. At George Washington's insistence, even the president is known simply as 'Mr President,' despite John Adams's month-long plea to Congress for some more exalted title such as 'His Majesty the President.')

In this society working for a living was a sign of lower status, just as it had been under the Athenian democracy in classical antiquity. Gentlemen were the highest non-noble freemen because they were rich enough not to have to work, which gave them time to develop manners, tastes, and other refinements needed in order to qualify as worthy of the company of nobility. One effect of the American Revolution was to eliminate the hereditary aristocracy, and thus it put all free persons on something closer to an equal legal status. A 1795 naturalization act required nobles to renounce their titles as a condition of US citizenship.

Following the American Revolution, the concept of self-ownership started to be used as a justification for more extensive political equality among white males. In 1787, James Madison claimed that "[a] man has property in his opinions and the free communication of them, he has property in . . . the safety and liberty of his person."[7] Where wage earners had been deemed unfree because they lacked property in land, they were seen now as holding property in their persons and in their labor. Selling labor was not much different from a selling one's wares as a craftsman. Laborers were entitled to respect, because they held the most important kind of property: ownership of oneself. Economic freedom now was not about owning an estate, but about having rights to choose one's occupation and place of residence. As a result, states began easing and eliminating property qualifications as a requirement for the right to vote and to hold office. By the 1860s, the United States had universal adult white male suffrage.

The new respect accorded to labor resulted partly from internalizing some of the ideals of the revolution, and partly it was a matter of necessity. When the American population was small, land was plentiful, so most white men became landowners. As population increased and the industrial economy began to accelerate, men increasingly found that their best option, at least in the short term, was to work for wages. With high turnover rates and significant labor mobility, it was implausible – at least in the US – to regard most factory workers as slave-like.[8] The employer–employee relationship became increasingly similar to what we know it to be today: a transaction. Although the US had plenty of 'unclaimed' land for homesteading – land in fact occupied by Native Americans – the east coast was becoming congested. Land was becoming expensive.

Nevertheless, as the nation wanted to see itself as constituted by free persons, indeed as the freest nation in history, something had to give. What gave was the view that landed property was necessary for freedom. The West was supposed to prevent the formation of an underclass. It did not succeed, so the response was to change the ideology of what constitutes a class.[9]

This transformation led in turn to a rethinking of the value of work. From ancient Athens onward and right into early American history, the dominant view was that *needing* to work signified having lesser status. However, in ante-bellum America, and especially in the North and the West, the (Puritan) idea spread that idleness was a vice and productivity was a virtue.[10] Some western Europeans may view as odd today the American tendency to identify oneself with one's work and to think that personal merit depends partly on productivity. Still, historically, these attitudes developed in the culture as a result of egalitarian impulses: they honored the common rather than the rich person.

Today, many philosophers on the left are suspicious of the idea of self-ownership.[11] Some worry about claims of self-ownership being used to justify rights that reinforce an economically and politically unequal status quo. Nevertheless, self-ownership rhetoric in nineteenth-century US helped to make possible the universal (white) male suffrage, and was also used in the argument for black equality. The actual historical effect of the self-ownership thesis was not to enshrine the status quo but to correct it, even as measured by the standards of contemporary critics of self-ownership.

Slavery

Perversely, chattel slavery persisted in Britain and in the United States – nations whose self-conceptions were defined by freedom. Jefferson and Madison seemed especially aware of this contradiction. Foner describes both of them as slave owners "who despised slavery."[12]

They helped to forge a political union that would protect slavery for seventy years.

We have discussed how innovations and inventions have increased positive freedom for all, by widening the range of options and capacities. Eli Whitney's 1793 cotton gin may be an exception to the rule. Southern plantations had used slave labor before; but the gin made cotton production more efficient, and thus it made large-scale cotton production possible. The immediate effect was to increase the demand for slaves. The northern states eliminated slavery – in part, no doubt, because their economy had little use for slaves. Without the cotton gin to increase the returns from slave labor, slavery might quietly have dwindled away.

Michael Munger and Jeffrey Grynaviski hypothesize that racism in the American South was a response to slavery more than a precondition of it.[13] Americans bought slaves in west Africa because that is where the sellers were. They bought black slaves because black slaves were what west Africans were selling.[14]

Christian southerners had a problem: they needed to reconcile their faith's basic tenets with their patently murderous commitment to the slave trade. The problem was slavery, not race per se, but race offered a handy excuse. The view spread that blacks needed to be enslaved because they couldn't handle freedom. Women likewise were deemed to be prone to hysteria, swayed by passions, incapable of sound reasoning, and too pure-hearted for politics.

Such attitudes form a self-serving ideology, but this doesn't make the beliefs insincere. Indeed, sincerity is part of what makes an ideology self-serving. By and large, oppressors believe their own rhetoric.[15] They defend their turf, never doubting that defending their turf is a matter of principle (see Chapter 6).

Some people, of course, ought to be treated like children: in particular, people who really are children. So the paternalistic thought is not always wrong. In part, this is what makes the thought so dangerous. When one passionately longs to do something at someone else's expense, it is human nature to believe one's own excuses, no matter how transparent they may be. In particular, oppressors find a way to believe that oppression is good for the oppressed, and thus not truly oppressive. (Anyone too obviously worse off is classified as having no right to complain, or is deemed not worse off in relation to a morally 'correct' baseline.)

Although slaves have always been classified as being of barbarian origin, slavery in the New World was distinctively racist. Philosopher Kwame Anthony Appiah and Henry Louis Gates, director of Harvard University's W. E. B. Dubois Institute, observe: "A stark racial component distinguished this modern Western slavery from the slavery that existed in many other times and places: the vast majority of slaves consisted of Africans and their descendants, whereas the vast majority of masters consisted of Europeans and their descendants."[16] Historian Larry Koger acknowledges that, "[i]n Louisiana, Maryland, South Carolina, and Virginia, free blacks owned more than 10,000 slaves, according to the federal census of 1830."[17] Koger documents widespread underreporting, suggesting that the actual number may be three times higher. Even so, the number confirms the contention of Appiah and Gates that the vast majority of slave owners were European.[18]

During the early years of the American Revolution, northern blacks petitioned to abolish slavery by using the same arguments that colonials had used to justify the revolution. Colonials had brandished the metaphor of slavery to argue for independence, yet many seemed indifferent to literal slavery. Still, following the revolution, northern states began to abolish slavery.

In 1791, the abolitionist author Thomas Clarkson collaborated with William Wilberforce, a British member of Parliament, to introduce a bill to abolish England's slave trade. The bill was easily defeated, but Wilberforce and Clarkson would not quit, although each of them suffered from debilitating illnesses. Wilberforce introduced the bill again, more or less annually, until it finally passed the House of

Commons in 1807, having already been approved by the House of Lords. A bill to abolish slavery itself in England was passed in 1833, three days before Wilberforce's death. Frederick Douglass would remark later that, although the United States took pride in having won freedom from tyrannical Britain, it was less free than Britain. At least Britain did not have a sizeable population of people in bondage.

Slavery was not an institution peculiar to the British Empire. However, an anti-slavery ideology is in many respects a western idea. Foner writes:

> ... if traditional African societies knew the desire not to be a slave, the modern idea of freedom was born in the West. In the world from which the slaves had been forcibly removed, where individuals existed within a wide network of communal and kin relationships, and social identity depended on being anchored in a web of power and authority, personal freedom was an oxymoron. By invoking the Revolution's ideology of liberty to demand their own rights and defining freedom as a universal entitlement, blacks demonstrated how American they had become, even as they sought to redefine what American freedom in fact represented.[19]

French immigrant Régis de Trobriand became a naturalized US citizen in 1861 and joined the Union Army. He first saw battle at Gettysburg in 1863. Every third soldier was killed; de Trobriand was commended for bravery under fire. Later on he would write that, after Abraham Lincoln signed the Emancipation Proclamation on September 22, 1862,

> [i]t was no longer a question of the Union as it was that was to be re-established. It was the Union as it should be – that is to say, washed clean from its original sin. . . . We were no longer merely the soldiers of a political controversy . . . we were now the missionaries of a great work of redemption, the armed liberators of millions of men bent beneath the brutalizing yoke of slavery.[20]

This proclamation, we must admit, was not the end of America's schizophrenia regarding the idea that all men are born equal. The proclamation did not abolish slavery in the lands controlled by the Union Army, but only in those counties of particular states that were deemed to be in armed rebellion against the authority and government of the United States. Thus Lincoln's Secretary of State William Seward admitted: "We show our sympathy with slavery by emancipating slaves where we cannot reach them and holding them in bondage where we can set them free."[21] Still, England and France decided not to intervene on the South's behalf, notwithstanding the Confederacy's constitutional right to secede, lest the Europeans be seen by history and by themselves as taking the side of slavery. The Union eventually won the war. The thirteenth amendment to the US Constitution would officially abolish slavery throughout the realm on December 18, 1865. Slavery was over, although its aftermath casts a shadow over American society to this day.

Reconstruction and Jim Crow

During the post-Civil War Reconstruction, the US passed further amendments that guaranteed equal protection to all citizens, giving them the right to vote regardless of race. Blacks had won a number of formal freedoms. Foner claims that blacks at that time compared their story to that of Exodus. They were like the emancipated Jews being delivered to "the Promised Land of American Freedom."[22] However, while the situation of most blacks improved, the Black Codes of 1866, the Jim Crow Laws of 1876 onward, and pervasive discrimination and abuse meant that the story of deliverance was, like the story of Exodus, at best only loosely based on fact. Frederick Douglass said that, without the right to vote, blacks were stigmatized; for lacking the franchise signifies inferiority. Yet, as Douglass also understood, having the franchise is no more than an aspect of equal citizenship.

Booker T. Washington

Booker T. Washington, like Douglass, was born into slavery and illiteracy. With Douglass's death in 1895, Washington became the most celebrated spokesperson for, and educator of, African Americans. In 1865, after the end of the Civil War, General Samuel Chapman Armstrong established a school to educate black soldiers, and eventually founded the Hampton Institute. In 1872, at the age of sixteen, Washington showed up at Hampton's doorstep, penniless. He convinced Armstrong to let him work his way through school. Hampton's mission was to teach black students a trade, to train students as teachers of black students, and to inculcate the virtues of citizenship: professional pride and self-discipline above all. Washington learned these lessons surpassingly well, and eventually brought them to the school he himself founded, the Tuskegee Institute. He taught his students to be non-militant, to work for their own prosperity, and to be concerned above all with what was in their power as individuals. Coming to be regarded as the equal of whites was, in Washington's view, unrealistic in the foreseeable future; but *deserving* to be regarded as anyone's equal was very much within a student's reach. Washington's view was thus inspiring. He instilled optimism and equipped his students to earn the right to be proud of themselves.

W. E. B. Dubois

On the other hand, there was ample reason for righteous anger with the world as it was – reason to refuse to reconcile oneself to making the best of an unfair deal. For this reason Washington's one-time friend, W. E. B. Dubois, eventually became a critic of Washington's approach. In *The Souls of Black Folk* (1903), Dubois acknowledged that "[e]asily the most striking thing in the history of the American Negro since 1876 is the ascendancy of Mr. Booker T. Washington"; but, having acknowledged Washington's admirable sincerity and considerable success, Dubois also complained that Washington overemphasized the trades ("triumphant commercialism") at the expense of the arts. Above all, to Dubois's mind, Washington was teaching his students to be satisfied with a lot that was manifestly unsatisfactory, and thus "Mr. Washington's counsels of submission overlooked certain elements of true manhood."[23]

In Dubois's view, Washington was teaching blacks to be grateful that they were citizens at all, albeit on unfavorable terms, at a time when the "fire of freedom" should still be burning in their veins.[24] Washington was embraced by blacks, Dubois admitted, but largely because whites had embraced him first. Dubois concluded that,

[s]o far as Mr. Washington preaches Thrift, Patience, and Industrial Training for the masses, we must hold up his hands and strive with him, rejoicing in his honors and glorying in the strength of this Joshua called of God and of man to lead the headless host. But so far as Mr. Washington apologizes for injustice, North or South, does not rightly value the privilege and duty of voting, belittles the emasculating effects of caste distinctions, and opposes the higher training and ambition of our brighter minds – so far as he, the South, or the Nation, does this – we must unceasingly and firmly oppose them. By every civilized and peaceful method we must strive for the rights which the world accords to men, clinging unwaveringly to those great words which the sons of the Fathers would fain forget: "We hold these truths to be self-evident: That all men are created equal; that they are endowed by their Creator with certain unalienable rights; that among these are life, liberty, and the pursuit of happiness."[25]

Dubois himself, however, was by no means a separatist, and was capable of impressive gestures of forgiveness. Even as he was criticizing Washington, he hastened to add that white southerners of the present "are not responsible for the past, and they should not be blindly hated or blamed for it."[26] Dubois went on to found the National Association for the Advancement of Colored People in 1909; in the process he drew censure from African Americans for including whites who sought to join the cause.

It is a conundrum. It is easy to find fault with either man – Washington and Dubois – but at the same time it is hard to blame either of them. What better thing can one do than to do the best one can, starting from wherever one has to start? On the other hand, aren't there days when the right thing to do is to forget about improving one's circumstances in incremental ways and take a stand against injustice instead, no matter what the consequences may be?

Presumably both Washington and Dubois saw themselves as fighters, and perhaps each one saw the other as shying away from the main fight. Appiah and Gates plausibly assert that Dubois's criticism of Washington made blacks in general feel more free to speak their minds in the ensuing years.[27] There is something to be said for living a meaningful life, which for some means an inspired and inspiring life, which for some means fighting for a worthy cause. Paradoxically, the feeling that goes with being in a position to say, "Here I stand; I can do no other," is a feeling of freedom.

Jim Crow

The Jim Crow Laws were state and municipal laws that defined and enforced racial segregation.[28] One such law, from the Birmingham City Code of 1944, states:

> It shall be unlawful to conduct a restaurant or other place for the serv-
> ing of food in the city, at which white and colored people are served
> in the same room, unless such white and colored persons are effec-
> tually separated by a solid partition extending from the floor upward
> to a distance of seven feet or higher, and unless a separate entrance
> from the street is provided for each compartment.[29]

Jennifer Roback has traced the history of the Jim Crow Laws, finding that the economics of the streetcar business weighed heavily against providing separate compartments. Streetcar companies, driven as they were mainly by the economics, had a history of actively resisting and campaigning against Jim Crow Laws. Note: *Anti*-segregation politicians sometimes were accused of being in the pockets of the streetcar companies.[30]

Women's Rights

It is somewhat ironic that, during the revolutionary period, Liberty was depicted as a goddess, when her flesh-and-blood sisters were all in chains. Early British feminist thinker Mary Wollstonecraft wrote *A Vindication of the Rights of Woman* in 1792. It was not exactly an egalitarian work. Wollstonecraft agrees that women are mentally inferior to men in her society. However, she says, this is because women do not receive the same education: reason is cultivated in men and neglected in women. Women are taught to be concerned with gossip and fashion rather than philosophy.

It is easy to think of women's rights as just being about equal voting power or the right to hold office. This is what springs first to the contemporary mind. We remember the Seneca Falls convention, or the suffrage movement of the 1920s. But the truly central issues of Wollstonecraft's time (which extend to this day in many parts of the world) were more grim. Women were largely forbidden from owning property, especially after they married. Wollstonecraft's character Maria from the novel *The Wrongs of Woman* complains: "marriage has bastilled me for life."[31] Later, Maria says of her husband:

> Thus he did pillage me and my family, and thus frustrate all of my plans of usefulness. Yet this was a man I was bound to respect and esteem, as if respect and esteem depended on an arbitrary will of our own! But a wife being as much a man's property as his horse, or his ass, she has nothing she can call her own. He may use any means to get at what the law considers his, the moment his wife is in possession of it, even to the forcing of a lock . . .[32]

Wollstonecraft's writings were initially well received, but later on she was reviled, when William Goodwin's biography of her disclosed that she had had an illegitimate child and numerous extramarital affairs. Her contemporaries became less willing to listen to her ideas once they associated them with promiscuity.

It is hard to imagine a more appalling violation of self-ownership than to lack the right to decide when and how to have sex.[33] In the early nineteenth century, the fight for sexual rights largely meant the right to refuse sex. By the end of the nineteenth century, it encompassed the right to use birth control. (This crosses over into issues of free speech: many obscenity laws such as the Comstock Law of 1873 were used to prevent pamphlets on contraception from being mailed.) By the twentieth century, the fight came to involve the right to enjoy sex as men did and, later, to enjoy casual sex without acquiring a stigma. In 1973, *Roe* v. *Wade* made abortion a legal right for women in the United States. A few European countries had already decriminalized abortion, and a number of them did so in the following years.

Nineteenth-century American feminists tended to be abolitionists and prohibitionists. Other support for prohibition came from Christians on the right and from progressives on the left. In practice, prohibition in the US from 1919 to 1933 was a disaster: it led to a massive black market in alcohol and associated gang violence. However, from the standpoint of liberty, it makes sense that early feminists would have supported prohibition. They sought to render women freer by making their husbands less drunk and thus less abusive.

Domesticity

People used the idea of domesticity to justify restricting women's rights. A man's place was considered to be the public life of politics and commerce; a woman's role, the private life of household management and child rearing. Still, of necessity, the practice of women not working outside the home was largely confined to the middle and upper classes. The culture of domesticity was often backed by laws restricting women's hours or the types of jobs they could hold. As any economist would expect, when laborers are not free to choose between many types of employment, they end up with low wages, long hours, and poor conditions. This was true both of women who stayed home and women who worked outside the home.

When we think of, say, the Lowell textile mills in ante-bellum America, we might balk at the long hours and sweaty conditions. Still, oppressive though the system was by today's standards, the alternatives tended to be worse, so would-be workers continued to flock to the mills. The nineteenth-century feminist Mary Livermore (editor of *The Agitator* and, later, associate editor of *Woman's Journal*) wrote frequently about women's limited professional opportunities. Of course, it is only because we are making progress that our ancestors' circumstances can look appalling by comparison to current and still rising standards.

Women's progress in securing economic freedom was unsteady. For instance, during the Great Depression, many states passed laws restricting women's hours not for the purpose of preventing their exploitation but in order to allow men to take their jobs. Foner notes that the Social Security Act and many other New Deal institutions were primarily aimed at protecting white males, often at the expense of minorities and women.[34]

Some argue today that women working as homemakers should be paid a wage, since they do legitimate work. One current interpretation of this idea is that governments should provide the wage. But such a scheme could be funded by general taxes only by transferring money from rich families to poor families, or from two-earner families to one-earner families, or from people who work for wages to people who don't. The original form of the call for housewives to be due a cash income was more honest, because it addressed the alleged point, namely the disparity between husbands and wives; Abigail Scott Duniway, publisher and editor of *The New Northwest* from 1871 to

1887, argued that married women should have equal rights as their husbands over the family income. This idea seems to have taken more of a hold in the law (given the way alimony works) and in popular practice. Today, husbands and stay-at-home wives are treated as having formed an economic partnership.

Voting: Who needs it?

In the American women's suffrage movement of the 1910s, the idea of domesticity was artfully used to argue for expanding rather than restricting women's rights. In order for women to raise good citizens, people needed to create a better environment by making food safer, schools more effective, and crime rates lower. Granting women voting rights would make the government more sensitive to these issues, since women were more sensitive to them than men.[35]

The fight for civil rights often centered around the franchise – the right to vote. What is so important about this right? Perhaps people are misinformed about the efficacy of individual votes. People chant, "Every vote counts!" But, once one does the arithmetic, it's hard to see this as more than a feel-good slogan. Economist Geoffrey Brennan and political philosopher Loren Lomasky have determined that the value of an individual vote drops slowly as the number of voters increases, and sharply with even a tiny anticipated majority.[36]

Political theorist Brian Barry once remarked that, even if one's vote has a low probability of being decisive, it must have high value when the stakes are high. Not so. Suppose the difference between two candidates, call them D and E, is easily quantified: If D wins, this will result in $33 billion more GDP growth over the next year. Suppose candidate D enjoys a tiny lead in the polls: 50.5 percent of voters favor him, while 49.5 percent of voters favor E. Finally, suppose the number of people voting will be the same as in the 2004 US presidential election (122,293,332 voters). You cast a vote for D. What is your vote worth? Using Brennan and Lomasky's formulae, the expected value of your individual vote is 4.77×10^{-2650}, that is to say, approximately zero.[37] If the difference between D and E were worth $33 billion to you *personally*, even then the value of your vote would remain approximately zero.

Hence the value of the right to vote consists in something else. It is not that individual votes have much practical utility. It is, rather, that the right to vote is a badge of equal personhood.[38] The Nazis made Jews wear the Star of David as a badge of inferiority. The right to vote is a metaphorical badge of equality. When Martin Luther King talked about being able to look people in the eye, this is what he had in mind.[39]

Moreover, even if the payoff of an individual vote is virtually zero, consider Joe Legislator deciding whether to support legislation patently hostile to women or blacks. Suppose the entire group has the right to vote against him if he should give them grounds for mobilizing against him en masse. The thought is bound to make him pause.[40]

The Cold War

Immediately after the Second World War, some northern states passed laws forbidding discrimination in hiring practices. In 1948, President Truman ordered military desegregation, prohibited discrimination in federal hiring, and took a stance on behalf of black liberty on the grounds that, if the United States were credibly to call itself the leader of the free world, it needed to "correct the imperfections" in its democracy.[41]

During this time, America was experiencing setbacks in other civil liberties. In its effort to defeat or contain Soviet communism, it began imitating some of the very practices that made the Soviet system so morally offensive. In a speech before the Republican Women's Club of Wheeling, West Virginia, senator Joseph McCarthy claimed to have a list of communist party members who were working for the State Department, and later he claimed that communists had significant influence in the government and media. The fear of communism turned into a worry that communists were everywhere, like unseen germs. This generated a bullying and paranoid culture (although some of McCarthy's accusations turned out to be true). Private companies began requiring oaths of loyalty to the US from employees. Universities fired professors suspected of being members of the communist party. (A decade later, when the era of rabid anti-communism had waned, perhaps partly as a reaction, communist sympathy would be at its apex in universities.) The Smith Act, passed in 1940, forbade advocating the overthrow of the US government and was used to criminalize and imprison members of the communist party. The act was overthrown in *Yates* v. *United States* (1957), as the court found that it violated first amendment rights.

McCarthy was by all accounts a demagogue who used anti-communist propaganda to promote himself. But, insofar as he genuinely cared about freedom, we see in him a paradox that is by no means unique to his person or to his time. He was using illiberal *means* in an attempt to promote liberal *ends*. Throughout history, we find people fighting for long-term freedom by surrendering civil liberties now. The tradeoff always seems compelling in the midst of a crisis. But seldom have illiberal means actually made the world more free.

What was the Cold War against?

As we discuss civil rights in the US, the so-called 'leader of the free world,' in the twentieth century, it is worth pausing to get some perspective by comparing how civil rights fared in the USSR, the leader of the unfree world. Traditionally, scholars had placed Josef Stalin's mass murders at 20 million;[42] Rummel believes the figure of 40 million to be more accurate.[43] Mao was responsible for perhaps 70 million deaths. Stéphane Courtois and his co-authors estimate the worldwide communist death toll to be about 95 million people.[44]

Lenin's attempts at collectivization failed. Peasants worked around the system or simply refused to produce grain. At least five million died from famine.[45] For Lenin, mass starvation was an opportunity.

In a letter to Vyacheslav Molotov written on March 19, 1922, he rejoiced that the peasants, reduced to cannibalism, would not oppose the wholesale execution of the clergy. At the same time Lenin waged war on commerce, hyperinflating the currency until it was worthless.[46] However, War Communism – Lenin's attempt to instantiate complete central planning – was a failure. To avoid a counterrevolution, he instituted the New Economic Policy, which allowed for some private enterprise. In a letter of March 3, 1922, to L. B. Kamenev, he said: "It is a mistake to think the *NEP* has put an end to terrorism. We shall return to terrorism, and it will be an economic terrorism."[47]

Peasants were a major problem for the Soviets, both in theory and in practice. In pure Marxist theory, the peasants were a problem because *they shouldn't have been there*. The revolution was supposed to come when almost all peasants had become urban workers. They were a problem in practice because they were an *enemy class*. Czars had liberated peasants and granted them land. (When they granted land to villagers communally, as often happened, the land was still the village's exclusive property.) As landowners, villagers were, technically, a bourgeoisie. And they acted like it. Forcing them to give up their land and to join farming collectives took an iron fist. Moscow's fist was not hard enough until Stalin seized power. The peasants rebelled at first. Many responded to the order to collectivize by killing all of their livestock. Riots were crushed with armored cars and even with aircraft. 'Stealing' was brutally suppressed: any unauthorized private appropriation of food guaranteed either a trip to the gulag, or, if one was lucky, execution.[48] One result was the Holodomor, often popularly referred to as the Terror Famine or the Ukrainian Holocaust. Somewhere between four and ten million Ukrainians died of hunger.

Lenin used show trials and forced confessions as a means of blaming communism's failures on supposed saboteurs. Stalin was worse; he invented a quota system for confessions. Moscow would announce that a certain number of people were to be found guilty, and the KGB and police agents in the various cities would produce the requisite number. Moreover, during collectivization (1929–33), Stalin paid villagers, workers, and party members to denounce one another. A villager need only accuse another villager of counter-revolutionary activities: the accuser would receive a monetary reward and temporary safety. Everyone had the same incentive: to denounce first, on pain of being oneself denounced. It was a war of all against all.[49]

We can compare the experience of the Soviet Union to that of the American South after the Reconstruction. Southern whites wanted to keep blacks in their place. As with democides, good estimates of lynchings are hard to find. However, historians agree that, while thousands of blacks may have been lynched in the last decade of the nineteenth century, the number of lynchings per decade decreased dramatically over the next seven decades. Economist Steve Levitt argues that the best explanation for this phenomenon is that "all those early lynchings worked."[50] In the case of the USSR, the explanation might be the same. Between Lenin and Stalin, the population had been terrorized for thirty-six years. The survivors were those who had learned to obey.

Thurgood Marshall

Post-war America remained a divided country. Female participation in the work force (including industrial jobs) increased during the Second World War and would continue to increase afterward. However, the 1950s saw a resurgence, aided by television family sitcoms, of the ideal of women's domesticity. There remained a distinction between men's and women's jobs.

Shelley v. *Kraemer*

As the twentieth century dawned, the rights of blacks had made few advances since the end of Reconstruction. The ruling of *Plessy* v.

Ferguson in 1896 asserted the right to segregate streetcars, and effectively made the Jim Crow era constitutional. It upheld the constitutionality of segregation on the grounds that separate public facilities could still be equal facilities, and so segregation did not entail inequality before the law.

Certain states in the South legally required segregation. Others, mostly in the Northeast, legally forbade it. A few such as Kansas made segregation optional by school district, and others – for instance New Hampshire, which lacked any sizable black population – simply had no laws regarding it. Beyond legal segregation there was *de facto* discrimination, which made it difficult for blacks to get high-paying jobs or good education.

In 1911, thirty out of thirty-nine owners in a St Louis neighborhood signed a covenant barring the sale of their parcels to non-whites. In 1945, the owner of one such parcel sold to Shelley, an African American family. Neighbors sued to stop Shelley from taking possession. The trial court dismissed the suit on a technicality, ruling that the covenant was valid only on condition that all the neighborhood owners sign, and not all had done so. The Supreme Court of Missouri reversed the decision, arguing that the people who signed the agreement had a right to do so, and their exercising such a right violated no provision of the constitution. Shelley, who was by then occupying the property, counter-sued, saying that the covenant did indeed violate the US Constitution's fourteenth amendment, which guarantees to each citizen "equal protection of the laws." *Shelley* v. *Kraemer* went to the US Supreme Court, which ruled in 1948 that private racist covenants are constitutional, but *public enforcement* is not. Private covenants per se do not implicate the state, but public enforcement of private covenants does. (This was the same year when President Truman desegregated the armed forces and prohibited discrimination in federal employment.)

Shelley terminated half a century of segregation via covenant. The idea of covenant is neutral in the abstract, but in practice it was used to exclude African Americans. *Shelley* signaled that the courts would scrutinize actual patterns of discrimination, not just formalities. Today people have a right to enter covenants or exchange easements with neighbors, but they cannot bind future generations by creating racist covenants that *run with the land*. Being a racist is one thing; binding future owners to uphold a racist covenant is another. If a covenant is designed to run with the land, the issue is not just one of contract any more. It has become a property issue. In property law, *limiting doctrines* prevent the idiosyncratic wishes of previous owners from running with the land.[51] Contractors can agree to whatever idiosyncratic deal they want, but their agreement does not bind the future buyers of their property. When restrictions that run with the land are challenged, those who wish to preserve them must make a case to the effect that such restrictions aim at making the community a better place and are reasonably expected to be of value to subsequent owners. Could racist covenants be reasonably expected to be good for subsequent white owners? Perhaps; but suppose a court agreed that a community would be better for unspecified subsequent white owners by virtue of enforced legal covenants that exclude blacks. The state would be enforcing covenants prejudicial to black citizens on the supposition that excluding blacks is a reasonable way of making the community a better place. This is precisely what the fourteenth amendment's 'equal protection' clause forbids.

The lawyer who argued Shelley's case was Thurgood Marshall. Marshall, whose grandfather had been a slave, had been refused admission to the University of Maryland on grounds of race. After graduating from Howard University in 1933, his first major case was a successful suit against the University of Maryland for denying admission to Donald Gaines Murray on grounds of race. (H. L. Mencken, a pundit with a conservative reputation, would applaud Marshall's victory, deeming "brutal and absurd" the university's objection to the "presence among them of a self-respecting and ambitious young Afro-American well prepared for his studies by four years of hard work in a class A college.")[52]

Brown v. Board of Education

Marshall was just getting started. In the 1950s, the NAACP worked with him to litigate a number of cases where blacks sued their school districts for requiring their children to attend all-black schools. They argued that the black schools were inadequate and, more importantly, that the very fact of segregation was psychologically crippling. The case of *Brown v. Board of Education of Topeka* (1954) was combined with others and eventually went to the Supreme Court, where the justices found, in a 9–0 decision against segregated schooling, that, as a matter of historical fact, 'separate' is not 'equal.' At best, someone who believed that equality and separation were compatible would have to admit that separation was a failed experiment. (Since the emergence of the Black Panthers and Malcolm X, there have been black separatists who sincerely believe that 'separate' is a black person's best shot at anything approximating 'equal.' Between *Plessy* and *Brown*, though, the profession of 'separate but equal' was a sham.)

Brown v. Board of Education put an end to legalized school segregation; but it was to be decades before all schools would be in compliance with the *Brown* mandate. Three years after *Brown*, in the famous case of Little Rock Central High School, military force was needed in order to enforce desegregation. Most other public and private institutions remained legally segregated. Beyond this fact, mere legal equality was not enough. The whole culture needed to change. *Brown* v. *Board* did not change the country or the world immediately. The desegregation mandate of *Brown* v. *Board* was not being put into practice with anything remotely assembling 'all due haste.' But the wheels were turning.[53]

In 1961, President Kennedy appointed Marshall to the Second Circuit Court of Appeals. All of Marshall's many rulings on behalf of immigrant rights, the rights of defendants to a fair trial, and so on were upheld by the Supreme Court.[54] In 1967, Marshall would become the first (but not the last) black member of the Supreme Court.

Civil rights in 1960s America

It often appears that a culture is poised for a change, but brave individuals are needed as a catalyst. On December 1, 1955, Rosa Parks of Montgomery, Alabama, was arrested for refusing to give up her bus seat to make room for white passengers. At the age of twenty-six, Martin Luther King, Jr became famous as the vocal leader of the Montgomery Bus Boycott. The boycott was planned by E. D. Nixon. It would last over a year, until the US Supreme Court ordered bus desegregation. King advocated non-violent resistance and helped to organize marches, sit-ins, and protests against segregation and discrimination. In March 1963, he helped to organize the March on Washington for Jobs and Freedom, which drew a quarter million people and at which King made his famous "I Have a Dream" speech.

In 1964, the Civil Rights Act was passed into law. It forbade discrimination in hiring, housing, voter registration, and the like and it put an end to segregation in public places (including restaurants and other privately owned facilities). The law was not well enforced at first. A year later, on "Bloody Sunday" (March 7, 1965), police attacked 600 civil rights marchers as they crossed the Edmund Pettus Bridge in Selma, Alabama, just a few blocks from where their march had begun. Seventeen marchers were hospitalized. News channels around the country showed videos of the police beatings. Two days later, King, who had not been present at the first march, led a second one on the same route. Later that day, a white minister from Boston who had participated in the march was beaten, and he died a few days later. Support for the civil rights movement grew.

In the mid- to late 60s, King turned his attention to the North, to protesting against Vietnam, and to fighting for a "poor people's bill of rights." In his eyes, racism, poverty, and militarism were connected, so that eliminating one meant eliminating the others. King thought that the solution to poverty was, in the short term, a bill to give jobs to poor workers, and, in the long term, a movement toward social democracy.

On April 3, 1968, James Earl Ray shot King at the Lorraine Motel in Memphis, where King had been staying to support black sanitation workers, who were on strike. King's death would lead to nationwide race riots. Today King is remembered as a martyr for civil rights and equality, though much of his economic agenda is whitewashed in the national memory. During his lifetime, the FBI attempted to discredit him, for instance by looking (unsuccessfully) for evidence of his involvement in the communist party.

Non-violent resistance, direct action, and civil disobedience were the staples of King's activism. His philosophy was that violence would not solve the problem; it would only invite oppressors to use even greater force to crush the oppressed. (With violent protesters it is easy to justify ignoring the cause they uphold, because one can claim that the protesters are themselves lawless.) King believed that direct action was necessary rather than negotiating, writing letters, and the like – because the former can create "a crisis and foster such a tension that a community which has constantly refused to negotiate is forced to confront the issue. It seeks so to dramatize the action that it can no longer be ignored."[55] Further, King thought that "freedom is never given voluntarily from the oppressor; it must be demanded."[56] Civil disobedience meant refusal to comply with unjust laws, for example by using white-only facilities. King was often accused of extremism, but he retorted that there is nothing wrong with using extremism in the cause of justice. He prodded the fainthearted by pointing out that the person most dangerous to the black's cause was not the southern racist but the white moderate, who believed that blacks should be free but wanted them to wait for a gradual change.

King inspired a change, but problems remain. Black Americans as of 2006 had a poverty rate of 21.6 percent compared to 8.0 percent for white Americans.[57] Both rates have risen since 2000, although the black rate has fallen sharply since 1959 (the earliest year for which we have data), when it stood at 54.9 percent.[58]

Glenn Loury writes that the United States, despite having only 5 percent of the world's population, houses 25 percent of the world's inmates.[59] One in a hundred American adults is currently in prison, and one in nine black males aged 20–34 is currently in prison.[60] Loury frequently asks his students to reflect on such numbers and to consider: What sort of nation do we want to be? Do we want to be a nation where so many go to jail, where the corrections system employs more people than Walmart, General Motors, and Ford combined? Can we call ourselves a free country when one in a hundred American adults is behind bars?

Crime rates were skyrocketing between 1960 and the mid-90s, Loury notes, so it was not entirely unreasonable for policy-makers and politicians to think that they should respond with an increasingly active and punitive justice system. Loury remarks that, even though white high-school seniors report higher drug-use rates than those of their black counterparts, the war on drugs has been aimed at inner cities and at poor blacks, who are far more likely to be arrested, prosecuted, and imprisoned for drug use and who tend to receive harsher sentences. Loury comments:

> Incarceration begets more incarceration, and incarceration also begets more crime, which in turn invites more aggressive enforcement, which then re-supplies incarceration . . . three mechanisms . . . contribute to and reinforce incarceration in neighborhoods: the declining economic fortunes of former inmates and the effects on neighborhoods where they tend to reside, resource and relationship strains on families of prisoners that weaken the family's ability to supervise children, and voter disenfranchisement that weakens the political economy of neighborhoods.[61]

Still, in 2009, the US inaugurated Barack Obama, a black man, as president. Obama's main rival for the Democratic Party nomination was a woman – Hillary Clinton. The Republican Party also nominated a woman, Sarah Palin, for Vice-President.

Measuring progress sometimes seems almost as hard as making progress in the first place. Here is an indication of progress, though.

In 1900, life expectancy in the US was 47 years for white males and 33 years for black males. By the year 2000, life expectancy was 75 years for white males and 68 years for black males.[62]

One can look at the gap between 68 and 75 years and infer that something is still wrong: equality still eludes us. We have heard people say that the increase in life expectancy does not even count as progress, because the only thing that counts as true progress is true equality. But if, on the contrary, the gap between 68 and 75 matters, then so does the gap between 33 and 68. If raising life expectancy from 68 to 75 years would be a worthy achievement, then so was raising life expectancy from 33 to 68 years.

Civil rights in the twenty-first century

One of the current and very active frontiers of civil liberty in the United States concerns equal rights for homosexuals. As late as 1975, the US Civil Service banned gays and lesbians from holding civilian federal jobs. In 1993, President Bill Clinton tried – and failed – to eliminate the ban on gays in the military. Still, things have improved on many fronts. Television shows with openly gay or lesbian protagonists or hosts are now popular. In the 2004 case of *Goodridge* v. *Department of Public Health*, the Massachusetts Supreme Court ruled that it was unconstitutional under the Massachusetts Constitution to forbid gay marriage. Thus Massachusetts became the first state to legalize full-blown marriage between same-sex couples. An increasing number of states (mostly in the northeast and west coast) allow civil unions, which offer gay couples many (but not all) of the benefits of marriage. In May 2008, California's Supreme Court found the ban on same-sex marriage to be unconstitutional. California became the second state to legalize gay marriage. However, during the elections of November 2008, Proposition 8, which amended California's constitution so as to ban gay marriage, received the majority of votes. As of August 2009, six US states have legalized same-sex marriage.

Recent events seem to be forcing Americans to decide what sort of nation they aspire to be and how far they are willing to go in the quest for national security. In 2001, following the terrorist attacks on the World Trade Center, Congress passed the Patriot Act. This law greatly expanded the federal government's powers to monitor US citizens – including the power to conduct "sneak and peek" wiretaps and to allow surveillance (such as obtaining an individual's library records) on the basis of "probable cause," without search warrants granted by judges. Meanwhile, in Britain there are reportedly 4.2 million surveillance cameras – roughly one for every fourteen people.[63]

Discussion

1 Does there ever come a time when it is a good idea to use illiberal means to achieve liberal ends?

2 When, if ever, is the best response to injustice to swallow it and to make the best of it? Is there such a thing as an injustice not worth fighting over? When does an injustice become so severe that stopping it is a goal worth living and dying for? (Consider the grievances mentioned in America's Declaration of Independence. Did such injustices, if injustices they were, suffice to warrant a revolution?)

3 What is equality before the law? Is it possible to have equality before the law when some defendants are so much better than others at obtaining effective legal counsel? In view of the fact that there will never be any such thing as perfect equality before the law, how close must an approximation be to be close enough? How much liberty, if any, should we give up for the sake of that approximation?

4 Martin Luther King dreamt of a world in which his children would be judged not by the color of their skin but by the content of their character. What do you suppose he meant? How do you suppose

he would have weighed the pros and cons of having different college admission standards for different races?

5 There are two popular arguments against same-sex marriage among laypeople. One argument says that marriage is, by definition, between a man and a woman, and has been so for all of human history. The other says that gays already have equal rights with heterosexuals, because both homosexuals and heterosexuals have a right to marry someone else – of the opposite sex. What, if anything, is wrong with these arguments?

Acknowledgments

For helpful comments, we thank Nathan Ballantyne, Ian Carter, Troy Causey, and Stephen Davies.

Notes

1. King 1963.
2. Estlund 2007, 40.
3. Aristotle 1996, 12–28, passim.
4. Foner 1998, 163 et passim.
5. Ibid., 9.
6. Ibid.
7. Ibid., 17.
8. Ibid., 67.
9. We don't mean to suggest that disdain for wage earning disappeared in 1860. Even into the twentieth century, working for wages was regarded as less respectable than self-employment or working for a professional salary. Thanks to Steven Davies for this point.
10. Foner 1998, 67.
11. See Cohen 1995, especially chapter 10.
12. Foner 1998, 35.

13. Munger and Grynaviski 2008. This is not to say that racism is an American invention. Ethnocentrism, racism, the extermination by colonists of indigenous peoples, and similar phenomena have proved to be pretty much universal throughout history.

14. Obadina (2000) says:

> Estimates of the total human loss to Africa over the four centuries of the transatlantic slave trade range from 30 million to 200 million. At the initial stage of the trade parties of Europeans captured Africans in raids on communities in the coastal areas. But this soon gave way to buying slaves from African rulers and traders. The vast majority of slaves taken out of Africa were sold by African rulers, traders and a military aristocracy who all grew wealthy from the business.

See also Bowser 1974. M'bokolo (1998) gives the following account:

> As for slavery within African society itself, everything appears to indicate that it grew in parallel with the Atlantic slave trade and was reinforced by it. It similarly gave rise to many forms of resistance: flight, open rebellion, and recourse to the protection afforded by religion (attested in both Islamic and Christian countries). In the Senegal valley, for example, the attempts by certain monarchs to enslave and sell their own subjects gave rise, at the end of the 17th century, to the Marabout war and the Toubenan movement (from the word *tuub*, meaning to convert to Islam). Its founder, Nasir al-Din, proclaimed that "God does not permit kings to pillage, kill or enslave their peoples. He appointed them, on the contrary, to preserve their subjects and protect them from their enemies. Peoples were not made for kings, but kings for peoples." Further south, in what is now Angola, the Kongo peoples invoked Christianity in the same way, both against the missionaries, who were compromised in the slave trade, and against the local powers. At the beginning of the eighteenth century a prophetess in her twenties, Kimpa Vita (also known as Doña Beatrice), turned the slave traders' racist arguments on their head and began to preach that "there are no Blacks or Whites in heaven" . . . The desire for freedom, and freedom itself, did not come to the Africans from outside, whether from Enlightenment philosophers, abolitionist agitators or republican humanists. They came from internal developments within the African societies themselves.

15. Or perhaps they don't believe their claims, but think they do. They might be self-deluded. (Thanks to Julia Driver for helpful discussions of this idea.)

16. Appiah and Gates 2004, 372.

17. Koger 1985, 1.

18. The same 1830 federal census indicates that the total number of slaves in the United States was over 2 million, which implies that the 10,000–30,000 owned by free blacks adds up to 1–2 percent of the total.

19. Foner 1998, 35.

20. Regis de Trobriand, *Four Years with the Army of the Potomac*, Boston, Ticknor, 1889, pp. 391 and 396. Note that, although the Emancipation Proclamation as a practical matter put the Union on a path to abolishing slavery altogether, it officially abolished slavery only in the confederate states. Lincoln said repeatedly that he was not particularly concerned about freeing slaves. His agenda was to preserve the Union, to repudiate the right of the several states to secede, to strengthen the federal government, and to protect domestic industry from foreign competition. See DiLorenzo 2002.

21. Quoted in Guelzo 2004, 222.

22. Foner 1998, 101.

23. Dubois 1903, 44. We thank Troy Causey for the observation that Dubois was a Harvard PhD who spent most of his years in the most progressive parts of the country, *talking* about hard-line activism. By contrast, Washington was born a slave, worked in salt furnaces and coal mines, put himself through school working as a janitor, then moved to the deep South to run the Tuskegee Institute – at a time and place where a person could be lynched for turning black students into better tradesmen than their white competitors. Dubois was himself, beyond doubt, a heroic figure; but, for him as for anyone else, to question Washington's manhood was preposterous.

24. Dubois 1903, 33–44.

25. Ibid.

26. Ibid., 33.

27. Appiah and Gates 2004, 424.

28. The name 'Jim Crow' apparently comes from a popular 1830s song that caricaturized African Americans.

29. As recorded by Schmidtz at the Civil Rights Institute in Birmingham.

30. See Roback 1984 and 1986.
31. Wollstonecraft 2007, 137. The Bastille was a notorious prison in pre-revolutionary Paris. As mentioned above, Voltaire was among its more notorious inmates.
32. Ibid., 140.
33. One item that men considered theirs and could forcibly take was their wives' bodies. Women had few rights, if any, to refuse sex. Foner (1998, 83) writes:

> The emphasis in abolitionist literature on the physical violation of the slave woman's body helped give the idea of self-ownership a concrete reality, a literalness that encouraged application to free women as well. The law of domestic relations presupposed the husband's right of sexual access to his wife and courts were reluctant to intervene in physical chastisement so long as it was not "extreme" or "intolerable." The idea that women should enjoy the rights to regulate their own sexual activity and procreation and to be protected by the state against violence at the hands of their husbands fundamentally challenged the notion that claims for justice ... stop at the household's door.

34. Ibid., 207. See also the essay on "Guarantees" in Schmidtz 2008, or the chapter on "Mutual Aid" in Schmidtz and Goodin 1998.
35. Foner 1998, 156.
36. Lomasky and Brennan 2000, 66. See also Brennan and Lomasky 1993, 56–7 and 119. In the latter, the authors outline what is now considered the best way of calculating the value of individual votes (though their formulae are not without controversy). Suppose there are two candidates, D and E. We can calculate the utility of my vote as $U_i = p[V_i(D) - V_i(E)]$, where U_i is the utility of my vote for D, p is the probability of my vote being decisive, and $[V_i(D) - V_i(E)]$ represents the difference in the value of the two candidates. The probability of my vote being decisive is a function of two other variables: (1) the number of people voting in the election; and (2) the anticipated proportional majority enjoyed by one of the candidates. A candidate has an anticipated proportional majority when, going into the election, she is already a favorite, is leading in the polls, and so on. Technically speaking, the notion of 'anticipated proportional majority' designates the probability that a random voter will vote for the leading candidate.

37. By comparison, suppose we said that a lottery ticket must have a large value when the prize is large, even if the probability of the ticket winning is low. Again, this is not so. If one has a 1 in 146,107,962 chance of winning the Powerball Jackpot, then a $1 ticket for the largest jackpot in history ($365 million) has an expected value of about $2.50 gross. If the jackpot is taxed and then paid as an annuity over 29 years, the expected value of a $1 ticket drops to about 37 cents.

38. In the introduction we said that we thought of institutions as being more like hammers than like paintings: they are to be judged by their functionality rather than by their symbolism. Here, however, we are speaking approvingly of the symbolic value of the right to vote. We, too, care about what institutions symbolize. We could add now that granting everyone equal voting rights tends to lead to better results than not. Any institution that decides who gets to vote and who does not is ripe for abuse.

39. Holmes and Sunstein (1999, 164) note: "Neither King nor [Thurgood] Marshall can plausibly be accused of promoting a cult of victimhood. On the contrary, they are generally thought to have helped establish greater independence for African Americans. . . . Their advocacy of rights was part and parcel of their reformist dynamism and refusal to assume a passive stance."

40. We thank Christopher Martin for the thought.

41. Foner 1998, 258.

42. Conquest 1991, 5.

43. Rummel 1997. See also Amis 2002.

44. Courtois, Werth, Panné, Paczkowski, Bartosek, and Margolin 1999.

45. Apologists were quick to blame the weather. The year of the famine, 19221–2, also saw a drought, but Russia had seen many severe droughts without such catastrophic famines.

46. Note that, although Lenin was beloved by western intellectuals, he had no love for the intellectual class. Intellectuals *disagree*, and in the process draw attention. But tyranny grows in darkness, so there is no place there for honest scholarly or journalistic inquiry. In a September 15, 1919 letter to Maxim Gorky, Lenin (1919, no page number in online document) said that intellectuals are not "the brains of the nation. In fact they are not its brains but its shit."

47. Lenin 1976, 497.

48. One excellent account of collectivization is Conquest 1987.

49. Indeed, much as Lenin loved terror, Stalin loved it even more. Stalin loved to 'terrorize the terrorizers.' In the Great Terror of 1936–8, he had a huge numbers of members of the Communist Party tried and executed for counterrevolutionary activities. Former torturers were tortured. The army was purged, with all but a handful of the top officers executed. See Amis 2002, 129.

50. Levitt and Dubner 2005, 62.

51. Schmidtz 2010 (forthcoming).

52. Source: http://marshall.ucsd.edu/prospective/marshall.shtml, accessed 07/24/09.

53. One anomalous note. As Thomas Sowell describes Washington DC's Dunbar High School,

> Dunbar was an African American high school whose students' standardized test scores in 1899 averaged higher than those of most white high school students in the district. The school was composed overwhelmingly of urban black students from poor households and had an all-black staff, including the principal, Mary Jane Patterson, who in 1862 became the first African American woman to earn a college degree. Principal Patterson's influence, along with that of other well-educated African American teachers, resulted in Dunbar graduates who outperformed the national averages consistently for some eighty-five years. From 1870 to 1955 most of Dunbar's graduates went on to higher education, many to Harvard and other elite institutions. The accomplishments of the school's alumni have been admirable. These alumni include the first African American graduate of Annapolis, the first African American woman to receive a Ph.D. in America, the first African American federal judge, the first African American general, the first African American cabinet member, and the first African American U.S. senator since Reconstruction. (Evers and Clopton 2006, 115)

On the story of Dunbar, see also Sowell 2005, 204–8. Department of Education official Williamson Evers says that things came apart after *Brown* v. *Board*, partly because the school in effect went from being a magnet school to being a local school (Evers and Clopton 2006, 116).

54. Source: http://chnm.gmu.edu/courses/122/hill/marshall.htm (accessed 07/24/09).

55. King 1963.
56. Ibid.
57. US Bureau of the Census Statistical Abstract, Table 693, accessed 7/26/2009 at www.census.gov/compendia/statab/tables/09s0693.pdf.
58. US Bureau of the Census, Historical Poverty Tables, Table 2, accessed 7/26/2009 at www.census.gov/hhes/www/poverty/histpov/hstpov2.html.
59. Loury 2007.
60. Liptak 2008.
61. Fagan, West, and Holland 2003, as quoted in Loury 2007.
62. See http://www.elderweb.com/home/node/2838 (accessed 07/24/09), citing data from the US Census Bureau's Current Population Reports.
63. This was brought to our attention by Ian Carter. See "Britain is a Surveillance Society," BBC News, November 2 2006, at http://news.bbc.co.uk/1/hi/uk/6108496.stm (accessed 07/24/09).

Chapter 6

Psychological Freedom, the Last Frontier: 1963

THESIS: *Freedom of the will is not an on/off switch, something you either have or not. Instead, real-world freedom of the will is an ongoing achievement that comes in degrees, and not to everyone to the same degree. Moreover, our wills can be more free in some circumstances than in others. Because our cultures and systems of government affect people's inclination and ability to make up their own minds, the most intriguing versions of the free will problem today are personal, social, and political, not metaphysical.*

Our liberty today is, in so many ways, unprecedented. Where shall we live? What will we do for a living? Shall we be members of traditional religions? Of traditional families? To a degree that previous generations could scarcely have imagined, we answer such questions pretty much as we please. In these respects, the future has never seemed so underdetermined and unconstrained.

Yet, when we focus on well-off members of free societies – people who are stunningly free of economic, cultural, and political shackles – we find evidence not so much of people basking in their liberation as of people shackled from within – shackled by their own anxieties, neuroses, defense mechanisms, and so on.[1] It seems that we are adept at snatching defeat from the jaws of victory. This 'last frontier' of freedom is the topic of the present chapter.

The preceding chapters discussed humanity's halting progress in removing external impediments to our positive freedom.[2] This progress has diminished one external impediment after another;

but the end result is not so much, or not only, that all impediments have disappeared; rather, we are now in the best position we have ever been to see that there are impediments other than the obvious ones. The most perfect success at removing external impediments to our positive freedom would leave us still needing to confront this last frontier: internal obstacles.

Political theorist C. Fred Alford interviewed approximately fifty young adults and found them largely uninterested in traditional political, civil, and economic freedoms. Apparently liberty in our society is so secure that young people typically take it for granted. Alford's interviewees, who, to judge by the criteria discussed in our introduction, are among the freest people ever to have lived, tended not to regard themselves as especially free. They felt oppressed by unfulfilled desires and by their dependence on friends, family, and co-workers. For them, what we call psychological freedom has become *the* issue.[3]

From Metaphysics to Psychology

Ever since people began to conceive of their world as law-like, the free will issue has been one of philosophy's most gripping topics. How do we reconcile the apparent fact that we live in a world where every event has a cause with the apparent fact that there are agents – beings who have options and who can *will* themselves to act in one way rather than another?

To be sure, when we treat the paradigm of an event as the transfer of momentum that occurs between billiard balls, free will seems mysterious, even miraculous. But this nineteenth-century picture of physics is no longer current (at least among physicists). Skepticism today is less of a worry about choice being inexplicable in terms of physics, and more of a worry about evidence from psychology to the effect that we are not as autonomous as we think. Even if we set aside metaphysical skepticism, this latter worry remains.

No one is skeptical about our ability to experience pain, yet there are skeptics when it comes to our ability to experience choice.[4] Why?

Neither pain nor choice has been explained in terms of physics. If there is a difference between them, it is not one that is explicable in purely physical terms. One apparent difference is that we can be mistaken about whether we are choosing, but not about whether we are in pain. It is not clear how much of a difference this is; but, whatever difference there is, it is to be explained in terms of psychology, not physics. In any case, if there is any miracle here, it concerns something even more fundamental than the ability of conscious beings to choose. (We could have said 'to choose freely,' but the fact that there is choice *at all* is already a mystery.) The real miracle is that there is such a thing as consciousness. In any case, the traditional metaphysical concern about free will is not our present concern. We mention it only to sharpen the contrast: what we are considering here is a newly emerging (and by no means merely academic) form of the free will puzzle.

Alvin Goldman revolutionized epistemology when he set aside the Cartesian problem of proving that we are not dreaming, and focused instead on scientific evidence regarding the question of what makes some belief-forming processes more reliable than others. The same thing is happening again with the free will problem. The free will puzzle, for the twenty-first century, is not about finding room for choice in a world that seems deterministic. Not that we have solved that problem; rather, we simply have a more interesting problem today: a genuine practical problem that calls for, and allows for, a genuine practical response. The problem is, for each of us, to find within ourselves tools for self-control in a world that seems less deterministic, more chaotic, and more prone to the emergence of genuine ontological novelty than it seemed once to be – a world that is largely unpredictable even at the macro-level.[5]

The puzzle of self-control

The first key, of course, to having self-*control* is to have a self; and recent psychological research suggests that this is harder than it looks.[6] In particular, it appears now that minds are less unified than we once thought. Evolutionary psychology suggests that minds are not thoroughly unified things, but rather collections of subroutines that evolved somewhat independently, as responses to specific problems, and that exist as outcomes of separate selection processes. The mind as a whole was not selected for, and exists only in the sense in which societies exist. In other words, there is something to which the term 'mind' refers in the same way in which there is something to which the term 'society' refers, but that something is not a substance.[7] There is a certain unity to either concept, yet each refers less to a thing we observe than to a chosen way of understanding what we observe.

Neither are minds as transparent as we once thought. We have suspected ever since Freud, and now we have ample reason to believe, that some of what goes on in our minds is hidden from us. Jonathan Haidt likens the human mind to a rider sitting on an elephant. The 'rider' is our conscious mind. We think the rider is in charge, but often the elephant has a goal of its own. Moreover, the rider is always constructing a narrative to justify the path he thinks he has chosen. The rider is unaware that the elephant often makes the decisions that matter, and the rider's story is often just a story.[8]

We take it for granted that there are events – let us call them *choices* – that we control in a way that we don't control other events.[9] Moreover, our choices make a difference. Things can go better or worse for us, and how well things go depends partly on what we choose to do. In turn, our ability to *care* about how things go implies that we can have a *reason* for choosing one way rather than another. So do we (ever) control ourselves well enough to do what we have reason to do? Cutting even closer to the philosophical bone, do we control ourselves well enough to believe what we have reason to believe? Suppose not. Suppose our beliefs are just events that happen to us, and the felt experience of deciding what to believe after weighing evidence is a delusion. In that case we have no reason to take our beliefs seriously – including our belief that we lack free will.

Psychologists today are saying that there are impediments to our approaching the world with a mind as open as we would like. (We use the word 'we' here in an impersonal sense, but this is a humbling personal reflection as well.) In most cases we take it for granted that the research discussed here was conducted by authors who are not themselves in the grip of the biases they purport to have discovered. The good news is this: the premise that any researcher can construct an unbiased case for, and thus can have good reason to believe in, the sort of biases we discuss presupposes that they are not inescapable.[10]

We take it to be as well confirmed as an empirical fact can be that we (including the psychologists who produced the research we discuss) make choices – including choices about how to weigh experimental evidence – more or less freely. (If we do not choose more or less freely whether to view evidence against free will as empirically well confirmed, then we have no reason to take our view seriously.) But we say 'more or less' for a reason. Our conjecture, in a nutshell, is as follows:

(a)   Freedom of the will is not an on/off switch, something you either have or not.[11] Instead, real-world freedom of the will is an ongoing achievement.

(b)   Freedom of the will is achieved in degrees, and not everyone achieves it to the same degree.

(c)   Moreover, not only are some wills more free than others, but any given individual's will is more free in some circumstances than in others.

(d)   It is because our culture and system of government affect people's inclination and ability to make up their own minds that the most fascinating and important versions of the free will problem today have more to do with psychology and politics than with metaphysics.

In this chapter, we confine ourselves to a handful of the most notorious lines of research. In part, we discuss these studies precisely because they are notorious. However, the worries they suggest seem to us to be genuine, not merely widely regarded as genuine.[12] None of these findings underwrites metaphysical skepticism about the general idea of free will, but the results considered together do suggest an alternative (and politically portentious) psychological basis for a measure of skepticism, implying that threats to the autonomy of our wills are various, serious, and real.

Shackled by Social Pressure

Milgram

Perhaps the most disturbing of all psychological experiments, Stanley Milgram's 1963 study seemingly shows that we have a propensity to obey orders even when we believe that what we are being ordered to do is immoral (for instance to deliver life-threatening shocks to a fellow human being), and even when we want to disobey. Social pressure, it seems, makes us cowards – something profoundly at odds with the picture we would like to have of ourselves.

Milgram brought in a subject; introduced the subject to another one, who was in fact an actor; and told both subjects that they were part of a study of learning. Milgram assigned to the first subject the role of teacher, and to the actor the role of learner. The teacher's assignment was to ask questions and to deliver an electric shock to the learner for any wrong answer. The shocks supposedly began at 15 volts and increased by 15-volt increments to 450 volts. The higher voltage settings had warning labels such as "Danger: Extreme Shock" and, after that, "XXX." The teacher, after observing the learner hand-cuffed to a chair and hooked up to electrodes, was taken to another room and told to begin the test. The learner/actor began giving incorrect answers according to a script, and the punishment commenced; the learner eventually complained of a heart condition, then began screaming to be released as the voltage mounted toward what the teacher's control panel described as increasingly dangerous shock levels. If and when the teacher expressed concern, the lab director, again according to script, ordered the teacher to continue. When the learner refused to answer, then apparently collapsed, the teacher was ordered to treat non-answers as incorrect answers.

About 65 percent of subjects kept going, sending what appeared to be ever more lethal shocks into their presumably unconscious fellow subject.[13] Subjects typically did not want to obey, and often seemed on the edge of hysteria. Some pleaded with the lab director to halt the experiment. Many, being incapable of openly repudiating the director's authority to order the apparent torture and execution of innocent subjects, withdrew into questions about who was responsible. The lab director assured them that he, the lab director, was the one responsible. Once their quasi-defiant challenge about responsibility was so easily met, subjects knew they had asked the wrong question. However, unable to summon the courage to assert themselves more honestly, they froze in the headlights of that authoritarian pressure, and obeyed. Afterwards, in debriefing, the lab director asked the teachers whether there was anything the learner could have said that would have made them stop. Some subjects seemed to be astonished, as if the idea of simply deciding to stop had not occurred to them. They had lost sight of the real issue – namely that they had been causing pain to an innocent person and had been unequivocally asked to stop.[14] They got wrapped up in what was, to them as well as to observers, a spurious question about whether they would be responsible. The real question was not whether they would be responsible for the train wreck but whether they could prevent it.

In a fiendishly clever follow-up, G. A. Shelton familiarized students with the Milgram experiments, asked them whether today's more skeptical citizens would be as obedient today, and then recruited them to help her put the question to a test by running a follow-up experiment.[15] She asked the students to pose as lab directors. The experiment seemed to unfold according to the standard design. But this time the teacher, too, was a collaborator. After a while the teacher began, according to script, to report being under excruciating stress, begging the lab director to terminate the experiment. Yet 22 of Shelton's 24 lab directors, unaware that they were the real subjects, dutifully followed to the hilt Shelton's instructions to play the lab director role, saying: "No, the experiment requires that you continue. Please administer the shock and go on to the next question."[16]

Asch

Here is an even more chilling thought: when people go along with the crowd, what if it isn't just their actions that go along, but their beliefs as well? Only slightly less notorious than the Milgram experiments, those of Solomon Asch suggest that being in the presence of a seemingly unanimous opinion can warp our judgment even when the issue is an uncontroversial perceptual matter that is right in front of our faces.

In Asch's experiments, eight to ten students were shown lines of obviously differing lengths and were asked which line most closely matched a standard length. Only one member of this group was an actual subject; the rest were collaborators. At some point, the collaborators began unanimously to select the wrong line. How did the real subject react? About 25 percent of them stuck to their own judgment and never conformed, but about 37 percent caved in, coming to agree completely with the group.[17] Control groups who responded privately, in writing, had one fifth the error rate.

Did the conforming subjects know that the lines they picked did not match the standard? Were they only pretending to agree with the group? Or did they actually come to see the world differently? Recently, researchers repeated a version of the experiment using functional magnetic resonance imaging.[18] By monitoring the brain, they might be able to tell whether subjects were making an 'executive decision' in order to conform to the group or whether their perceptions actually changed;[19] and these later results suggest that many subjects actually come to see the world differently in order to conform to the group. This pressure seemingly distorts their perception, not just their will.[20] In a different version of the experiment, when the group consisted of real subjects with only one collaborator consistently out of line, subjects were annoyed, reacting to the collaborator with complacency, amusement, or disdain.[21]

In the face of such evidence, it is unclear how confident we should be about our ability to assess accurately any evidence at all, including the evidence just reviewed. The effect of social pressure – of other people's expectations in general – appears to cut deeply indeed.[22]

Note that we are talking about situations where subjects had no incentive to comply. They were not trying to humor an authority figure or anyone who could hurt them. The task was not complex. Moreover, it took only three or four collaborators to induce the maximum error rate. No one saw group estimates as irrelevant.[23] Most subjects thought that the problem is not with the majority but with themselves. But subjects were far more resistant to the pressure of a non-unanimous majority – that is, to a group where one out of the several collaborators gave the right answer.[24] This suggests more generally that autonomy in the face of social pressure is not a simple matter of individual versus collective will. It is also a matter of having allies from whom one can draw emotional support in the face of social pressure from particular directions, or perhaps it is a matter of being able to fall between the cracks of opposing group pressures.

People may intuitively recognize a prevalent form of discrimination as being wrong, but they may avoid admitting it even to themselves. Sometimes self-interest is part of the explanation, but not always. By analogy, when a deer is 'caught in the headlights' and fails to avoid an oncoming truck, this does not mean the deer prefers being hit by a truck. Rather, the deer cannot bring itself to move despite the lack of external impediments. Sometimes people are similarly frozen in the headlights of a seemingly monolithic social pressure. Social pressure is a key element in sustaining racist, sexist and other discriminatory cultures, and at the same time it helps to explain why such societies change: that is, even when people look the other way and are unwilling or unable to be the first to break ranks and lead the charge against sexism, racism, drunk driving, littering, and so on, these same people may be quick to follow a rebel's example. Social pressure can keep the lid on; but, when the pendulum starts to swing, social pressure can catalyze the revolution.

Shackled by Self-Deception

Confirmation bias

The phrase 'confirmation bias' is used to refer to various related phenomena. For example, it seems that we tend to be overly impressed with evidence supporting our existing beliefs and relatively inattentive to evidence weighing against our existing beliefs. We also tend to *look for* evidence supporting existing beliefs rather to than to seek disconfirming evidence. Moreover, we quickly become bored (or worse) by evidence in favor of views we reject; we cannot be bothered to evaluate its cogency.[25] Moreover, we are heartened by arguments against such views, giving them every benefit of the doubt. We are, it seems, not built to manifest the spirit of science. According to Jonathan Haidt, we tend to use reasoning not to find the truth but to find reasons to believe what we prefer to believe.[26] To evolutionary psychologist Robert Wright, the human brain is "a machine for winning arguments" – that is, for seeking victory, not truth.[27] It aims to convince others as well as itself.

Interestingly, Francis Bacon, one of the inventors of the scientific method, explicitly recognized an affinity between superstition and what we now call confirmation bias.

> The human understanding when it has once adopted an opinion (either as being the received opinion or as being agreeable to itself) draws all things else to support and agree with it. And though there may be a greater number and weight of instances to be found on the other side, yet these it either neglects or despises, or else by some distinction sets aside and rejects; . . . And such is the way of all superstition.[28]

Of course, it is one thing for *lawyers* to be self-consciously engaged in an adversarial process aimed at constructing the best possible case for their client, even if the best case has nothing to do with weighing the evidence impartially. It is another thing for philosophers or scientists to do the same without self-awareness, then to conclude that anyone who disagrees is either deluded or dishonest.

To be clear about how disturbing this should be, suppose that a pair of identical clones were given identical information sets. Confirmation bias implies that these clones would reach different conclusions if the identical bits of information were presented in a different order. Prior bits of information, provisionally accepted as true, become hurdles to our accepting later bits of information that weigh against the bits already accepted. But later bits of information, rejected now on the grounds that the evidence for them is not compelling enough to warrant rejecting the bits already accepted, would nevertheless have been accepted, had they been received first. Neither clone makes any clear mistake, yet they reach different conclusions. Their only clear mistake occurs when they start to think that only a deluded or dishonest person could draw a different conclusion from the evidence presented.[29]

Psychologist Drew Westen published an experiment on a related theory – motivated reasoning – which holds that the brain tries to converge on beliefs that produce maximum positive feelings and minimize negative feelings. His subjects were loyal Republicans and Democrats. Subjects were shown a statement made by a celebrity, followed by information that made the celebrity seem hypocritical. Then the same subjects were presented with an 'exculpatory statement.' For instance, a test run had a quotation by Walter Cronkite saying that he would never do TV work again after retiring; this was followed by footage showing that he did TV work after retiring; and this was finally followed by an explanation that the work was a special favor. In the experiment, the celebrities were identifiable as Republicans or Democrats. Democrat subjects strongly agreed that the famous Republicans contradicted themselves, but only weakly agreed that the Democrats contradicted themselves. Republican subjects, likewise, readily accepted exculpatory statements from Republicans, but not from Democrats. Functional magnetic resonance imaging (fMRI) showed that a subject's pleasure centers were activated both when she was condemning members of the other party and when she was denying evidence against members of her own party.[30]

Kahneman and Tversky on anchoring and adjustment

When we estimate how much a piece of new information deviates from a baseline expectation, our estimates tend to be conservative. Suppose that some subjects are shown a typical person, perhaps 5 feet, 6 inches tall, and asked to estimate that person's height in comparison to a 5 foot benchmark: they tend to estimate something in between – that is, between 5 feet and 5 feet, 6 inches. Asked to estimate how that same person's height compares to a 6 foot benchmark, here too they tend to estimate something in between – in this case between 5 feet, 6 inches and 6 feet. The benchmark serves as an anchor; subjects are cautious about straying from it. We surmise that they seek to improve on the accuracy of the baseline measurement. And if the point is to improve on the accuracy of the baseline measurement, then the rational thing to do is to avoid overshooting; one aims instead to land somewhere between the baseline and the correct measurement. The problem is that, when the baseline is arbitrary, there is no reason to use it as a baseline.

Now, to speculate, suppose that a professor asks students to estimate something far more complex, like how much the correct view on the morality of stem cell research differs from the professor's own view. Most professors try to be open-minded. Many succeed; they don't require their students to be clones and are truly satisfied when a student seeks a middle ground and goes away seeming to have learned something. But the search for a middle ground can be a bias in itself, subject to potential compounding when the student goes on to another class, splitting the ideological difference yet again, with a new professor. Suppose the new professor's position on stem cell research resembles that of the previous professor. By the time one graduates, one has become a clone after all, with views indistinguishable from those of professors with whom one has repeatedly compromised. No overt pressure is needed. We want to stress that this does not require or presume that the professors are villains. On the contrary, the point is that they may well be individually innocent and nearly (if not entirely) blameless, for they have no inkling of the kind of pressure they apply in concert.

A closely related obstacle to people being free to make up their own minds has to do with the phenomenon of *framing effects*. Before we make a decision, we need to have our alternatives in mind. Typically, we consider our alternatives under a description. For example, the glass we are choosing is half full or half empty. The glass is what it is, of course, so it should not matter how we describe it. The problem is that it does matter; the way we feel about an alternative depends on the way we describe it. To follow Tversky's and Kahneman's example, suppose you face the outbreak of a lethal disease that is about to kill 600 people. You have two options. Following the first option would save 200 out of 600 with certainty. The second has a one-third chance of saving all 600. Given this choice, 72 percent of subjects say they would rather be sure that they saved 200. So far, so good. But now consider a second scenario. Again, you are responding to a disease that is about to kill 600 people; and, again, you have two options. Following one option would result in 400 out of the 600 dying with certainty. The second option offers a two-thirds chance that all 600 will die. Confronted with this choice, 78 percent of subjects say they would rather gamble with 600 lives than choose the certainty of 400 dying. The two scenarios are, of course, two ways of describing the same problem.[31]

Perhaps there is no right or wrong way to frame the problem. Even so, the worry remains: if the problem does not change, then what a student is likely to think about it should not turn on arbitrary details of how a teacher describes the problem. But, apparently, it does.

Confabulation

Jonathan Haidt reports on Don Batson's less famous but truly depressing study of, ostensibly, how unequal rewards affect team-work. Subjects were told they were part of a team of two, but would never meet their partner. They would answer skill-testing questions together, and, if they answered correctly, they would win a prize. A second aim of the study, subjects were told, was to examine how unequal power-sharing affects teamwork. Accordingly, they were instructed that the prize could not be divided but had to be awarded only to one of the two team members; the other would get nothing. Each individual subject was told privately that it was solely up to him or her to decide which of the two would get the prize. Subjects were given a coin, to use if they wanted to assign the prize by ran-dom chance, and were told that their partner would in any event be told that the prize would be allocated by chance. Subjects were then left alone to choose how to assign the prize.

About half of the subjects did not use the coin; of those, 90 per-cent awarded the prize to themselves. The other half of the subjects did flip the coin, yet they too – 90 percent of them – awarded the prize to themselves. Weeks earlier, Batson had given the subjects questionnaires. Subjects who seemed from these questionnaires to be most concerned about morality were the most likely ones to flip the coin; yet they were no more likely than the others to allocate the prize to their partner.

So, Haidt says, although professed moralists flip the coin, "when the coin flip comes out against them, they find a way to ignore it and follow their own self-interest. . . . Batson's subjects who flipped the coin reported (on a later questionnaire) that they had made the deci-sion in an ethical way."[32] Evidently, quite a few were lying; but Haidt suspects that many of them did not know they were lying.[33] They were lying first of all to themselves. Haidt says that we are fairly accurate in our perceptions of others; it is self-perceptions that are distorted.[34] In the coin-flip experiments, the decision to go with self-interest is made (recalling Haidt's metaphor) by the elephant. The rider spins a yarn about fairness and equality, but in many cases, often in ways patently hypocritical to an outside observer, the yarn is just a yarn.[35]

Shackled by Discontent

The hedonic treadmill

We are not free to continue to be happy with our past successes. What was once a source of satisfaction – a promotion, pay raise, new toy, new music – ceases to thrill us after a while. What if our achievements never do more than leave us fleetingly happier than our baseline disposition? From an evolutionary perspective, the winding down of our response to what has become the status quo is prosurvival, insofar as it preserves our sensitivity to novel stimuli. But, although there is this evolutionary advantage to our propensity to revert to our baseline condition, there is also a problem with it when it comes to managing the felt quality of life. The phenomenon of reversion to a hedonic baseline limits how long we hang on to the euphoria accompanying any particular gain.[36] We evolved to be alert to change in our environment rather than to remain excited by what is not changing. So we seem condemned to always wanting more. We have to turn to the next project, setting our sights on what we have not achieved yet. Thus satisfaction tends to be ephemeral, no matter how much we achieve.

Intuitively it is better to be rich than to be poor, other things being equal; but there is a limit to what money can buy. This much is common sense. It has been reported – and this is sometimes called the Easterlin Paradox – that, even though GDP has massively increased in the developed world over the past sixty years, people are not much happier now than when they were relatively poor.

What exactly does 'not much happier' mean? In this case, it means people were invited to rate their happiness, or degree of life satisfaction, on a scale of one to ten. Generations ago, average people judged themselves to be happier than average, and accordingly circled seven or eight. Today, average people still consider themselves to be happier than average, and still circle seven or eight. Does this mean that people are no happier? No. It implies only that average people do not rate themselves higher *relative* to neighbors and colleagues.

In fact, the Easterlin Paradox is grounded in reports that people do not circle higher numbers as they, or their countries, get richer. As a matter of fact, people today *do* circle higher numbers. There is mounting evidence that life satisfaction is strongly correlated with wealth and GDP. Nobel laureate Daniel Kahneman concludes from more recent data:

> The most dramatic result is that when the entire range of human living standards is considered, the effects of income on a measure of life satisfaction (the "ladder of life") are not small at all. We had thought income effects are small because we were looking within countries. The GDP differences between countries are enormous, and highly predictive of differences in life satisfaction. In a sample of over 130,000 people from 126 countries, the correlation between the life satisfaction of individuals and the GDP of the country in which they live was over .40 – an exceptionally high value in social science. Humans everywhere, from Norway to Sierra Leone, apparently evaluate their life by a common standard of material prosperity, which changes as GDP increases. The implied conclusion, that citizens of different countries do not adapt to their level of prosperity, flies against everything we thought we knew ten years ago. We have been wrong and now we know it.[37]

As was recounted by David Leonhardt in the *New York Times*, Japan was the main example originally offered in support of the Easterlin effect. Strikingly, the number of people who circle 10 *dropped* in Japan since the 1950s, even as their GDP was increasing seven-fold. Such a drop is curious to say the least. What could explain it?

As Leonhardt explains, what happened is that the definition of 10 changed. In the late 1950s and early '60s, pollsters told subjects that 10 meant: "Although I am not innumerably satisfied, I am generally satisfied with life now." Many people agreed, and circled 10. But in 1964 the most positive answer of 10 was said to mean: "Completely satisfied."[38] Some still said yes, but a lot of people who might have agreed that they were generally, even if not completely, satisfied, and thus would have circled 10, were not circling 10 now.

So the drop between the late 1950s and 1964 was not a drop in the number of people who felt *completely* satisfied. Neither was it a drop in the number of people who felt *generally* satisfied. All we learned was this: more people think of themselves as generally satisfied than as completely satisfied.[39]

Suffice it to say, data is not (and may never be) conclusive, and what researchers think about a topic is not likely to be driven by the data. Our wanting to believe one thing rather than another, then finding a reason to believe, is only human.

Still, despite Easterlin's paradox turning out to be a myth, it remains common sense that, although money *can* buy happiness, it is by no means *guaranteed* to do so. The translation of rising wealth into rising happiness is not automatic at an individual level. Happiness takes work. Even if national statistics reveal that the tide of wealth does indeed make for happiness as a general rule, whether any given individual's happiness rises with that tide will continue to be an open question. Some individuals will fail to capitalize on the opportunities that wealth creates. There are many ways in which people are adept at snatching defeat from the jaws of victory.

Comparisons and envy

We have a tragic penchant for reconceiving win–win games as zero-sum games or worse. Rather than worrying about how we are doing in absolute terms, we worry about being well off relative to our peers. It is possible for all people to improve their absolute circumstances in terms of wealth and health, but it is not possible for one person to gain in *status* without another person dropping. Wealth is absolute; status is relative. Insofar as we come, incorrectly, to see other people's gains as our losses, we tend to create adversarial systems and to choose policies that harm us all.[40] Our concern for status is not all bad, but being preoccupied by it is bad both for oneself and for anyone having to put up with one's dreary complaints about one's status.

Pundits and many serious scholars alike worry about rising inequality. Perhaps it is realistic to be pessimistic about this, but our pessimistic reading of the literature is that, if there is no such thing as being permanently satisfied by any given level of wealth, there is no such thing as remaining satisfied by any given level of equality either. The astounding increases in life expectancies for the developed world's poor (having doubled over the past century and being now within a few years of the life expectancies of the richest) should be celebrated. That many egalitarians do not celebrate this achievement, and that some cannot bring themselves even to acknowledge it, indicates that wealth and fame are by no means the only currencies in terms of which humans can be insatiable.

Busy, really busy

We, and many of our readers, could spend all day, every day, dealing with email, and – for those of us who teach at a university – writing recommendation letters, refereeing for journals or for tenure review committees, or fund raising. (Members of other professions will have analogous lists.) We have not yet mentioned real work such as teaching and writing. Neither have we mentioned doing what we need to do to keep our homes, cars, and personal relationships in good working order. The stress is nebulous, yet the oppressiveness of it is tangible, sometimes brutally so.[41] Being free is not supposed to feel like this![42]

Solutions

Social pressure

First, suppose we accept at face value the evidence that we are biased. What, if anything, follows? Should we be in the business of debiasing people? If so, who exactly should the 'we' be? Given how biased the debiasers themselves would be – that is, taking the data at face value – the practical upshot is by no means a clear call for intervention.[43]

Solving the problem of social pressure, if a solution exists at all, is substantially a personal matter rather than a matter of institutional design. Obviously, educational systems make some difference, so when we say 'substantially' we do not mean 'exclusively.' Yet we also suppose that the main difference moral education can make is simply to prepare students for the test. And the main preparation is for students simply to be aware that the test is coming and to imagine what form it may take – to be aware that Milgram experiments, or situations like them, are not rare.

A person has to realize that, in most situations, nothing important is at stake. We feel the pressure to conform, and the pressure creates cognitive dissonance because there is no apparent reason for us to feel as pressured as we do.[44] We resolve the dissonance by talking ourselves into believing the stakes are high, so as to make the pressure we feel seem rational. In truth, it often makes no difference whether we agree or disagree, so we may as well report what's on our mind in a civil, humble, non-threatening way.

The hedonic treadmill

One of the most important things we can do in life is to stop, take stock, and count our blessings. Apparently we do not do that naturally. When we count our blessings, we swim against a psychological tide. We can do it, but not automatically. It takes work. It's a personal problem: how to stay in touch with our capacity for healthy grati-tude, for smelling the flowers. The treadmill makes us less able than we should be to appreciate the benefits of living in a free society.

Intuitively, money does not buy happiness. Obviously, there are people who are relentlessly envious, insatiable, or otherwise self-destructive; but, just as obviously, there are people who pause daily to count their blessings, and those who stop to count tend to be happier when they have more to count. The trick is to be in the habit of counting blessings in relation to a fixed baseline. Insofar as it is within our power, we must discipline ourselves to count our bless-ings, and we must resist our tendency to discount blessings as they become familiar.

Being unsatisfied

Haidt reports that satisficers are happier than maximizers. Intuitively, this seems inevitable. *Nothing brings happiness unless you are content with it.*[45] But Haidt also reports it as an experimental finding that maximizers get less pleasure per dollar spent.[46]

Haidt shows that, among the external circumstances which gen-uinely matter, there are a few simple things. Two words of caution. First, although Haidt's list is prosaic, there is nothing trivial about these findings. They affect our life expectations, and even our life expectancies, in dramatic ways. Second, these factors obviously don't affect everyone the same way, but we are well advised not to give in to the all-too-typical urge to classify ourselves as atypical. There may be exceptions; but, as a rule:

1 It pays to minimize noise levels. Traffic noise and so on is a health-compromising stress even if we learn to ignore it.
2 It pays to minimize the time we spend commuting by car. We may think we are accustomed to it. We may even think we enjoy it. But we aren't and we don't. Every mile regularly commuted correlates to higher blood pressure.

3   It pays to minimize the time we spend in circumstances where we do not see ourselves as volunteers. (Background noise and traffic are stresses partly because we don't control them.)

4   Perhaps most importantly on Haidt's list, it pays to avoid conflict and to resolve it quickly when it does occur, especially at home. Haidt claims that chronic conflict with a spouse is a sure way to reduce happiness. There is no such thing as adapting to unresolved conflict with total success; it damages every day, even those days when we do not see other person. (We suggest a corollary to this point: respond to loved ones with compassion. They are only human, which means they face many obstacles to their autonomy. They are not wired to be rationally autonomous 100 percent of the time, and it is not their fault.)[47]

Shackled by the Dearth of Shackles

We want to mention one last apparent wedge between our objective liberty, understood in some quantifiable sense, and our subjective and qualitative experience of freedom. Namely, we have the time and energy to consider only so many options, and sometimes our set of options expands beyond that point.

Barry Schwartz states that people do better with six options than with more or less. Thus, if you are from Eastern Europe (or, in Schmidtz's case, from rural Canada) the first time you visit an American supermarket, you are overwhelmed at all the different yogurt flavors. Let us concede for argument's sake that you would be better off having only six choices. But the very fact that you would be better off with fewer choices motivates you to learn to ignore the noise.

When choosing a restaurant, you do not consider every restaurant within driving distance. Why not? Because, if you tried, you would be overwhelmed. You consider your half dozen favorites, plus one or two restaurants you've heard about but have not tried. We *quickly* learn to ignore anything that for us is not a real contender. Restaurants you've found disappointing disappear from your mental menu, and what you have left is a short list of real contenders. If Schwartz is right, the number ends up being six. In any case, the number is whatever your personal comfort level allows. The length of your list is not given by external constraints. The constraint is self-imposed. (One genuine problem for satisficers, though, has been created by the pace of the modern marketplace. The problem is this: what once was known to be a satisfactory alternative may no longer be in stock next time we go shopping. Items are 'discontinued' at a sometimes frustrating rate.)[48]

There are such things as smart shoppers, but smart shoppers are experienced shoppers.[49] Much of the research reported by Schwartz shows something different from what Schwartz thinks it shows: it shows not what it is like to have *more than six options*, but rather what it is like to be *inexperienced*. (We readily admit that feeling inexperienced can indeed be uncomfortable.)

Summarizing, Schwartz describes situations where we confront the unfamiliar. We note that the second visit to the supermarket is not like the first, and that a free society allows people to try again, and to learn. Schwartz would take that away. He has his reasons. He is not obviously wrong. But this is not how we would do it; not how John Stuart Mill would do it; not how a liberal society would do it. Putting some of these points together, the emotional distress we feel about shopping is yet another facet of our experience that reverts to a hedonic baseline, and what we are soon left with is mainly the objective improvement in our circumstances that comes from having better options. Research on the hedonic treadmill tells us that we are built to be sensitive to novelty. Familiarity dulls our reactions. Schwartz is gripped by the attractions of limiting other people's opportunities to experiment with new alternatives.[50] Would that make us happy? Conceivably. We might be under less stress of a particular kind – we would have more of the stress that comes from being treated like children, less of the stress that comes from being free and responsible. But the latter kind of stress is also, to some degree, the spice of life.

There is another issue. Schmidtz once said to Schwartz:

> I was scheduled for brain surgery in Tucson in March of 2003. A week or so later, when I found out I had the option of going to a more celebrated surgeon in Phoenix, it was the worst day of my life. It was literally a life and death decision. Until then, I was as composed as a person could be under the circumstances. I realized my life was in my surgeon's hands, so I had turned my mind to sewing up the loose ends of my life. Then, unexpectedly, I had an alternative. As you [Schwartz] might accurately have predicted, it felt horrible to have that extra alternative, and to be in a position of needing to make that life and death choice. But what your analysis misses is that, however horrible it felt to be forced to choose among that expanded set of options, I was still better off, indeed (it is clear in retrospect) vastly better off.

In sum, Barry Schwartz is talking about how it *feels* to have important choices to make, which is a different question from whether we are better off having those choices to make. A high-school student today might have to agonize over which college to apply to from among hundreds of options. Then he or she might have to choose from among several acceptance letters. By contrast, Schmidtz's parents went to elementary school long enough to learn to read and write, and then they were back on the farm. Life was simpler then; but life is better now.

We think Schwartz would agree with much of this. Schwartz repeatedly says that he is not against options; he appreciates their value. When the time comes to sum up for the popular press, though, Schwartz overreaches.[51] In the process, he ignores a further political point: namely that, if people are no good at running their own lives, letting them run other people's lives does not solve the problem.[52] We must not make the heroic leap from the premise that we are not good at making choices for ourselves to the false conclusion that we are better at making choices for others, or at electing people who are better at making choices for others.

The idea that the people around us are neither as rational nor as wise as they think will always be a hypnotically powerful message. People are gripped by the reassurance that, no matter how inadequate they feel, others are worse (because others are oblivious to their inadequacy). A recent review of two books in this genre is titled "Free to Choose but Often Wrong."[53] Here is one way in which we go wrong: we grossly exaggerate how bad it is to be wrong.[54] Exaggerating the downside of being wrong – of paying for, and having to learn from, our mistakes – beguiles us into shifting onto others the responsibility to choose on our behalf. But the biases discussed here are democratic. They afflict us all, and only a vigilant humility can contain the damage they do.[55] Even if it is best to have fewer options, this implies only that we need to simplify by limiting our range of options, as in fact we do every day. It does not imply that it is best for someone else to limit our options for us.

We *vastly* underestimate how complicated life was in the 'good old days,' but, in any case, as societies evolve, new kinds and levels of complexity emerge. Perhaps more than ever, today's college graduates must not only figure out how to support themselves; they must also figure out what sort of self they want to support. The basics of earning a living are not much of a struggle any more. At the American poverty line, a typical person's main caloric struggle will be to avoid obesity rather than starvation – which says something about how far society has come. Today we have time to face the fact that making progress, thereby creating and confronting new frontiers, causes anxiety. And we have made a lot of progress.

The point of having more options, of course, is not simply to have more, but to increase the likelihood of having a good option. We can entertain, as a possible ideal, having just one perfect option – say, the best surgeon who ever lived. The question is, in the real world, what is the best approximation of this ideal: having just one option, having the option of (internet) shopping from a world of alternatives, or something in between? (Many people are frustrated the first time they try to search the internet or to use any new technology. Older people often choose to forgo the new technology. The young rarely do.) The best approximation to being presented with the best alternative might be to live in a world that is constantly creating new alternatives (sometimes improving on old alternatives, sometimes not), then leaving people alone to choose among as large a subset of that world of opportunities as they can handle comfortably. In particular, this will be preferable to being presented with a *fait accompli*, chosen by a bureaucrat for reasons known only to that bureaucrat and to the corporations to whom the bureaucrat grants a monopoly privilege.[56]

Revisiting Mill

Such worries underscore John Stuart Mill's conception of the value of liberty: to free our minds, we need to live in a marketplace of ideas, a climate of opinion where unanimity is conspicuously absent.[57] Part of Mill's point is that we want students not to face a united front. Recall the problem of anchoring and adjustment; if some professors ask students to justify evaluations as (metaphorically speaking) deviations from six feet, we want other professors to be asking students to judge in terms of deviation from five feet. Sometimes we might even want students to be overwhelmed for a time – if this means facing more than six choices about what to believe.

We must at the same time resist the temptation to react to contrary opinions by copping out: by concluding that all opinions are mere opinions, and that there is no truth of the matter. As Mill would have insisted, we must take responsibility for putting ideas into testable form as best we can, then learn from experience that not all opinions are equal. A free society lets Copernicus disagree with Ptolemy, but it does not stop there. It also leaves the rest of us free to figure out – indeed responsible for figuring out – who is right.

One final thought about figuring out who is right, and about the shackles of chronic or gratuitous conflict. In intellectual and personal life, *not needing to be right* is a massively underrated freedom. People who do not insist on treating discussions as competitions to be won or lost are people who are still growing. They tend to be more likable, and they probably learn more.

Discussion

1 A group the size of a college class is more than large enough, it seems, to be capable of triggering misperception in Asch-style experiments. Do you ever notice how different some people are in a small group as opposed to a large group? Do you notice how differently they feel about speaking? What should be done about this?

2 How much time do you suppose people spend reading or discussing views with which they intensely disagree? Should they spend more? (How much time do you spend?)

3 When, if ever, should intolerance be tolerated?

4 People today in the developed world are literate. They have a life expectancy approaching 80 years. So they can anticipate 75 years of literate life. Has this fact made them more free?

Acknowledgments

Thanks to Richard Arneson for organizing a symposium on "New Directions in Classical Liberalism" at the American Philosophical Association meeting in Pasadena in 2008, and to co-presenter Gerald Gaus and commentator Peter Vallentyne for their contributions to that session. Thanks to Michael Byron for inviting a version of this chapter as the 2008 Veroni Lecture at Kent State. Thanks also to audiences at the University of Toronto, Florida State University,

Florida State College of Law, and Georgia State University. We received help from Rob Atkinson, Michael Bishop, Andrew J. Cohen, Chris Freiman, Brian Galle, Walter Glannon, Loren King, Tahira Lee, Michael McKenna, David McNaughton, Eddy Nahmias, Tamara Piety, George Rainbolt, Piers Rawling, Clifford Sosis, Kevin Vallier, Peter Vallentyne, Lesley Wexler, and Chris Zarpentine.

Notes

1. Kate Johnson observes in conversation that we are implicitly talking about a Maslow hierarchy of values. We worry about psychological freedom only when, and only because, we have won the more fundamental battles. Michael McKenna notes in conversation that this is a matter of degree. A person who is dodging bullets is not thinking about whether his wants are truly authentic; but a person in prison may be.

2. Here we construe positive freedom as a matter of having 'real choices' in the sense defined in our Introduction, that is, as having options together with the capacity to exercise them effectively. For reasons explained in the Introduction, we avoid defining positive freedom in terms of the capacity to get what we want, but at the same time we wish in this chapter to emphasize rather than ignore the fact that circumstances – which arguably include our expanding set of options and capacities – can warp our wants, can blind us to what we most want, and so on.

3. See Brennan 2006.

4. One possible explanation for the asymmetry: we cannot possibly be wrong in thinking that we are aware of being in pain, but we could be wrong in thinking that we are aware of making a choice. Or the pain just is the awareness, whereas choice is something beyond mere awareness; and that is where the possibility of error arises. Our point is precisely that we cannot possibly be wrong in thinking that there are phenomena, such as consciousness of being in pain, whose inexplicability in terms of physics is never treated as a reason for doubting their existence.

5. See, in general, Ismael 2006; see also Bargh and Ferguson 2000. The latter article argues that even higher mental processes are themselves

best understood from a scientific perspective as being governed by deterministic processes. The authors surely understand themselves to be making an empirical claim, supported by evidence, but their hypothesis is not testable in any obvious way.

6. In Gabrielle Taylor's (1987) analysis, integrity is about "keeping oneself intact." A life of integrity is a unified life. Integrity is a form of freedom. It is the power to continue having a self in the moment. It, too, is an achievement, not a given.

7. See Cosmides and Tooby 1992.

8. Research suggests that we are prone to what is called a *pessimistic bias*: a tendency to believe that the past is better than it really was, that the past is better than the present, and that the present is better than the future will be. And we tend to be wrong about all this. See Jouini and Napp 2006.

    There is also research suggesting that depressed people are more realistic than others and that pessimists are more realistic than optimists. Much of the literature is transparently slanted toward confirming depressing hypotheses about human nature. Our main purpose is neither to debunk these attempts – which themselves seek to debunk more inspiring pictures of human nature – nor to depress, or to reassure pessimists that pessimism is realistic. We simply aim to be realistic about how free human beings can be.

9. Michael McKenna notes that, if we think of choices as intentional efforts to settle uncertainty, then many of our actions could count as being subject to self-control even if they do not involve choice in that narrow sense. McKenna tells us in correspondence that, if I see an elderly woman in need of help crossing the street, I straightaway move to help her. I did so freely, intentionally, but I did not first choose to help her (for I was not uncertain about whether I should) and then help; I simply helped. Yet my intention is under my control. (I could have defused it if I wanted, say if I came to believe the woman was a Nazi war criminal.)

10. Do those who deny that humans are capable of rational judgment forfeit their claim to be taken seriously? (After all, those who make such judgments thereby assert that their judgments are not rational.) Transcendental arguments seem too cute, somehow; but, even so, the answer seems to be yes.

11. To be clear, acquiring the ability to drive an automobile is part of a developmental continuum (perhaps one that empirically exhibits more or less dramatic developmental steps), but the law still has to pick an arbitrary age limit and treat the state of being qualified to drive as if it were an on/off switch. There may well be analogs in the realm of free will of the idea of being *qualified* to drive, but that is not our topic here. We are treating the capacity to steer ourselves, as it were, as analogous to our capacity to steer an automobile.

12. Gigerenzer (2008) asks important questions about some of the data we present here, and about the computational standards for judging human rationality presumed by some of these experiments.

13. When Milgram asked for predictions in 1963, Yale undergraduates predicted an obedience rate of 1.2 percent. Forty Yale faculty psychiatrists predicted a rate of 0.125 percent. See Blass 1999, 963.

14. Philosophers are aware of this literature, but haven't talked about it much. However, see the work of Nahmias 2007 or Nelkin 2005.

15. Shelton 1982. What we report here conforms to Blass 1999.

16. In 1971, Philip Zimbardo selected twenty-four middle-class male undergraduates to inhabit a simulated prison for two weeks, randomly assigning them to roles of prisoner and guard. In their first encounter, the guards strip-searched the prisoners. Guards went on to develop increasingly sadistic routines, depriving prisoners of sleep and food, assigning degrading chores, and requiring prisoners to simulate having anal sex. When Zimbardo was informed that the 'prisoners' were planning to walk out, he himself phoned the police to ask for help with preventing a 'prison break.' The police declined, and only later did Zimbardo come to see his own behavior as bizarre. Originally planning a two-week experiment, Zimbardo called it off after six days (2007, 211). By his own account, Zimbardo was more than a little carried away with his role of warden. At least one participant said that the guards were just students following Zimbardo's orders and acting out his fantasies about how to intensify the prisoners' humiliation. Zimbardo seemed so bent on confirming his theory – namely that situations and role expectations determine behavior – that he wound up playing a role similar to that of Milgram's lab director. His student guards, then, were arguably no more spontaneous than Milgram's 'teachers' were.

17. Asch 1955, 37 and 1952, 457–8.

18. Berns, Chappelow, Zink, Pagnoni, Martin-Skurski, and Richards 2005.

19. Ibid. In this study subjects were given a mental rotation task: they had to determine whether two images on a computer screen represented different objects or merely the same object, rotated in space. The baseline error rate was a mean 13.8 percent. The error rates in the presence of wrong information given by a group of confederates, and by a computer, were 41 percent and 32 percent, respectively (ibid., 248). When asked why they went along with the group, 82.8 percent of the genuine subjects said that on some trials they were sure they were right, and, serendipitously, so was the group. 58.6 percent said that on some trials they were not sure but decided to go with the group. 3.4 percent said they were sure they were wrong but decided to go with the group nonetheless. The presence of external information was shown to decrease activity in the occipital and parietal parts of the brain, which are known to govern perceptual tasks. The authors say: "it was striking that the effects of social conformity were detected only in the most posterior aspects – the occipital and parietal lobes." "The lack of concomitant activity changes in more frontal areas was highly suggestive of a process based, at least partially, in perception. Of course, changes in frontal activity could have occurred below our detection threshold, but with 32 participants, we think this unlikely" (ibid., 251).

20. Presumably there is a major evolutionary advantage to being able to track the truth without distortion. But presumably there is also a major evolutionary advantage to being able to 'go along to get along.'

21. Asch 1952, 480.

22. We should note that several experiments have attempted to replicate Asch's results, and some (but only some) have failed. See Perrin and Spencer 1980 and Lalancette and Standing 1990. When everything has been said, the pressures to conform are undeniably varied and serious, but we also see ample evidence that the pressures are by no means dispositive. Resistance is a very real option.

23. Part of the problem is social epistemology. Even if all we want is to have the truth rather than to conform, the fact that a bunch of seemingly normal, intelligent people disagree with me is, after all, a reason to think that I have made a mistake. So it is not entirely unreasonable for Asch's subjects to think that their eyes are messed up.

24. Asch 1952, 477. What a shame, then, when people with minority views don't speak out. Perhaps we should have someone in every classroom whose job is vocally to disagree with the professor every day or so. The story of the Emperor's new clothes, Asch reflects, is a story of baseless consensus (ibid., 450). What went wrong in this parable is that everyone kept their mouth shut.

25. Of course, there are many more overtly hostile or disrespectful reactions in addition to boredom. Creationists aren't *bored* by evidence for Darwinian evolution. Instead, they are intrigued by the levels of self-deception they think they see in evolutionists. In a way, boredom is nevertheless the more worrisome reaction, because the bias in it is more subtle and harder to control.

26. Haidt 2006, 65.

27. Wright 1994, 280.

28. Bacon 1998, 7.

29. Why are we like that? Otto von Neurath says we are like sailors rebuilding our boat in the open sea. So, as we are patching holes, we encounter driftwood and other materials in an arbitrary order. It' is not arbitrary to work with what you have. But, once you have incorporated one piece of driftwood and built other patches around it, it is often not worth ripping it out when a new and better piece comes along.

30. See Westen, Kilts, Blagov, Harenski, and Hamann 2006. Jason Brennan first learned of this study when he was reading a political blog. The blogger – a Democrat – said he believed the results to be true of the Republicans, but not of the Democrats. The blogger was not trying to be ironic.

31. Tversky and Kahneman 1981.

32. Haidt 2006, 62.

33. Ibid., 63.

34. Ibid., 66.

35. Haidt says in a personal communication that a lot of our reasoning goes on after we have already made up our minds. We are reasoning our way toward excuses. Or perhaps it is not as bad as it sounds. If our logic has led to a conclusion that is utterly surprising, it is not a bad thing to be continuing to reason: in other words, to question the unexpected conclusion. But this probably is not what Haidt is talking

about, because to reach a conclusion in the tentative sense just described and to *make up one's mind* are not the same thing.

36. Daniel Kahneman presumably has no particular loyalty to, or even familiarity with, the ancient eudaimonist way of conceiving of happiness; yet he infers from his experimental findings that "the goal of policy should be to increase measures of objective well-being, not subjective measures of satisfaction or happiness" (Kahneman 2003, 4, as reported in Wilkinson 2007, 13). Lest this be misunderstood, let us stress that Kahneman does not look to Aristotle for clues as to how to define what he calls "objective happiness." Instead, he defines objective happiness as the MRI-measurable momentary experience of pleasure, averaged over time. So, there is a certain sort of objectivity in what Kahneman is calling objective, but it is not a normative claim of objective worthiness in the way that would interest an Aristotelian. We thank Brian Galle for helpful discussion.

37. See Kahneman 2006.

38. Leonhardt (2008) contains a striking map correlating reported life satisfaction with per capita GDP.

39. Angus Deaton (2008, 60) reports that several factors help to explain why recent surveys would show a linear relationship where earlier surveys found no relationship (past a certain point) between national income and life satisfaction. First, earlier surveys included only a small handful of the poorest countries; many of the countries included in the second survey help to smooth out the curve. Second, the earlier survey sampled literate urban people in the poorer countries, ostensibly with the intention of working with individuals more comparable to those surveyed in the richer countries: this was by way of controlling variables other than the difference in GDP. But, by doing so, the earlier survey was comparing the most satisfied people in the poorest countries to average members of richer countries. Once such effects were controlled, the appearance of a kinked relationship between satisfaction and wealth (rising, then flattening) disappeared, according to Deaton.

40. Chris Freiman (in conversation) notes that envy and equality are not the only issues for us to worry about. Brighouse and Swift (2006) talk about positional goods (such as certificates or licenses the primary value of which is to give us an advantage in job applications) in their work

on non-egalitarian rationales for equality. We agree that this is a real issue and we applaud the approach. It makes for a different kind of treadmill and we should not ignore it.

41. Are we really busier? Ramey and Francis (2006) claim that leisure hours were the same in 2000 as in 1900. They note that we have reduced work hours, increased domestic labor hours, and increased education hours. So we are busier learning and taking care of our homes than we were, but we spend the same amount of time doing nothing. When Schmidtz thinks about the farm he grew up on and the farmers he knew, and about what they and their wives had to do to make it through the day, it is hard to imagine being more busy than they were. Nowadays children seem to be supervised around the clock. Back then, parents did not have time for that. When children shot each other or got their arms chopped off in a piece of farm machinery, perhaps after getting drunk, that was life. Our parents focused on the task in front of them. Today, we suspect, people are not more *busy* as much as more *distracted*.

42. Goodin, Rice, Parpo, and Eriksson (2008) claim that the spare time we have left after the hours we spend working, sleeping, and so on is less important to our life satisfaction than the amount of *discretionary* time we have. They define discretionary time as the amount of time we have left after the amount of time we strictly *need* to spend working, sleeping, and so on. Thus many people work longer hours than strictly necessary, but if they are choosing autonomously to spend their discretionary hours working, they tend to be more satisfied than workers who have no discretion in the matter.

43. We thank Lesley Wexler for the thought.

44. Cognitive dissonance is another notorious threat to our ability to trust our own thinking. We will not discuss the issue here, but see Chen 2008.

45. Haidt 2006, 25. A *satisficer* is someone who seeks satisfactory solutions that may or may not be optimal. Normal people in normal situations typically search their decision space in satisficing rather than optimizing mode. For example, if you are looking for an apartment, you look for something that meets your needs (with respect to price, location, number of bedrooms, and other amenities). Once you find something that meets your needs, you take it, and you save your scarce time for

other areas of your life where your search for satisfactory solutions has not yet been a success. See Schmidtz 2008.

46. Haidt 2006, 102.

47. One further thought on externals that matter: one of the best experiences we could have is the experience of total immersion in a deeply challenging yet manageable task; see Haidt 2006, 95. This total immersion is what Csíkszentmihályi (1997) calls 'flow': a state where the end of the action is the action itself, a state where there is no other place to be, just pure absorption – being at home in the moment.

48. Another point, slightly technical but still practically important: maximizers can be bogged down by an excess of options, insofar as they keep searching for more options, uncomfortable with the thought that the option they chose might not have been the best available. Satisficers have no such problem insofar as, no matter how large the set of options is, they stop searching when they find something that is enough to meet the need that sent them searching.

Philosophers argue about whether adopting satisficing strategies is compatible with being a maximizer. It does not matter; what matters is that failing to adopt satisficing strategies is not compatible with being humanly rational. See the essay on "Choosing Strategies" in Schmidtz 2008.

49. Needless to say, it does not go both ways. Not all experienced shoppers are smart shoppers.

50. Part of Schwartz's point is that advertisers deliberately bury us in options, thus manipulating us into making suboptimal choices. Now, we don't suppose that Schwartz is reporting the results of any particular scientific research. He is reporting his intuitions, honed in as they are by his reading of John Kenneth Galbraith. Of course, Schwartz's main claim is intuitively plausible. It is not plausible, however, to infer that we would be less subject to manipulation if the government took firm control of deciding which advertisers we could handle.

51. Gregg Easterbrook 2004 makes many of the same points as Schwartz 2003. He does not overreach, though, and perhaps this partly explains why his book does not have the notoriety of Schwartz's.

52. Bryan Caplan's *Myth of the Rational Voter* is one of the more recent entries in the literature debunking human rationality; but, unlike

almost all of the others, Caplan extends the implications of such human folly from the economic to the political sphere (much as James Buchanan extended insights about rational self-interest from the economic to the political sphere). Caplan focuses on four so-called biases: the bias that blinds us to the mutual benefits of trade in general; the bias that blinds us to the benefits of trading with foreigners in particular; the bias that makes us see job creation per se as a good thing; and the bias that blinds us to evidence of our steadily improving quality of life (to a point that many find such evidence *upsetting*).

53. David A. Shaywitz, "Free to Choose but Often Wrong," *Wall Street Journal* (June 24, 2008). Given the measured and mildly skeptical tone of the review, we suspect that the title of the review was chosen by an editor at the newspaper rather than by the author himself.

54. Lewis Thomas has a charming essay called "To Err Is Human." He claims that the ability of human beings to jump to conclusions unwarranted by the data is what makes such beings great. It is by doing things that do not fit the data – by trying to confirm our biases, by finally admitting that the attempt is not working, and by starting to wonder why – that we make progress. Thomas concludes by asking how we should organize our community given that we are now a single, planet-spanning human community.

> We can assume, as a working hypothesis, that all the right ways of doing this are unworkable. What we need, then, for moving ahead, is a set of wrong alternatives much longer and more interesting than the short list of mistaken courses that any of us can think up right now. We need, in fact, an infinite list, and when it is printed out we need the computer to turn on itself and select, at random, the next way to go. If it is a big enough mistake, we could find ourselves on a new level, stunned, out in the clear, ready to move again. (Thomas 1979, 40)

55. It seems so odd to say that it does not matter if poor people feel satisfied with their lot in life – dismissing this as advertiser-induced false consciousness – while simultaneously holding that a few rich people's feeling overstressed changes everything. People feel good about positive change. If they do not understand how much better they should feel about being born at the end of a century in a country where life

expectancy nearly doubled, this does not change the fact of how much better it is.

56. See Scheibehenne, Greifeneder, and Todd (2009) for a recent, comprehensive survey of the literature on the 'too much choice' effect. They find a discrepancy between the growing number of publications attesting to the effect and empirical data showing no effect, or even the opposite effect. They infer from their own studies that the effect is less robust than was previously thought; it manifests itself in thought experiments where subjects have to justify their choices, but in general it is hard to detect.

57. The Espionage Act of 1917 had made it a criminal offense to criticize the US government. The concept of the 'marketplace of ideas' was explicitly articulated for the first time in the dissenting opinion of Associate Justice Oliver Wendell Holmes, Jr (joined by Louis Brandeis) in the US Supreme Court case *Abrams* v. *US* (1919):

> Persecution for the expression of opinions seems to me perfectly logical. If you have no doubt of your premises or your power and want a certain result with all your heart you naturally express your wishes in law and sweep away all opposition . . . But when men have realized that time has upset many fighting faiths, they may come to believe even more than they believe the very foundations of their own conduct that the ultimate good desired is better reached by free trade in ideas – that the best test of truth is the power of the thought to get itself accepted in the competition of the market, and that truth is the only ground upon which their wishes safely can be carried out. That at any rate is the theory of our Constitution.

Bibliography

Acton, John Edward Dalberg (1907) "The History of Freedom in Christianity," http://oll.libertyfund.org/index.php?option=com_content &task=view&id=561&Itemid=283.

Acton, John Edward Dalberg (1985) *Selected Writings of Lord Acton*, Indianapolis: Liberty Classics.

Amis, Martin (2002) *Koba the Dread*, New York: Miramax.

Anderson, Perry (1996) *Lineages of the Absolutist State*, London: Verso.

Annas, Julia (1993) *The Morality of Happiness*, New York: Oxford University Press.

Appiah, Kwame Anthony and Henry Louis Gates (2004) *Civil Rights*, Philadelphia: Running Press.

Aristotle (1996) *The Politics and the Constitution of Athens*, trans. Jonathan Barnes, ed. Stephen Everson, New York: Cambridge University Press.

Armstrong, Karen (1994) *A History of God*, New York: Ballantine.

Asch, Solomon E. (1952) *Social Psychology*, New York: Prentice-Hall.

Asch, Solomon E. (1955) "Opinions and Social Pressure," *Scientific American* 193, no. 5: 31–5.

Bacon, Francis (1998) "Francis Bacon, *New Organon* (1620)," in *Modern Philosophy*, eds. Roger Ariew and Eric Watkins, Indianapolis: Hackett Publishing, pp. 4–7.

Bacon, Francis (2000) *The New Organon*, New York: Cambridge University Press.

Bargh, John A. and Melissa J. Ferguson (2000) "Beyond Behaviorism: On the Automaticity of Higher Mental Processes," *Psychological Bulletin* 126: 925–45.

Barlow, Jack (2002) "Cicero's Defense of Property Rights," Claremont Institute. Posted October 10, http://www.claremont.org/publications/ pubid.248/pub_detail.asp#footnote2.

Barron, John (1974) *Secret Work of Soviet Secret Agents*, New York: Bantam.

Barry, Brian (2008) "Reply to Goodin, Schmidtz, and Arneson," *Ethics*, 118: 687–710.

Bastiat, Frédéric (1995) "What Is Seen and What Is Unseen," in idem, *Selected Essays on Political Economy*, trans. Seymour Cain., ed. George B. de Huszar, Irvington-on-Hudson, NY: The Foundation for Economic Education, Inc., pp. 1–50.

Baumol, William J. (1990) "Entrepreneurship: Productive, Unproductive, and Destructive," *Journal of Political Economy* 98: 893–921.

Benn, Stanley (1988) *A Theory of Freedom*, New York: Cambridge University Press.

Bergson, Abram (1961) *The Real National Income of Soviet Russia since 1928*, Cambridge, MA: Harvard University Press.

Berlin, Isaiah (1997) "Two Concepts of Liberty," in idem, *The Proper Study of Mankind*, New York: Farrar, Straus, Giroux, pp. 191–242.

Berman, Harold (1983) *Law and Revolution: The Formation of the Western Legal Tradition*, Cambridge: Harvard University Press.

Berman, Harold (2003) *Law and Revolution II: The Impact of the Protestant Revolution on the Western Legal Tradition*, New York: Cambridge University Press.

Berns, Gregory S., Jonathan Chappelow, Caroline F. Zink, Giuseppe Pagnoni, Megan E. Martin-Skurski, and Jim Richards (2005) "Neurobiological Correlates of Social Conformity and Independence During Mental Rotation," *Biological Psychiatry* 58: 245–53.

Bewes, Wyndham Anstis (1986) *The Romance of the Law Merchant*, Littleton, CO: Fred B. Rothman and Co.

Blanqui, Jérôme-Adolphe (1837) *Histoire de l'économie politique en Europe depuis les anciens jusqu'à nos jours*, Paris: Guillaumin.

Blass, T. (1999) "The Milgram Paradigm after 35 Years: Some Things We Now Know about Obedience to Authority," *Journal of Social Psychology* 29: 955–78.

Bloch, Marc (1961) *Feudal Society*, Chicago: University of Chicago Press.

Booker, Cory (2001) "School Choice and Government Reform: Pillars of an Urban Renaissance," *Manhattan Institute Civic Bulletin* 25, www.manhattan-institute.org/html/cb_25.htm.

Bosanquet, Bernard (1970) "Personal Freedom Through the State," in *Freedom: Its History, Nature, and Varieties*, eds. Robert E. Dewey and James A. Gould, London: Macmillan, pp. 190–200.

Bowser, Frederick P. (1974) *The African Slave in Colonial Peru, 1524–1650*, Stanford: Stanford University Press.

Brainard, Elizabeth (2006) "Reassessing the Standard of Living in the Soviet Union: An Analysis Using Archival and Anthropometric Data," Discussion Paper 5525, Centre for Economic Policy Research, <www.cepr.org/pubs/dps/DP5525.asp>.

Brennan, Geoffrey and Alan Hamlin (1995) "Economizing on Virtue," *Constitutional Political Economy* 6: 35–56.

Brennan, Geoffrey and Loren Lomasky (1993) *Democracy and Decision: The Pure Theory of Electoral Decision*, New York: Cambridge University Press.

Brennan, Jason (2006) "The Experience of Freedom," review of C. Fred Alford, *Rethinking Freedom* (New York: Palgrave Macmillan, 2005), *Review of Politics* 68, 687–9.

Brennan, Jason (2007a) "Dominating Nature," *Environmental Values* 16: 513–28.

Brennan, Jason (2007b) "Rawls' Paradox," *Constitutional Political Economy* 18: 287–99.

Brighouse, Harry and Adam Swift (2006) "Equality, Priority, and Positional Goods," *Ethics* 116: 471–97.

Buchanan, James (2003) "Politics without Romance," *Policy* 19: 13–18.

Buckle, Stephen (1991) *Natural Law and the Theory of Property: Grotius to Hume*, New York: Oxford University Press.

Burns, Ric, James Sanders, and Lisa Ades (1999) *New York*, New York: Knopf.

Butterfield, Herbert (1980) *Toleration in Religion and Politics*, New York: Council on Religion and International Affairs.

Cameron, Rondo and Larry Neal (2003) *A Concise Economic History of the World*, New York: Oxford University Press.

Carter, Ian (2003) "Liberty," in *Political Concepts*, eds. R. P. Bellamy and A. Mason, Manchester: Manchester University Press, pp. 4–15.

Carter, Ian (2007) "Positive and Negative Liberty," in *The Stanford Encyclopedia of Philosophy* (Winter 2007 edition), ed. Edward N. Zalta, http://plato.stanford.edu/entries/liberty-positive-negative/.

Chen, Keith (2008) "Rationalization and Cognitive Dissonance: Do Choices Affect or Reflect Preferences?" *Cowles Foundation Discussion Paper No. 1669*, <http://www.som.yale.edu/Faculty/keith.chen/papers/CogDisPaper.pdf>.

Christiano, Thomas (2008) *The Constitution of Equality*, New York: Oxford University Press.

Cicero, Marcus Tullius (1991) *On Duties*, New York: Cambridge University Press.

Cipolla, Carlo M. (1956) *Money, Prices, and Civilization in the Mediterranean World: Fifth to Seventeenth Century*, Cincinnati: University of Cincinnati Press.

Cohen, G. A. (1995) *Self-Ownership, Freedom, and Equality*, New York: Oxford University Press.

Comte, Charles (1817) "De l'organisation sociale considérée dans ses rapports avec les moyens de subsistence des peuples," *Le Censeur Européen* 2: 1–66.

Conquest, Robert (1987) *The Harvest of Sorrow*, New York: Oxford University Press.

Conquest, Robert (1991) *The Great Terror: A Reassessment*, New York: Oxford University Press.

Constant, Benjamin (1988) "The Liberty of the Ancients Compared with that of the Moderns," in idem, *Constant: Political Writings*, ed. Biancamaria Fontana, New York: Cambridge University Press, pp. 309–28.

Cosmides, L. and J. Tooby (1992) "Cognitive Adaptations for Social Exchange," in *The Adapted Mind*, eds. J. Barkow, L. Cosmides, and J. Tooby, New York: Oxford University Press, pp. 163–228.

Courtois, Stéphane, Nicolas Werth, Jean-Louis Panné, Andrzej Paczkowski, Karel Bartosek, and Jean-Louis Margolin (1999) *The Black Book of Communism: Crimes, Terror, Repression*, Cambridge, MA: Harvard University Press.

Covey, Cyclone (1966) *Roger Williams: The Gentle Radical*, New York: Macmillan.

Cowen, Tyler (1998) *In Praise of Commercial Culture*, Cambridge: Harvard University Press.

Csíkszentmihályi, Mihaly (1997) *Finding Flow: The Psychology of Engagement with Everyday Life*, New York: Basic Books.

Danford, John W. (2000) *Roots of Freedom*, Wilmington, DE: ISI Press.

Darwin, Charles (1958) *Autobiography of Charles Darwin*, New York: Norton.

Darwin, Charles (1979) *The Origin of Species*, New York: Random House.

Davies, Stephen (2003) *Empiricism and History*, New York: Palgrave Macmillan.

Davis, Lance E. and Robert E. Huttenback (1988) *Mammon and the Pursuit of Empire: The Economics of British Imperialism*, New York: Cambridge University Press.

De Bracton, Henry (1915) *De legibus et consuetudinibus Angliae*, New Haven: Yale University Press.

De Soto, Hernando (2000) *The Mystery of Capital*, New York: Basic Books.

De Tracy, Antoine Destutt (1970) *A Treatise on Political Economy*, ed. Thomas Jefferson, New York: Augustus M. Kelley.

Deaton, Angus (2008) "Theoretical and Empirical Approach to Consumer Demand under Rationing," in idem, *Essays in the Theory and Measurement of Consumer Behavior*, Cambridge: Cambridge University Press.

DeLong, Brad (2002) *Macroeconomics*, New York: McGraw-Hill.

Dietz, Mary G. (1986) "Trapping the Prince: Machiavelli and the Politics of Deception," *American Political Science Review* 80: 777–99.

DiLorenzo, Thomas J. (2002) *The Real Lincoln*, New York: Three Rivers Press.

Dubois, W. E. B. (1903) *The Souls of Black Folk*, Chicago: McClurg.

Easterbrook, Gregg (2004) *The Progress Paradox*, New York: Random House.

Easterly, William (2006) *The White Man's Burden*, New York: Penguin.

Ensminger, Jean E. (2001) "Experimental Economics: A Powerful New Tool for Theory Testing in Anthropology," in *Theory in Economic Anthropology*, ed. Jean Ensminger, Lanham, MD: AltaMira Press, pp. 59–78.

Ensminger, Jean E. (2004) "Market Integration and Fairness: Evidence from Ultimatum, Dictator, and Public Goods Experiments in East Africa," in *Foundations of Human Sociality: Economic Experiments and Ethnographic Evidence from Fifteen Small-Scale Societies*, eds. J. Henrich, R. Boyd, S. Bowles, C. Camerer, E. Fehr, and H. Gintis, New York: Oxford University Press, pp. 356–81.

Estlund, David (2007) *Democratic Authority*, Princeton: Princeton University Press.

Evers, Williamson M. and Clopton, Paul (2006) "High Spending, Low Performing School Districts," in *Courting Failure*, ed. Eric Hanushek, Stanford: Hoover Institute, pp. 103–94.

Fagan, Jeffrey, Valerie West, and Jan Holland (2003) "Reciprocal Effects of Crime and Incarceration in New York City Neighborhoods," *Fordham Urban Law Journal* 30: 1551–602.

Folsom, Burton W., Jr (1987) *The Myth of the Robber Barons*, Herndon, VA: Young America's Foundation.

Foner, Eric (1998) *The Story of American Freedom*, New York: Norton.

Frankl, Viktor E. (1997) *Man's Search for Meaning*, New York: Pocket.

Gaus, Gerald F. (1997) "On the Difficult Virtue of Minding One's Own Business: Towards the Political Rehabilitation of Ebenezer Scrooge," *The Philosopher* 5: 24–8.

Gaus, Gerald F. (2000) *Political Concepts and Political Theories*, Boulder, CO: Westview.

Gaus, Gerald F. (2004) *Contemporary Theories of Liberalism*, Thousand Oaks: Sage.

Gaus, Gerald F. (2010) Coercion, Ownership, and the Redistributive State," *Social Philosophy and Policy* 27, forthcoming.

Gelderblom, O. and J. Jonker (2005) "Origins of Paper Money in China," in *Origins of Value*, eds. W. Goetzmann and K. Rouwenhorst, New York: Oxford University Press, pp. 177–88.

Gigerenzer, Gerd (2008) *Rationality for Mortals: How People Cope with Uncertainty*, New York: Oxford University Press.

Glenn, H. Patrick (2005) *On Common Laws*, New York: Oxford University Press.

Goetzmann, W. and K. Rouwenhorst, eds. (2005) *Origins of Value*, New York: Oxford University Press.

Goodin, Robert E., James Rice, Antti Parpo, and Lina Eriksson (2008) *Discretionary Time*, Cambridge: Cambridge University Press.

Goolsbee, Austan (2007) "'Irresponsible' Mortgages Have Opened Doors to Many of the Excluded," *New York Times*, March 29.

Grantham, George (2008) "The Prehistoric Origins of European Economic Integration," Montreal: Departmental Working Papers, McGill Economics Department.

Green, T. H. (1986) "Liberal Legislation and Freedom of Contract," in idem, *T. H. Green*, eds. P. Harris and J. Morrow. Cambridge: Cambridge University Press, pp. 194–212.

Grier, Robin M. (1999) "Colonial Legacies and Economic Growth," *Public Choice* 98: 317–35.

Grotius, Hugo (2005) *The Rights of War and Peace*, Indianapolis: Liberty Fund.

Gould, Stephen Jay (1982) *The Panda's Thumb*, New York: Norton.

Guelzo, Allen C. (2004) *Lincoln's Emancipation Proclamation*, New York: Simon and Schuster.

Haakonssen, Knud (1985) "Hugo Grotius and the History of Political Thought," *Political Theory* 13: 239–65.

Haidt, Jonathan (2006) *The Happiness Hypothesis*, New York: Basic Books.

Hasnas, John (1995) "The Myth of the Rule of Law," *Wisconsin Law Review* 1995: 199–233.

Hasnas, John (2005) "Hayek, the Common Law, and Fluid Drive," *New York Journal of Law and Liberty* 1: 79–110.

Hayek, Friedrich (1945) "The Use of Knowledge in Society," *American Economic Review* 35: 519–30.

Henderson, M. Todd (2008) "From Seriatim to Consensus and Back Again: A Theory of Dissent," in *Supreme Court Review 2007*, eds. Dennis J. Hutchinson, David A. Strauss, and Geoffrey R. Stone, Chicago: University of Chicago Press, pp. 283–344.

Herman, Arthur (2001) *How the Scots Invented the Modern World*, New York: Three Rivers Press.

Hill, Roland (2000) *Lord Acton*, New Haven: Yale University Press.

Hobbes, Thomas (1994) *Leviathan*, Indianapolis: Hackett.

Hodgson, Marshall G. S. (1993) *Rethinking World History: Essays on Europe, Islam, and World History*, Cambridge: Cambridge University Press.

Holmes, Stephen and Cass R. Sunstein (1999) *The Cost of Rights: Why Liberty Depends on Taxes*, New York: W. W. Norton and Company.

Holt, J. C. (1992) *Magna Carta*, Cambridge: Cambridge University Press.

Horan, R., E. Bulte, and J. Shogren (2005) "How Trade Saved Humanity from Biological Exclusion: An Economic Theory of Neanderthal Extinction," *Journal of Economic Behavior and Organization* 58: 1–29.

Horan, R., E. Bulte, and J. Shogren (2008) "Coevolution of Human Speech and Trade," *Journal of Economic Growth* 1, http://www.springerlink.com/content/xrg7828x64780x85/fulltext.pdf.

Hume, David (2000) *Enquiries Concerning Human Understanding and the Principles of Morals*, ed. L. A. Selby-Bigge, New York: Oxford University Press.

Ismael, J. T. (2006) *The Situated Self*, New York: Oxford University Press.

Jacobs, Jane (1970) *The Economy of Cities*, London: Vintage Publishers.

Joffe-Walt, Benjamin (2004) "Women Tell of Brutal Rapes in Secret Camp," *San Franscisco Chronicle* [updated May 27, 2004; cited January 24, 2008], http://www.sfgate.com/cgi-bin/article.cgi?file=/chronicle/archive/2004/05/27/MNGBT6SHP71.DTL.

Johnston, David (1989) *The Rhetoric of Leviathan*, Princeton: Princeton University Press.

Jouini, Elyes and Clotilde Napp (2006) "Is There a Pessimistic Bias in Individual Beliefs? Evidence from a Sample Survey," *Theory and Decision* 61: 345–62.

Kahneman, Daniel (2003) "Objective Happiness," in *Well-Being: The Foundations of Hedonic Psychology*, eds. Daniel Kahneman, Ed Diener, and Norbert Schwartz, New York: Russell Sage Foundation, pp. 3–25.

Kahneman, Daniel (2006) "The Sad Tale of the Aspirational Treadmill," in *The World Question Center* 2006, ed. John Brockman, http://www.edge.org/q2008/q08_17.html#kahneman.

Kant, Immanuel (1996) "The Groundwork of the Metaphysics of Morals," in idem, *Practical Philosophy*, trans. and ed. Mary J. Gregor, New York: Cambridge University Press, pp. 37–108.

Kaufman, Walter (1979) *Critique of Religion and Philosophy*, Princeton: Princeton University Press.

Kautsky, John H. (1997) *The Politics of Aristocratic Empires*, New Brunswick: Transaction Publishers.

Kekes, John (2010) "The Right to Private Property: A Limited Justification," *Social Philosophy and Policy* 27, forthcoming.

King, Martin Luther, Jr (1963) "Letter from Birmingham Jail," http://www.africa.upenn.edu/Articles_Gen/Letter_Birmingham.html.

King, Peter (2007) "Damaged Goods: Human Nature and Original Sin," *Faith and Philosophy* 24: 247–67.

Koger, Larry (1985) *Black Slaveowners: Free Black Slavemasters in South Carolina, 1790–1860*, Columbia: University of South Carolina Press.

Kramer, Samuel Noah (1981) *History Begins at Sumer*, Philadelphia: University of Pennsylvania Press.

Krech, Shepard (2000) *The Ecological Indian*, New York: W. W. Norton.

Krouse, Richard and Michael McPherson (1988) "Capitalism, 'Property-Owning Democracy,' and the Welfare State," in *Democracy and the Welfare State*, ed. Amy Gutmann, Princeton: Princeton University Press, pp. 79–106.

Lalancette, M. F. and Standing, L. G. (1990) "Asch Fails Again," *Social Behavior and Personality* 18: 7–12.

Lenin, V. I. (1919) "Letter from Lenin to Gorky, Sep. 15, 1919," in *Library of Congress Revelations from the Russian Archives*, <http://www.loc.gov/exhibits/archives/g2aleks.html>.

Lenin, V. I. (1976) "Letter to L. B. Kamenev," in idem, *Lenin Collected Works*, Vol. 45, Trans. Bernard Isaacs. Moscow: Progress Publishers, 496–99.

Leonhardt, David (2008) "Maybe Money Does Buy Happiness After All," *New York Times*, April 16, <http://www.nytimes.com/2008/04/16/business/16leonhardt.html?_r=1&oref=slogin>.

Levitt, Steven D. and Stephen J. Dubner (2005) *Freakonomics*, New York: Harper Collins.

Levy, Debbie (2007) *The Signing of the Magna Carta*, Breckenridge, CO: Twenty-First Century Books.

Lindert, Peter H. and Jeffrey G. Williamson (1983) "English Workers' Living Standard During the Industrial Revolution: A New Look," *Economic History Review* 36: 1–25.

Lindsey, Brink (2007) *The Age of Abundance*, New York: Collins Business.

Liptak, Adam (2008) "1 in 100 U.S. Adults Behind Bars, New Study Says," *New York Times*, February 28. <http://www.nytimes.com/2008/02/28/us/28cnd-prison.html>.

Locke, John (1980) *Second Treatise of Government*, ed. C. B. MacPherson, Indianapolis: Hackett.

Locke, John (1996) *Essay Concerning Human Understanding*, ed. Kenneth Winkler, Indianapolis: Hackett Publishing.

Locke, John (2005) *Two Treatises of Government and a Letter Concerning Toleration*, eds. Ian Shapiro, John Dunn, and Ruth Grant, Stilwell, KS: Digireads.Com Publishing.

Lockwood, Shelley (1997) *On the Laws and Governance of England*, Cambridge: Cambridge University Press.

Lomasky, Loren and Geoffrey Brennan (2000) "Is There a Duty to Vote?" *Social Philosophy and Policy* 17: 62–86.

Lopez, Robert (1976) *The Commercial Revolution of the Middles Ages, 950–1350*, New York: Cambridge University Press.

Loury, Glenn (2007) "Why Are So Many Americans in Prison? Race and the Transformation of Criminal Justice," *Boston Review* 32, July/August, <http://bostonreview.net/BR32.4/article_loury.php>.

Luther, Martin (1958) "Secular Authority: To What Extent It Ought to Be Obeyed," in idem, *Martin Luther: Selections from His Writings*, ed. John Dillenberger, New York: Anchor Books, pp. 363–402.

M'bokolo, Elikia (1998) "The Impact of the Slave Trade on Africa," *Le Monde diplomatique,* April, <http://mondediplo.com/1998/04/02africa>.

MacCallum, Gerald (1967) "Negative and Positive Liberty," *Philosophical Review* 76: 312–34.

Maccasay, Lyndon (1924) "Review of the Romance of the Law Merchant," *Journal of Comparative Legislation and International Law* 6: 179–81.

MacCulloch, Diarmaid (2004) *The Reformation: A History*, New York: Viking.

Machiavelli, Niccolò (1964) *The Prince*, trans. Mark Musa, New York: St Martin's Press.

Maddison, Angus (1998) "Measuring the Performance of a Communist Command Economy," *The Review of Income and Wealth* 44: 307–23.

Maddison, Angus (2007) *Contours of the World Economy, 1–2030 AD: Essays in Macro-Economic History*, New York: Oxford University Press.

Makdisi, John A. (1999) "The Islamic Origins of the Common Law," *North Carolina Law Review* 77 (5): 1635–739.

Maloney, Michael T. and J. Harold Mulherin (2003) "The Complexity of Price Discovery in an Efficient Market: The Stock Market Reaction to the Challenger Crash," *Journal of Corporate Finance* 9: 453–79.

Marx, Karl and Friedrich Engels (1983) *Selected Works in Three Volumes*, Moscow: Progress Publishers.

Marx, Karl and Friedrich Engels (2002) *The Communist Manifesto*, New York: Penguin.

McCloskey, Deirdre N. (1992) *If You're So Smart: The Narrative of Economic Expertise*, Chicago: University of Chicago Press.

McFarlane, Alan (1997) *The Savage Wars of Peace: England, Japan, and the Malthusian Trap*, New York: Blackwell Publishing.

Meiggs, Russell (2008) "Cleisthenes of Athens," *Encyclopedia Britannica*, <http://www.britannica.com/eb/article-9024296/Cleisthenes-Of-Athens>.

Milgram, Stanley (1974) *Obedience to Authority*, New York: Harper and Row.

Mill, J. S. (1978) *On Liberty*, Indianapolis: Hackett Publishing.

Miller, David (1991) *Liberty*, New York: Oxford University Press.

Miller, Fred (1996) "Legal and Political Rights in Demosthenes and Aristotle," *Philosophical Inquiry* 27: 27–59.

Miller, John (2005) "Hugo Grotius," in *The Stanford Encyclopedia of Philosophy*, ed. Edward N. Zalta, <http://plato.stanford.edu/entries/ grotius/>.

Milne, J. G. (1943) "The Chronology of Solon's Reforms," *The Classical Review* 57: 1–3.

Mokyr, Joel (1990) *The Lever of Riches*, New York: Oxford University Press.

Morris, Christopher W. (1986) "Leviathan and the Minimal State: Hobbes' Theory of Government," in *Early Modern Philosophy*, eds. Georges Moyal and Stanley Tweyman, Delmar, NY: Caravan Books, pp. 373–95.

Muller, Herbert (1961) *Freedom in the Ancient World*, New York: Harper.

Mumford, Lewis (1961) *The City in History*, New York: Harcourt, Brace, and World.

Munger, Michael and Jeffrey Grynaviski (2008) "The Ideology of Racism in the Slave South," Durham, NC: Duke University (unpublished manuscript).

Myers, David (1993) *The Pursuit of Happiness*, New York: Avon Books.

Nahmias, Eddy (2007) "Autonomous Agency and Social Psychology," in *Cartographies of the Mind*, eds. Massimo Marraffa, Mario de Caro, Francesco Ferreti, New York: Springer, pp. 169–88.

Nardinelli, Clark (1990) *Child Labor and the Industrial Revolution*, Bloomington: Indiana University Press.

Nardinelli, Clark (2005) "Industrial Revolution and the Standard of Living," in *The Concise Encyclopedia of Economics*, ed. David R. Henderson, http://www.econlib.org/library/Enc/IndustrialRevolutionandtheStandardof Living.html.

Nelkin, Dana (2005) "Freedom, Responsibility, and the Challenge of Situationism," in *Free Will and Moral Responsibility, Midwest Studies in Philosophy* 29. Cambridge: Blackwell, pp. 181–206.

Nietzsche, Friedrich (1994) *On the Genealogy of Morals*, New York: Cambridge University Press.

Nixon, Richard M. (1962) *Six Crises*, Garden City, NY: Doubleday.

North, Douglas and Robert Paul Thomas (1976) *The Rise of the Western World: A New Economic History*, New York: Cambridge University Press.

Nye, John V. C. (2007) *War, Wine, and Taxes: The Political Economy of Anglo-French Trade, 1689–1900*, Princeton: Princeton University Press.

Obadina, Tunde (2000) "Slave Trade: A Root of Contemporary African Crisis," *African Economic Analysis*, <http://www.afbis.com/analysis/slave.htm>.

Ovchinnikov, I. V., A. Gotherstrom, G. P. Romanova, V. M. Kharitonov, K. Liden, and W. Goodwin (2000) "Molecular Analysis of Neanderthal DNA from the Northern Caucasus," *Nature* 404: 490–3.

Patterson, Orlando (1991) *Freedom: Freedom in the Making of Western Culture*, New York: Basic Books.

Perrin, S. and C. Spencer (1980) "The Asch effect – A Child of Its Time," *Bulletin of the BPS*, 33: 405–6.

Pettit, Philip (1997) *Republicanism: A Theory of Freedom and Government*, New York: Oxford University Press.

Philpott, Dan (2003) "Sovereignty," in *The Stanford Encyclopedia of Philosophy*, ed. Edward N. Zalta, <http://plato.stanford.edu/entries/sovereignty/>.

Pinker, Steven (2002) *The Blank Slate*, New York: Penguin.

Pipes, Richard (1999) *Property and Freedom*, New York: Vintage.

Plato (2004) *The Republic*, ed. and trans. C. D. C. Reeve, Indianapolis: Hackett.

Postgate, J. N. (1992) *Early Mesopotamia: Society and Economy at the Dawn of History*, New York: Routledge.

Powell, Jim (2000) *The Triumph of Liberty*, New York: Free Press.

Raaflaub, Kurt (2004) *The Discovery of Freedom in Ancient Greece*, Chicago: University of Chicago Press.

Raico, Ralph (2006) "Classical Liberal Roots of the Marxist Doctrine of Classes," <http://mises.org/story/2217>.

Ramey, Valerie A. and Neville Francis (2006) "A Century of Work and Leisure," *NBER Working Paper No. 12264*, http://www.nber.org/papers/w12264.

Rasmussen, Dennis C. (2006) "Rousseau's 'Philosophical Chemistry' and the Foundations of Adam Smith's Thought," *History of Political Thought* 27: 620–41.

Rasmussen, Dennis C. (2008) *The Problems and Promise of Commercial Society: Adam Smith's Response to Rousseau*, University Park: Pennsylvania State University Press.

Rawls, John (1971) *A Theory of Justice*, Cambridge, MA: Harvard University Press.

Rawls, John (1993) *Political Liberalism*, New York: Columbia University Press.

Rawls, John (2001) *Justice as Fairness: A Restatement*, Cambridge, MA: Harvard University Press.

Rawls, John (2007) *Lectures on the History of Political Philosophy*, Cambridge, MA: Harvard University Press.

Rawls, John and Philippe Van Parijs (2003) "Three Letters on *The Law of Peoples* and the European Union," *Revue de philosophie économique* 7: 7–20.

Richerson, Peter J. and Robert Boyd (2008) "The Evolution of Free Enterprise Values," in *Moral Markets*, ed. Paul J. Zak, Princeton: Princeton University Press, pp. 107–41.

Roback, Jennifer (1984) "Southern Labor Law in the Jim Crow Era: Exploitative or Competitive?" *University of Chicago Law Review*, 51: 1161–92.

Roback, Jennifer (1986) "The Political Economy of Segregation: The Case of Segregated Streetcars," *Journal of Economic History*, 46: 893–917.

Robinson, Eric (1953) "Matthew Boulton: Patron of the Arts," *Annals of Science* 9: 368–76.

Robinson, Eric W. (2004) "Herodotus, *Histories* (3.80–82)," in idem, *Ancient Greek Democracy: Readings and Sources*, Oxford: Blackwell, pp. 152–4.

Rose, Carol (1985) "Possession as the Origin of Property," *University of Chicago Law Review* 52: 73–88.

Rosenberg, Nathan and L. E. Birdzell Jr (1986) *How the West Grew Rich: The Economic Transformation of the Industrial World*, New York: Basic Books.

Rothschild, Emma and Amartya Sen (2006) "Adam Smith's Economics," in *The Cambridge Companion to Adam Smith*, ed. Knud Haakonssen, New York: Cambridge, pp. 319–65.

Rousseau, Jean-Jacques (1968) *The Social Contract*, trans. Maurice Cranston, London: Penguin.

Rummel, R. J. (1997) *Death by Government*, Somerset: Transaction Publishers.

Sachs, Jeffrey and Andrew Warner (1995) "Economic Reform and the Process of Global Integration," in *Brookings Papers on Economic Activity*, eds. W. Brainard and G. Perry, Washington: Brookings Institution, pp. 1–118.

Sandefur, Timothy (2005) "Sir Edward Coke and the Common Law," http://www.deltachiwindsor.com/history/edward.html.

Say, Jean-Baptiste (1964) *A Treatise on Political Economy, or the Production, Distribution, and Consumption of Wealth*, trans. C. R. Prinsep, New York: Augustus M. Kelley.

Scanlon, T. M. (1998) *What We Owe to Each Other*, Cambridge, MA: Harvard University Press.

Schaffer, Patricia (2000) "Laws in Ireland for the Suppression of Popery Commonly Known as the Penal Laws," <http://local.law.umn.edu/irishlaw/chron.html#anchor205594>.

Scheibehenne, Benjamin, Rainer Greifeneder, and Peter Todd (2009) "What Moderates the Too-Much-Choice Effect?" *Psychology and Marketing* 26: 229–53.

Schmidtz, David (2006) *Elements of Justice*, New York: Cambridge University Press.

Schmidtz, David (2008) *Persons, Polis, Planet*, New York: Oxford University Press.

Schmidtz, David (2010) "Property and Justice," *Social Philosophy and Policy* 27, forthcoming.

Schmidtz, David and Goodin, Robert (1998) *Social Welfare and Individual Responsibility*, New York: Cambridge University Press.

Schwartz, Barry (2003) *The Paradox of Choice: Why More Is Less*, New York: Ecco.

Seabright, Paul (2004) *The Company of Strangers*, Princeton: Princeton University Press.

Selgin, George (2008) *Good Money*, Ann Arbor: University of Michigan Press.

Shapiro, Daniel (2007) *Is the Welfare State Justified?* New York: Cambridge University Press.

Shaywitz, Daniel A. (2008) "Free to Choose but Often Wrong," *Wall Street Journal*, June 24.

Shelton, G. A. (1982) *The Generalization of Understanding to Behavior*, Vancouver: University of British Columbia (unpublished doctoral dissertation).

Sheridan, Richard B. (1981) "The Guinea Surgeons on the Middle Passage: The Provision of Medical Services in the British Slave Trade," *The International Journal of African Historical Studies* 14: 601–25.

Simpson, A. W. B. (1973) "The common law and legal theory," *Oxford Essays in Jurisprudence*, 2nd series, ed. A. W. B. Simpson. Oxford: Clarendon Press, pp. 77–99.

Smith, Adam (1976) *The Theory of Moral Sentiments*, ed. D. D. Raphael, Indianapolis: Liberty Fund.

Smith, Adam (1981) *An Inquiry into the Nature and Causes of the Wealth of Nations*, ed. E. P. Dutton, Indianapolis: Liberty Fund.

Sowell, Thomas (2005) *Black Rednecks and White Liberals*, New York: Encounter Books.

Spector, Horacio (2008) "Four Concepts of Liberty," Buenous Aires: Universidad Torcuato Di Tella (unpublished manuscript).

Spiegel, Henry (1983) *The Growth of Economic Thought*, Durham: Duke University Press.

Spinoza, Baruch (2005) *Ethics*, eds. Edwin Curley and Stuart Hampshire, New York: Penguin Press.

Taylor, Charles (1979) "What's Wrong with Negative Liberty," in *The Idea of Freedom*, ed. A. Ryan, Oxford: Oxford University Press, pp. 175–94.

Taylor, Gabrielle (1987) *Pride, Shame, and Guilt: Emotions of Self Assessment*, New York: Oxford University Press.

Thomas, Lewis (1979) *The Medusa and the Snail*, New York: Penguin.

Thurston, H. (1912) "Sir Thomas Beckett," in *The Catholic Encyclopedia*, Vol. 14, ed. Charles G. Herbermann, New York: Robert Appleton Company, pp. 676–8.

Trinkaus, E. (2007) "European Early Modern Humans and the Fate of the Neanderthals," *Proceedings of the National Academy of Sciences USA* 104, 7367–72.

Tullock, Gordon (2006) *Selected Works of Gordon Tullock*, Vol. 8, Indianapolis: Liberty Fund.

Tversky, Amos and Daniel Kahneman (1981) "The Framing of Decisions and the Psychology of Choice," *Science* 211: 4538.

Uglow, Jenny (2002) *The Lunar Men*, New York: Farrar, Straus, and Giroux.

US Census Bureau (2000) *Poverty in the United States: 2000*, Washington: US Department of Commerce, 2000, <http://www.census.gov/prod/2001pubs/p60-214.pdf>.

Van de Mieroop, Marc (2005) "The Invention of Interest," in *The Origins of Value*, eds. W. Goetzmann and K. Rouwenhorst, New York: Oxford University Press, pp. 17–30.

Vinogradoff, Paul (1924) "Feudalism," <http://socserv.mcmaster.ca/econ/ugcm/3ll3/vinogradoff/feudal> (original publication: *Cambridge Medieval History*, Vol. 3, pp. 458–84).

Von Glahn, Richard (2005) "The Origins of Paper Money in China," in *The Origins of Value*, eds. W. Goetzmann and K. Rouwenhorst, New York: Oxford University Press, pp. 65–90.

Wachsmann, Shelley (1998) *Seagoing Ships and Seamanship in the Bronze Age Levant*, College Station: Texas A&M University Press.

Ward-Perkins, Bryan (2005) *The Fall of Rome and the End of Civilization*, New York: Oxford University Press.

Westen, D., C. Kilts, P. Blagov, K. Harenski, S. and Hamann (2006) "The Neural Basis of Motivated Reasoning: An fMRI Study of Emotional Constraints on Political Judgment during the US Presidential Election of 2004," *The Journal of Cognitive Neuroscience* 18: 1947–58.

Wilkinson, Will (2007) "In Pursuit of Happiness Research: Is It Reliable? What Does It Imply for Policy?" *Policy Analysis* 590: 1–41.

Wittfogel, Karl (1957) *Oriental Despotism: A Comparative Study of Total Power*, New Haven: Yale University Press.

Wollstonecraft, Mary (2007) *Mary and the Wrongs of Woman*, New York: Oxford University Press.

Wood, Neal (1988) *Cicero's Social and Political Thought*, Berkeley: University of California Press.

Woodruff, Paul (2005) *First Democracy*, New York: Oxford University Press.

Wright, Robert (1994) *The Moral Animal*, New York: Vintage.

Wright, Robert (2000) *Nonzero*, New York: Vintage.

Veblen, Thorstein (1994) *The Theory of the Leisure Class*, New York: Dover.

Zagorin, Perez (2003) *How the Idea of Religious Toleration Came to the West*, Princeton: Princeton University Press.

Zak, Paul J. (2005) "Trust: A Temporary Human Attachment Facilitated by Oxytocin," *Behavioral and Brain Sciences* 28: 368–9.

Zak, Paul J. (2008a) "Introduction," in *Moral Markets*, ed. Paul J. Zak, Princeton: Princeton University Press, pp. xi–xxii.

Zak, Paul J. (2008b) "Values and Value: Moral Economics," in *Moral Markets*, ed. Paul J. Zak, Princeton: Princeton University Press, pp. 259–79.

Zak, P., M. Kosfeld, M. Henrichs, U. Fischbacher, and E. Fehr (2005) "Oxytocin Increases Trust in Humans," *Nature* 435: 673–6.

Zimbardo, Philip (2007) *The Lucifer Effect*, New York: Random House.

Zwolinski, Matt (2008) "The Ethics of Price Gouging," *Business Ethics Quarterly* 18: 347–78.

Zywicki, Todd J. (2003) "The Rise and Fall of Efficiency in the Common Law: A Supply-Side Analysis," *Northwestern University Law Review* 97: 1551–633.

Index